LITERACY AND POWER

The Latin American Battleground

David Archer
Patrick Costello

Earthscan Publications Ltd   London

First published 1990 by
Earthscan Publications Ltd
3 Endsleigh Street, London WC1H 0DD

Copyright © 1990 by David Archer and
Patrick Costello

British Library Cataloguing in Publication Data
Archer, David
  Literacy and power.
  1. Literacy. Sociocultural aspects
  I. Title II. Costello, Patrick
  302.2244

ISBN 1–85383–042–9

Production by David Williams Associates (081–521 4130)
Typeset by Selectmove Ltd., London
Printed and bound in Great Britain by
Guernsey Press Co. Ltd, Guernsey, C.I.

Earthscan Publications Ltd is a wholly owned and
editorially independent subsidiary of the International
Institute for Environment and Development (IIED)

David Archer has worked in secondary schools, further education, curriculum development, community video, development education and the unemployed movement in Britain. A co-founder of the Community Education Direct Research Unit (CEDRU), he has worked extensively in Latin America and also in India. He is now a literacy consultant and Latin America Desk Officer with ActionAid.

Patrick Costello studied politics and philosophy at Oxford, specializing in international relations and the philosophy of language. He joined CEDRU in 1987 to undertake research both in Britain and Latin America. He is currently the co-ordinator of the Guatemala Committee for Human Rights.

Contents

Everyone reads life and the world like a book. Even the so-called "illiterate". But especially the "leaders" of our society, the most "responsible" non-dreamers: the politicians, the businessmen, the ones who make plans. Without the reading of the world as a book, there is no prediction, no planning, no taxes, no laws, no welfare, no war. Yet these leaders read the world in terms of rationality and averages, as if it were a textbook. The world actually writes itself with the many-leveled, unfixable intricacy and openness of a work of literature. If . . . we can ourselves learn and teach others to read the world in the "proper" risky way, and to act upon that lesson, perhaps we . . . would not forever be such helpless victims.

Gayatri Spivak, *In Other Worlds*, 1987

Preface

In the 1960s a movement of popular education sprang up in Latin America based on the practical experiences of many small organizations seeking social and political change. Adult-literacy teaching was at the heart of the new methods, which conceived literacy not as the learning of a neutral technique but as the first step towards collective empowerment. This was one area, it seemed, where the so-called Third World had advanced, theoretically and practically, far ahead of the so-called First World. Research and evaluations of this movement by international agencies have rarely measured it on its own terms. Statistical analysis has proved inappropriate. Western academics have focused on the theoretical texts of the movement (by writers such as Freire and Illich) rather than on its practical impact in the South and its potential impact in the North.

In 1985, CEDRU (Community Education Direct Research Unit) was set up to help redress the balance and open up a dialogue between Latin America and the West in which Latin America took the lead. An initial research project involved work with the Ministry of Education in Nicaragua where the revolution of 1979 had given popular educators their first opportunity to implement their ideas on a national scale. In contrast, research in Colombia, Bolivia and Peru was with non-governmental groups who were working in opposition to the state. On the basis of this work a number of articles were published and an education pack was produced, based on the life of a Nicaraguan family, which attempted to put some of the ideas of popular education into practice both inside and outside the British education system.

The idea for this book arose out of an evaluation of that research. There was a need for more detailed investigation, to be situated in the experiences and histories of the learners rather than in the ideas and methods of the planners. This involved selecting a series of communities where literacy programmes were or had been in operation, including urban neighbourhoods, dispersed rural areas and refugee camps. The aim was to illustrate some of the political issues and problems of the continent through specific case-studies, highlighting the impact of popular education on people's daily struggles.

Case-study work began in October 1988 and ended in September 1989. We were helped by people and organizations throughout Latin America, whose generosity cannot be overstated. Living in the communities, we regarded informal meetings, in houses or under the shade of trees, as important as formal interviews with community leaders. The result, we hope, is a book that introduces Latin America as seen by some of its people, as much as it introduces the ideas of literacy and popular education: a work as much of popular education as about it.

Acknowledgements

Field-work/research team
1986: David Archer, Alan Murdoch
1988/9: David Archer, Patrick Costello, Tanika Gupta, Maggie Harvey.

Draft-reading: Dan Baron Cohen, Bella Costello, Tanika Gupta, Nilanjana Sarkar, Thangam Singh, Rachel Stringfellow.

Funding: Christian Aid, Oxfam, Third World First, CAFOD, Inner London Education Authority, Patrick Trust, Harold Buxton Trust.

Support:
Britain: Jaime Baez, Claire Ball, Debbie Bourke, Raff Carmen, Nick Costello, David Dixon, Benjamin Fernandez, Stella Gabriel, Eric Hall, David Hesmondhalgh, Steve Lewis, Mandy Macdonald, Josna Pankhania, Cary Pester, Robin Proctor.
   Mexico: Lucía Gómez, Deborah Eade, Juana Santos, Dr Millan, Padre Antonio, Miguel, the residents of San Miguel Teotongo, CONAMUP, ACNUR, COMAR, Heriberto Lopez, Finn Stepputat, INI, III.
   Guatemala: Herminio, Virgilio, Pedro (and ACUMAM), Ofelia, Dora Vasquez-Ramirez (and family), Fidel Rodas, the people of Cabrican, Guillermo Corado, FGER, IGER, Padre Edgar Mazariegos, Paula Worby, Infopress, Hilda Moran de García, CONALFA, PRONEBI, DAEA.
   Honduras: Rosa-Lila Rodriguez, Doris Hernández, Luciano Barrera, CNTC, the people of San Antonio de Jura, CEDOH, ACNUR, CRS, Adrian Fitzgerald, the refugees of Colomoncagua.
   El Salvador: Jorge Morales, ANDES 21 de Junio, Cesar Picon, UN, CRIPDES, PADECOMSM, PADECOES, the Archdiocese of San Salvador, ADEMUSA, IMU, Padre Ronald Hennessy.
   Nicaragua: Don Arnoldo Penas (and family), the people of Lechecuagos, Julieta (and family), Chilo (and family), Hermana Marguerita, the people of Batahola Norte; the Ministry of Education: Luis Alemán, Victoriano Artiaga, Pascual Ortiz, Juan Bautista Arién, Eduardo Baez; ANDEN, Silvio Vasillo, CNASP, Pauline Jones (NSC), Jane Freeland, Casa Oxford (Leon), Roberto Romero, Plutario Jimi Poveda, Danelia McCoy, Hazel Lau, Lucilla Low, Danilo Salamanca, CIDCA, Mirna Cunningham, Myrna Taylor, Alejandro Torres, Annie Manogue, Comandante Hercules,

Damasio Josef Alfred, Norman Reginald Francis, Charlie San Francis and all the people of Karata.

Ecuador: Elizabeth White, Jose and Pilar Cruzati Ayala (and family), the people of Santa Lucia, Lenny and Cathy Field, CAAP, Rosa María Torres, Carlos Poveda, Dr Alfredo Vera Arrata, Angel Nieto, Victor Eduardo Moreno Rodas, Santiago, Ruth Moya Torres, CEDIME, CIUDAD.

Bolivia: Margarita Callisayo, CDA, Juan Vargas, Suzanna Rance, Xavier Albó, CIPCA, Juan de Dios Yapita, ILCA, Carmen Beatriz Ruiz, CEPROMU, Arturo Moscoso Paredes, SENALEP, COB, CEBIAE.

Chile: Celia Fernandez (and family), Jose Rivero, UNESCO, Francisco Chiodi, Francisco Vio Grossi, CEAAL, Herman Mondaca, PROCESO, Valerio Fuenzalida, María Elena Hermosilla, CENECA, María Eugenia Letelier, TAC, EMA, Coty Silva, MOMUPO, Claudio, Augusto Gongora, Nueva Imagen/Teleanálisis.

France: Arthur Gillete, Jauregui de Ganza (UNESCO Paris).

United States: Emma Torres (UNDP), Ira Shor.

UNITED STATES

GUATEMALA
Pop. 8.6
Lit. 48%
Debt: 3.7

HONDURAS
Pop. 4.8
Lit. 60%
Debt: 3.4

NICARAGUA
Pop. 3.6
Lit. 88%
Debt: 6.5

MEXICO
Pop. 82.7
Lit. 84%
Debt: 120.6

COLOMBIA
Pop. 30.2
Lit. 88%
Debt: 16.1

EL SALVADOR
Pop. 5.1
Lit. 49%
Debt: 1.9

VENEZUELA
Pop. 18.7
Lit. 86%
Debt: 28.9

COSTA RICA
Pop. 2.8
Lit. 92%
Debt: 4.6

PANAMA
Pop. 2.2
Lit. 86%
Debt: 5.7

Santa Lucia •Quito
•Guayaquil

ECUADOR
Pop. 10.2
Lit. 84%
Debt: 10

BRAZIL
Pop. 144.4
Lit. 74%
Debt: 123.4

PERU
Pop. 21.2
Lit. 82%
Debt: 20.1

• La Paz

BOLIVIA
Pop. 6.9
Lit. 64%
Debt: 6

PARAGUAY

CHILE
Pop. 12.7
Lit. 92%
Debt: 22.7

•Santiago

URUGUAY
Pop. 2.9
Lit. 96%
Debt:

ARGENTINA
Pop. 31.9
Lit. 94%
Debt: 58.2

Pop. = Population (in millions) — mid 1988 estimates
   Source: UN Population and Vital Statistics Report (New York 1989)

Lit. = % of 'literate' population
   Source: Situacion Educativa de America Latina y El Caribe
      UNESCO-OREALC (Santiago 1988)

Debt = (US $ billions) — Total Debt 1987
   Source: OECD Financing and External Debt of Developing Countries
      (Paris 1989)

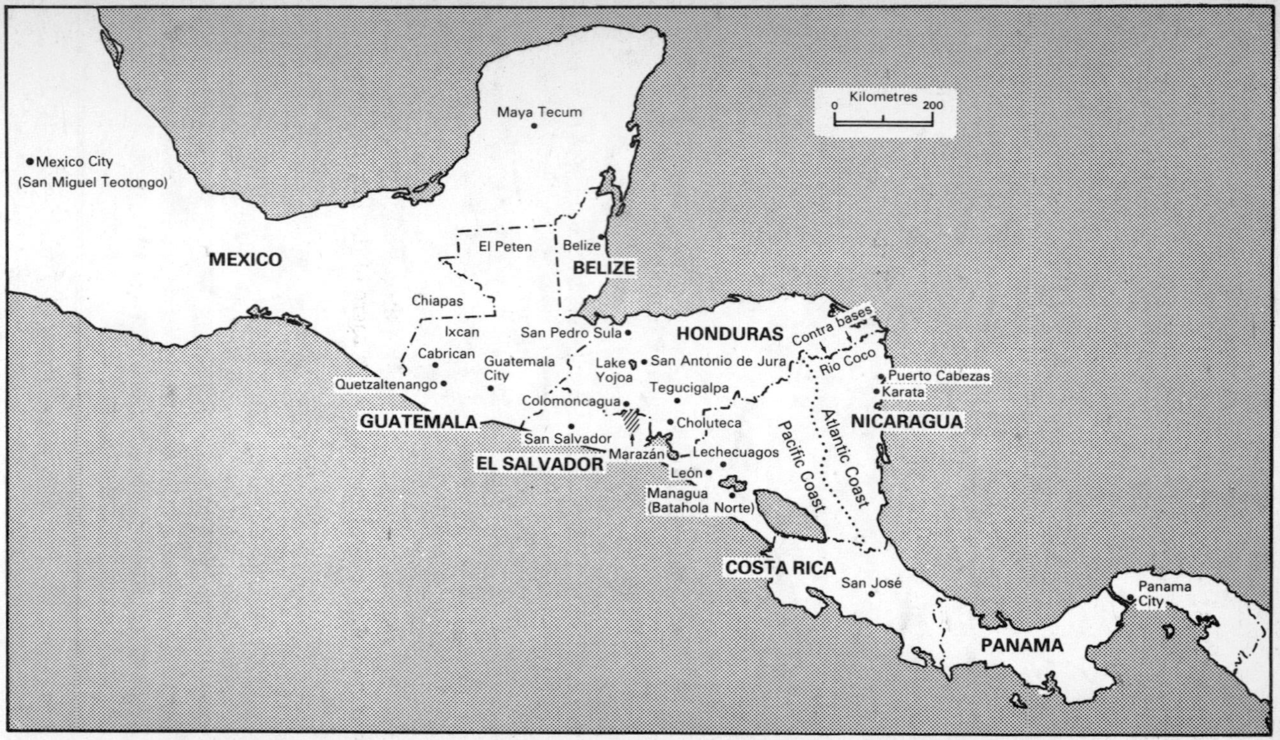
Kilometres
0
200
Mexico City
(San Miguel Teotongo)
Maya Tecum
MEXICO
El Peten
Belize
BELIZE
Chiapas
Ixcan
Cabrican
Quetzaltenango
Guatemala City
GUATEMALA
San Pedro Sula
HONDURAS
Lake Yojoa
San Antonio de Jura
Tegucigalpa
Colomoncagua
Choluteca
San Salvador
EL SALVADOR
Marazán
Lechecuagos
León
Managua
(Batahola Norte)
Contra bases
Rio Coco
Puerto Cabezas
Karata
Pacific Coast
Atlantic Coast
NICARAGUA
COSTA RICA
San José
PANAMA
Panama City

MAP 1

Glossary of Foreign Words

adobe – building material made from earth.

altiplano – plateau, literally "high plain".

barrio – urban neighbourhood, borough.

brigadistas – volunteer literacy teachers from the Nicaraguan and Ecuadorean campaigns.

campesino – peasant person who lives in rural areas. This word is sometimes used with derogatory intent (largely because of urban prejudice that all rural people are backward and ignorant). In Nicaragua the word has been reclaimed. In Bolivia, the Aymaran people prefer to be called *campesino* rather than *indio* (Indian), which is used more abusively.

castellanización – the process of converting Amerindian people to Spanish culture and the Spanish language (which is called *castellano* and not *espanol* in Latin America).

colonia – like *barrio*, a neighbourhood.

conquistador – the Spanish conquerors of the fifteenth and sixteenth century. It is interesting to note that one of the most renowned invaders, Pizarro, who was responsible for the massacre of the Incan empire, was illiterate.

junta – council/cabinet.

ladino – word most widely used in Guatemala to refer to descendants of the Spanish, as a term of abuse. It may be used to refer to people who have adopted "Spanish" or "Western" ways; hence *ladinized* and *ladinization*.

manzana – a measure of land (0.43 hectares), not to be confused with its other meaning (apple).

mestizo – term used in most of Latin America to refer to those people who are of mixed race between Spanish and Amerindian. The word does not carry the same abusive connotation as *ladino*.

popular – popular: but in the sense of "popular culture" rather than "liked by lots of people". The closest translation is probably "of the people", but in Latin American Spanish this is not a cliché.

quinua – high-protein root crop indigenous to the Andes.

Somocista – supporter of the Nicaraguan Somoza family dictatorship: the extremely rich élite of pre-revolutionary society.

I

REVOLUTION: WHAT IS POPULAR EDUCATION?

1. El Salvador, Colomoncagua: Words and bombs

> Through our years of exile we have learnt to read our history with our own eyes.
> *Mercedes (Salvadorean refugee in Colomoncagua camp, Honduras)*

In 1880, the law of extinction of communal lands ended the traditional indigenous way of life in the Central America republic of El Salvador. Those deprived of farmland by the law were forced to work on the big farms owned by the landlords who controlled both the means of production and the political structures of this small but densely-populated country. In this way, the wealth generated by the sale of cash crops – particularly coffee – on the international markets, found its way largely into the hands of 14 families, who have dominated the economy and political structures throughout this century. The boom after World War II provided surplus income for the development of the country, but the projects initiated at that time benefitted only the controlling elite.

> In many cases the projects were planned according to their convenience
> for a friend of the President, or an uncle or the brother of some official
> or a military chief. At no time did government plans take into account the
> opinions of the communities as to what their needs were.[1]

Lack of land forced thousands to migrate to neighbouring Honduras where unused land could be found more easily. In other areas – such as the rocky, mountainous region of Morazan – poor *campesinos* (peasants) grew maize and beans on small plots of poor land. Each year many were forced to supplement their income by migrating to work as day-labourers on the coffee, sugar and cotton harvests. The landless hired parcels of idle land from landlords who were happy to take half the value of the harvest as rent.

It was inequalities such as these, exacerbated by economic crisis in the late 1960s, that were responsible for the rise of popular movements demanding land reform, minimum wages and acceptable living conditions. There were other factors. The 1969 "Football War" with Honduras[2] had forced the Salvadorean settlers back home, increasing the pressure on land and sharpening the need for social change. A new generation of Catholic priests, radicalized by their day-to-day contact with injustice, used the Church to provide an important base for organization as well as the necessary moral justification for new social demands.

During the 1970s *campesino* organizations sprang up. In Morazan, the Christian organization FECCAS (Federation of Salvadorean Christian Campesinos) was an important forum for landless labourers demanding improved salaries and for small farmers seeking financial credit and a lowering of land-rents. There was little response from government, beyond the setting up of a counter-organization in the countryside called ORDEN, the Nationalist Democratic Organization:

> Behind a nationalist and reformist flag it [ORDEN] concealed its only
> reason for existing: a paramilitary body which, emerging from the heart of the
> peasantry, would put an end to the "subversion".[3]

The El Salvadorean constitution prohibits *campesino* organizations. The Church, particularly the Archdiocese in San Salvador, provided a cover for their work. Aware of this, by 1975, landlords were systematically excluding catechists (Catholic lay preachers) from work on the plantations, while members of ORDEN, who were informing on those actively involved in *campesino* movements and in some cases killing them, found jobs available everywhere.

> When the *campesino* can no longer be a *campesino*, he becomes a
> revolutionary. This has happened in El Salvador.[4]

Campesino movements in different parts of the country united and made links with student and urban-worker organizations in the cities. Actions such as land seizures, strikes on plantations and mass demonstrations became more frequent during the 1970s. Alongside these came the development of the armed struggle, initially as a response to ORDEN, but later, as different groups co-ordinated their action, as an integral part of a revolutionary movement. By the late 1970s, the popular movements were threatening to topple the ruling oligarchy. Guerrilla forces launched a "final offensive" in May 1980, confident that victory was in sight. Areas of the country were taken over as well as the poorer neighbourhoods of cities. Later in the year a united front of opposition parties and guerrilla armies was formed, the Farabundo Marti National Liberation Front (FMLN), in preparation for taking power.

The State's response was inhuman, involving a military strategy of selective massacre of the civilian population in areas such as Morazan where the movements were strong. Between 1980 and 1983, over 30,000 *campesinos* were killed.[5] An example is the destruction of El Mosote, a village in Morazan, where over 1,000 people died in one operation. The effects of such a brutal counter-insurgency strategy were extensive. Most immediately, it forced the guerrillas into camps up in the mountains so that, as the government's military campaign continued, the majority of the victims were people who may well have been sympathizers with the aims of the popular movements, or relatives of activists, but who were certainly not guerrillas. Next, it caused a huge displacement of people. Out of six million Salvadoreans, 1.2 million have been forced to move by the war, seeking refuge in other countries or in other regions within El Salvador.[6]

Before considering the plight of those who fled across the border, it is important to put what happened into context. In 1979 the Nicaraguan revolution had sent shockwaves through the US State Department, which feared that events in Nicaragua would act as an example to neighbouring countries, generating a "domino effect" throughout the region. Within the Republican Party, the nineteenth-century Monroe Doctrine – a statement of US refusal to allow any interference in its dealings with the Americas – was revived. Rather than warning off other colonial powers, Reagan's version was aimed at a new external enemy, international communism. Revival of Cold War rhetoric provided a convenient justification for US chauvinism, enabling the smashing of national liberation movements in Latin America which in fact had no contact with Cuba or the USSR.

In practice, the Central American strategy of the new Reagan administration consisted of turning Honduras into the military base and Costa Rica into the diplomatic mouthpiece for US policy (see map 1). Honduras became the base for the Nicaraguan Contras along one border and for control of the counter-insurgency strategy in El Salvador on another. Within Honduras, US military advisers trained Salvadorean, Honduran and Nicaraguan Contra military leaders. Under US influence, the Honduran and Salvadorean governments patched up the enmity that was a legacy of the Football War and signed the Lima Treaty which laid the groundwork for direct co-operation between the two armies in their attacks on the Salvadorean people.

> There exists between the armies of my country and El Salvador a clear
> understanding to confront the forces that threaten the democratic system.
> *Jose García, Honduran Minister of Defence, 16 June 1982*

On 13 May 1980, 250 Honduran soldiers set up stone trenches on one side of the River Sumpul which acts as a frontier between Honduras and El Salvador. The following morning, on the other side of the river, in the Salvadorean villages of San Jacinto and La Aroda, hundreds of Salvadorean National Guard, backed up with troops from the paramilitary ORDEN as well as two helicopters, massacred 600 defenceless people. Those who managed to escape to the river were forced back by the Honduran soldiers to the zone of the massacre, where they were murdered.[7]

People from other villages were more fortunate, but it can be understood why those who survived the journey into Honduras had not escaped the conflict. The Honduran army was collaborating in the massacres and accusing the refugees of being guerrillas. Significantly, the Hondurans had thrown Salvadoreans out of their country only 11 years earlier. The border area was still a disputed one and Honduras had never signed any international agreement on the treatment of refugees.

But for people who fled from the areas of conflict, Honduras was the only alternative.

> They destroyed our homes, our crops and massacred our people. We couldn't live there any more.
> *Mercedes, refugee, aged 25*

The first refugees came from Morazan in 1980. A group of about 600 arrived on 13 December and a further 400 the following day. They were received in the Honduran village of Las Flores, most of them women, children and old men who had been displaced by the violence. All of them had witnessed deaths and tortures.

> I lost my mother and sister. They were shot by the army. We travelled for ten days over the mountains hiding from the army to get here.
> *Trinidad, refugee, aged 30*

Many were suffering from malnutrition and the psychological trauma of their experiences. More groups arrived. Initially they were looked after by the local Honduran farmers who, in spite of the national boundaries, and in sharp contrast to their army, saw the Salvadoreans as their neighbours:

> Before the war, it was easier for us to go to markets and towns in El Salvador than ones in Honduras.
> *Ignacio, Colomoncagua farmer*

By mid-1981, over 18,000 people had crossed the border, nearly 6,000 of them from Morazan. Among them were a group of 100 children who had fled across the mountains, girls of 14 and 15 acting as mothers for the babies, feeding them coffee to replace their dead mothers' milk. With the help of the United Nations High Commission for Refugees (UNHCR), three camps were set up within Honduras, near the border villages of La Virtud, San Antonio and Colomoncagua. The Morazan refugees were settled at Colomoncagua. A road was built from the village to two hot, dusty valleys separated by a hill from which Morazan, only five kilometres away, could be seen. This arrangement suited the Honduran government as it meant that all the refugees from Morazan were in one place and therefore controllable.

Conditions in the camp were basic: families were living in tents and shacks made from empty food sacks. Water was extremely scarce in the semi-desert of the valley. Initial help in the form of food and clothes was provided by CARITAS, a Catholic humanitarian agency. The population was suffering from an ordeal that was still visible and often audible from their new home as the daily aerial bombardment of Morazan continued. There were relatively few adults: over half the refugees were under 15 years old.[8] However, as different aid agencies arrived, the refugees were insistent that they did not want to be treated as helpless or dependent and simply supplied with what they needed. They wanted to learn how to do things themselves.

CREATING A POPULAR EDUCATION

The micro-society of the camp offered possibilities of challenging traditional ways of organizing education. In most societies, formal education is organized in such a manner that at each stage more and more students are forced to drop out. The resulting educational pyramid reinforces the division of labour in society since only a small number of highly educated people form the elite that controls the vast number of less educated workers. In the camp, 50-year-old men, 30-year-old women, 12-year-old girls and 6-year-old boys were all at a similar educational level so it was possible to plan a truly *popular*[9] education that would prevent the emergence of any dominant group.

> We began teaching using charcoal as chalk and doors as blackboards . . . the teachers were the few refugees who were literate.
> *Mercedes, Education Committee*

> There were no schools, classes were in the road.
> *Veronica, CARITAS*

Nine out of ten refugees at Colomoncagua were illiterate.[10] Few had ever had access to education in Morazan where schools were considered a luxury for the privileged. Literacy skills were not valued highly in remote rural communities where they appeared to have little application. Nevertheless, when the first educational advisers arrived from CARITAS in 1981, they found basic education already working in the camp and refugees with a clear idea of what they wanted. The few literate refugees who were organizing the existing classes asked the assessors not to teach people directly. Instead, it was decided that the assessors would train the teachers already working, so that they could be more effective. In addition, CARITAS was asked to supply much-needed materials such as paper and pencils. Classrooms were built in every part of the camp, containing little more than blackboards and rough wooden benches.

At first, the schools set up in Colomoncagua taught only two grades. Although some students were ready to advance to third grade and higher, it was decided that they should not do so until everyone in the camp had completed second grade. More advanced students took on the responsibility of teaching the less advanced. Organized in this way, education took on a collective character.

> In classes, there is no fear of failure, or of not understanding. Really . . .
> there is no competition.
> *Veronica*

The distinction between student and teacher itself began to blur: after all, teachers were not part of a professional elite but shared the same background and experiences as their students. Moreover, the teachers were constantly learning valuable skills in the process of teaching, and the students, many of whom were adults, were often in a position to teach their teachers, many of whom were young.

For popular education to be successful, changes in structure had to be matched by equally radical changes in content. In Morazan, the few who had attended school learnt about a culture that was largely alien:

> We learnt about the city and modern life . . . but we never knew anything
> about it . . . it wasn't part of our reality.
> *Christina, teacher, aged 20*

By contrast, education in the camp took the refugees' own experiences as a starting point. Workbooks were produced which used themes such as agriculture, repression and the problems of life in the camp. But the changes had to go beyond the classroom. Within El Salvador most of the knowledge that was of use to *campesinos* was ignored by schools. Both education and society were based on an artificial elevation of the value of intellectual skills and the depreciation of manual ones. Part of popular education in the camp, then, had to be the development of practical manual skills to go with the new approach in the classroom. In Colomoncagua children – and many adults – spent their mornings in workshops learning different skills and the afternoons in schools developing them.

Just as the refugees didn't want foreign teachers, they also didn't want the agencies to supply and distribute the ready-made articles they needed. Initially, for example, clothes were supplied by CARITAS. Many of the sizes were too big, designed for well-nourished Europeans. It is a short step from adjusting to manufacturing clothing. Soon, the agencies were only supplying materials while refugees manufactured clothes in their own workshops. Over time, workshops were set up for the production of everything in the camp, from the beds people slept in to the toys the children played with, from metal pans and straw hats to violins and double-basses. The workers from Catholic Relief Services (CRS), another international agency, played the role of supplying necessary equipment and sharing their skills and knowledge:

> Last year, a potter arrived from Germany. Before he came, there were no

potter's wheels and all cooking utensils were made by hand. He worked with the Carpentry workshop designing and then manufacturing a wheel and taught a few people how to use it. After six months he left. Now, there are many wheels and everyone knows how to use them.
Veronica

Anything that is left here will be used by the people.
Francisco, CRS worker

In the middle of a rocky semi-desert and within earshot of the bombardment of their homes, the refugees were providing each other with a balanced education, useful to its pupils and intimately related to every aspect of their lives.

THE REPRESSION CONTINUES

To be a refugee between two countries that don't recognize that legal category is unfortunate but to have the added difficulty of being Salvadorean is almost suicide.[11]

The work of refugees and agencies was consistently viewed with suspicion by the Honduran military. Apart from suspecting them of aiding the guerrillas, the camp was a site in which international observers could observe and learn about the human rights violations being practised in the "war against international communism" on the other side of the border. There are countless examples of the violence inflicted on the refugees:

In April 1981, four refugees were captured by Honduran soldiers [in Colomoncagua] . . . Three of them were handed to the Salvadorean army. Their mutilated bodies were found a few days later, near the frontier.[12]

By the end of 1981, refugees were not allowed to travel more than fifty metres beyond the perimeters of the camp, not even to look for water. All agricultural projects were suppressed.

They accuse us of being guerrillas but we are mostly women and children.
Gabriela, refugee, aged 25

While international workers with the agencies had a certain amount of immunity, Honduran workers in the camp were frequently arrested and beaten up, accused of being communists and supporters of guerrillas. In addition the army wouldn't let any foreign workers live in the camp. They wanted no witnesses to their actions.

This treatment was politically motivated. In the village of Colomoncagua was another group of 300 refugees. They were also from Morazan but they had been given houses in the village, and food by the Honduran refugee commission CONARE. They had full freedom of movement and were suffering none of the treatment given to their neighbours in the valley nearby. These people were members of ORDEN, the Salvadorean para-military group responsible for death-squad activity. They had fled from northern Morazan in 1983 when the FMLN took full control over the area. What drove them out, ironically, was not any guerrilla reprisal but indiscriminate aerial bombing by the armed forces.[13]

The main aim of the repression against the Salvadoreans in the camp was to force them to relocate into the interior of Honduras. By moving them, not only could they be controlled more easily by the Honduran military but also there would be fewer witnesses to the co-operation between Honduran and Salvadorean armies in attacking the conflict areas in Morazan. In addition, it would prevent the continued flow of people into Honduras, trapping them in the war zone. At regular intervals since 1980 new refugees had arrived at night, often in large groups. To avoid detection by Honduran military patrols, some had to crawl for hours on their bellies in single file. Unsurprisingly the refugees didn't want to move further from their homes in Morazan.

> The Honduran armed forces don't want more refugees. They are
> accomplices of the events in El Salvador. That's why they want to move the
> camps.
> *Adonaldo, Public Relations Committee*

The refugees of La Virtud, the other big camp on the border, were forced to move. In early 1982, they were transported in cattle trucks to Mesa Grande, 40 kilometres from the frontier. They had been promised better conditions by UNHCR and CONARE, and an end to army harassment. They found that nothing had changed. After 22 deaths and 16 disappearances suffered in the process of moving, they had merely been brought further into a country whose authorities mistrusted them. Refugees continued to disappear: some were tortured, others killed. Later that year, a new move was planned. All the refugees were to be resettled in the east of the country. Once again they were told that conditions would be improved. At Colomoncagua, nearby San Antonio and at the relocated camp at Mesa Grande, there was a unanimous refusal to consider being moved.

> The army would have to kill us all. If they're going to kill us, let them kill us
> here.
> *Blanca, refugee, aged 30*

In 1985 the refugees in Colomoncagua had a visit from US military advisers who were looking at the possibility of establishing a military base on the site of the camp. This was part of a plan to surround the FMLN guerillas in their stronghold in northern Morazan. The site was ideal: it had strategic hills for observation and a convenient infrastructure (including electricity and water supply) that could have been converted into barracks with ease. Recognizing that plans to move the refugees forcibly were failing, the Honduran authorities, under US pressure, started to encourage voluntary repatriation to El Salvador. Once again the people of Colomoncagua refused.

> We will return to our country only when there is peace with justice.
> *Blanca.*

A trickle of people returned to El Salvador in response to army threats to cut off supplies and murder refugees. Then, in May 1985, the army encircled the camp permanently. For a week not even food was allowed through the army blockade. But the most serious attempt by the army to force the refugees to leave was on 29 August of the same year, a day now commemorated in the camp. A group of soldiers entered in a helicopter and captured ten refugees, killing three others and injuring 50 in the process:

> There were only three internationals in the camp that day. The army plan was to take ten leaders but there was so much chaos . . . bullets spraying round the camp . . . women were throwing themselves on the men to stop them being shot at . . . the young kids were unable to dodge the bullets . . . firing was indiscriminate . . . people were walking around with their guts hanging out. I was beaten up because I refused to let them arrest the people around me. A teacher was raped by some soldiers in front of her class of children. They arrested more than ten refugees . . . but their orders were to take only ten so they killed the rest outside the helicopter.
> *Adrian, CRS worker*

Three days later, the army returned. Within five minutes of them being sighted at the top of the hills, 8,000 people started hammering on the corrugated iron roofs of their barrack-like houses. The noise was deafening, a metallic roar echoing around the dusty valley. The soldiers stood on the hills, not knowing how to react, while UNHCR officials warned them that the mood in the camp was vengeful. They waited for the noise to subside but it continued, threatening death to anyone who entered. The sound was so loud that it whipped up the dust and left the camp shrouded in a protective, blinding haze. Fearful, the soldiers turned and left. From that moment an unspoken stalemate was operated. The encirclement remained but the soldiers were more wary of entering.

POPULAR EDUCATION AND RESISTANCE

> Educators are the motors of the camp.
> *Mercedes, Education Committee*

Popular education in the camp was maintained and extended. As the majority of refugees completed other grades, new levels were introduced. By 1988, 85 per cent were literate (the remaining illiterates were those refugees with sight defects) and in the same year a sixth grade of education was introduced. A technical school opened where classes in art, music and more advanced engineering were held. The written word had a big impact on all aspects of life in the camp. A library, set up by a refugee who was a librarian in her home town in Morazan, expanded with the aid of donations by visitors. The books were much read, particularly those on Salvadorean history. A small printing press was in operation producing regular newsletters for the sub-camps, as well as for the other camps in Honduras and for international news releases. Song-books were also printed, based on the work of the different music groups in the camp.

The written word was not the only means of communication in the camp. In the evenings, refugees listened to the FMLN radio, broadcast clandestinely from Morazan,[14] or watched the Salvadorean government news on an old black-and-white television around which people gathered in the open air. A gift of a video camera and projector meant that a film-making workshop could make films on different aspects of life at the camp. All visitors were interviewed. The films were shown at different times on screens in different parts of the camp to keep everyone informed.

In order to resist the attacks they were subject to, the refugees needed to be well organized. As the population became literate, they were able to participate in a complex web of committees. The camp was divided into nine sub-camps. Each sub-camp was divided into *colonias* of about 250 people. Each *colonia* elected representatives for housing, health, sanitation, children and food. These people were responsible for determining the needs of the *colonia*, on the basis of which production of clothing, furniture, pots and pans, hats and other things was organized. In addition, they elected sub-camp committees who in turn elected committees at the level of the whole camp. Alongside this formal structure other organizations were formed, including women's committees, youth groups, discipline groups (a problem with over 5,000 children in the camp), night patrols and committees to clean the latrines.

> The forms are always changing, but the process goes on. We are an assisted community but we have to work to make things. Nothing comes ready made. Everything depends on our work.
> *Virgilio, Education Committee*

Literacy was vital in all aspects of the working of these organizations, from the recording of minutes to the distribution of notices, from the running of store-rooms to the keeping of accounts.

Before arriving in the camp, the illiteracy rate amongst women was higher than that amongst men. Fewer women participated in village organizations. The burdens of domestic work and childcare left them with little time and therefore they were largely isolated from the social environment where literacy was relevant. In Colomoncagua, the equal involvement of men and women in popular education had a profound effect on these traditional roles. Women were in the majority on most of the committees. In the mechanics workshop, the manager and most of the participants were women. In one literacy class a 12-year-old girl in second-grade primary school was teaching the first written syllables to a group of mainly over-60s, who had just received glasses. This was not atypical.

As participation of women became the norm, domestic roles were challenged everywhere in the camp. Many tasks became social rather than individual responsibilities as women made their presence felt in public spheres. For example, the bringing up of children in Colomoncagua was largely collective with the availability of crèche facilities, *colonia* discipline committees and, of course, popular education itself which involved children in every activity in the camp. *Tortillas*, the maize pancakes that form the basis of all Central American diets, were made in a workshop rather than within the confines of each home. Although no men worked in the *tortilla* workshop, their creation was still a significant advance as it allowed many women to overcome the fear of the world beyond the home which they otherwise may have felt. In the small wooden huts where families lived, women were more often than not the head of the household. Some were single parents, but many others were living with men in informal "marriages" recognized by the community.

In a community where everyone was participating, and where everyone had attained a basic level of education, any attempt at repression came up against unified resistance. Selective kidnapping, torture and murder did nothing to weaken the resolve of the refugees to stay in Colomoncagua. If the majority had been illiterate then the removal of a few key leaders might have been enough to destroy the resistance of the camp but, as a population learning together, the refugees were not dependent on a handful of leaders. Nor were they dependent on any outsiders, as the teachers were themselves refugees. CARITAS assessors were there to provide a more general support and guidance. In 1989, for instance, they started giving training to teachers in the socio-economic problems of Central America, teaching methods and the philosophy of education.

> Really, we are not necessary . . . after this new project we won't be necessary at all. The plan is to train for self-sufficiency. If we all left now, they'd continue, though more slowly.
> *Tony, Caritas assessor*

The Honduran refugee commission, CONARE, was opposed to the popular-education programmes within the camp precisely because of the unity that they engendered. Even the United Nations Commission (UNHCR) was cautious, wanting to build a specialized school in the camp in order to train a few refugees as professional teachers who could then teach the rest. At another time they suggested sending a select group of refugees to Honduran schools in Tegucigalpa, and then to university, so that they could return to take charge of administration in the camp. CONARE took a different approach. In 1987, Colonel Turcios, its director, presented a plan to introduce 100 Honduran teachers to take over education in the camp. For the refugees, such plans were unacceptable: the camp would have lost its self-sufficiency.

> We said no, because we want teachers from our own community.
> *Mercedes, Education Committee*

The refugees feared that Honduran teachers would have encouraged integration into a different society. The children would have been taught with Honduran books and El Salvador would have become a parent's tale and an occasional memory for many of the young. CONARE were willing to deprive local Honduran communities of teachers, in the interests of breaking up popular education in the camp. They were even prepared to use violence:

> CONARE wanted to control the refugees. In 1987, the military were
> entering classes and threatening our teachers.
> *Virgilio, Education Committee*

Education in the camp, which promoted the equality of men and women, collective action and the unity to resist the concerted oppression of two armies, was also geared towards a return to Morazan. Knowledge developed through popular education could make a major contribution to the restructuring of their country. In this respect, building, cobbling, carpentry, clothes-making, electrical techniques and mechanical skill in general were as vital as musical, artistic, printing and administrative ones.

POPULAR EDUCATION WITHIN EL SALVADOR

From 1984, there were no representatives of state or army in the FMLN-controlled area of Northern Morazan. Aerial bombardment became a part of daily life. Even at night, flares were dropped by incoming bombers to light up the target areas. Schools were among the first buildings hit because of the visibility of their white roofs. An army encirclement prevented food, medical supplies or anything that could be used by guerrillas from entering the area. Even the Red Cross was prevented from entering for a while. The population, before the war over 100,000, declined through death and the escape of people to other countries, to an estimated 25,000.[15] As in Colomoncagua, however, the response was anything but passive. The villages set up local committees that took on responsibility for education, preventive health care (in the absence of medicines) and general administration. By constructing new communal organizations, they were able to train 60 literacy teachers and construct new schools.[16]

Elsewhere in the country, where the army had more of a foothold, a new strategy was developed, under the influence of US military advisers. The aim was to cover up the violations of human rights in areas of conflict in order to give an appearance of democracy and to legitimize the social-democratic Duarte government. In this way, Democrats in the US Congress would not object to the one million dollars a day needed to prop up the regime.[17] Death squad activity and massacres were largely replaced by "low-intensity" conflict, consisting of aerial bombing of crops suspected of being used to feed the guerrillas, coupled with "hearts and minds" campaigns in the villages.

> The plans implied that the people were stupid. The army arrived in villages
> . . . organized parties for children and meetings to discuss problems. The
> next day, the same people would be bombing us in helicopters.
> *Luis, Morazan resident*

In practice this did little to improve conditions in rural areas or regain people's confidence in the government. Those people displaced from the rural areas by the war remained in the towns in spite of appalling conditions. The following quote gives part of the history of a group of people from all over the country who fled to the capital, San Salvador, and who were living in makeshift housing on the outskirts of the city:

> After the earthquake [1986] we had to abandon our old shacks and we settled
> in the "Gardens of Remembrance" cemetery for twenty days. Then the army
> arrived and threw us off; we lived for a month in the green belt by the side
> of the motorway. There we formed a directive to look for a place to settle.
> Eventually we constructed new homes on a rubbish tip which we cleared.
> Now, we have a collective kitchen, we have installed running water and we
> are making a mural.
> *Community "October 10th"*

Communities like "October 10th" faced continual harassment by the army. Planes were used to intimidate residents by flying low overhead. The state deprived them of electricity, running water, drainage, health and education:

> Here illiteracy is part of the violation of human rights because the
> government cynically denies access to education.
> *CRIPDES worker*[18]

Illiteracy, officially 51 per cent, is actually closer to 75 per cent, and higher in rural areas.[19] While 3,500 teachers are unemployed, a million and a half children don't receive any schooling. Even state schools charge matriculation fees so many unemployed parents can't afford education for their children. Corruption is rife: in 1987, Buendia Flores, then Minister of Education, used construction materials for a school damaged by the earthquake to build his private home. There was no enquiry. The money from many government education programmes is used to finance the war or election campaigns. One widowed mother in "October 10th" jokingly showed us an exercise book given to her child at school with a picture on the front cover urging people to vote for the Christian Democrat presidential candidate in the 1989 elections, and said that it was the first time any of the children had received anything from the school.

Given the deficiencies in the state education system, many groups have taken the initiative in developing popular-education materials. The teachers' union ANDES (National Association of Salvadorean Educators) produce a literacy primer every year, with technical help from the university. ANDES's work is essential in the face of the government's failure to educate people,

> Fifty per cent of the national budget finances the war.
> *Jorge Morales, General Secretary ANDES*

Other groups are also active. The women's groups ADEMUSA and IMU[20] work with the women of communities such as "October 10th" organizing workshops on, for example, their role in the struggle for services. The Archdiocese of the Catholic Church in San Salvador has organized a radio-literacy programme for rural areas and the Lutheran Church is involved in the training of "popular teachers" and the preparation of educational materials for *campesinos*.

However, popular education groups are perceived as a threat by the Salvadorean state rather than as an independent initiative to fulfil an urgent need. Accused by the government of being guerrillas, many teachers have been killed by the army.

> There is a problem of security. If it has the name ANDES on the primer, it becomes a subversive document, so people get kidnapped . . . not because they have guns but because they have our primers. We are seen as subversive because we teach the people what to do when they hear the helicopters coming to bomb the community. Since 1980, 375 teachers have been killed and 97 have disappeared.
> *Jorge Morales*

ANDES was forced to move its offices 14 times in 18 months because of death-squad threats and police raids. In November 1988, a bomb was set off in the offices of the Lutheran church in San Salvador. Popular-education workers would not be military targets in El Salvador if the content of their education was not considered by the army to be an important "subversive" element.

The neglect of the urban and rural poor by the state education system and the work of popular-education groups in communities like "October 10th" have ensured a permanent source of support for the opposition movements. In the capital, bombs and machine-gun fire could be heard in the streets every night in the run-up to the 1989 elections. Each morning new graffiti appeared on walls that were already covered:

> The paint in the streets is the way the people educate themselves. This is part of education too.
> *CRIPDES worker*

In 1989, in the midst of this polarization, the United Nations was attempting to create a concerted approach to literacy teaching by "tolerating ideological pluralism" and forming a network of government and non-governmental groups to tackle the "technical" problem of illiteracy. They had some initial success in involving the Archdiocese in discussions with the Ministry of Education. However, the other groups were unacceptable to the government, and none of them participated in the network. In late 1989, this strategy encountered further difficulties:

> The UN office building in San Salvador was used by guerrilla snipers when rebels occupied the wealthy Escalon district. . . . Afterwards, soldiers entered the UN offices and smashed equipment, prompting the UN to pull its staff out of El Salvador and set up provisional offices in Guatemala. President Cristiani asked the UN to return and sent a delegation to Guatemala to offer assurances. But the soldiers ransacked the UN offices again, raising the question of who rules in El Salvador, the President or the military.
> The Independent, *12 December 1989*

In the refugee camp, the system of popular education was at odds with the education that CONARE wanted to introduce. Equally, within El Salvador, the work of popular education groups is in opposition to the education of the state. The UN's attempt to promote a dialogue between educators with different political goals itself involves taking a political position: one that detaches education from its social context. The reaction of the army shows how difficult, if not impossible, it is to develop plans that attempt to bypass the conflict. Dialogue between educational groups is only possible to the extent that it is possible between the two sides in the war.

> Educational practice and its theory cannot be neutral.
> *Paulo Freire*[21]

THE FUTURE

The United Nations' difficulties in creating a dialogue are a symptom of a much deeper political and military crisis. After ten years of war, the United States – in spite of supporting the government with over a million dollars a day – has failed to impose "democracy". In the 1989 elections, only 17 per cent of Salvadoreans eligible to vote,[22] voted for ARENA whose founder and controlling force, Major Robert D'Aubuisson, is widely known as the man behind the death squads that murdered Archbishop Romero in 1980.[23] Yet ARENA is now ruling the country with an absolute majority. This creates a dilemma for US policy makers. By continuing to support the government, they will be under pressure from Congress and human rights groups for supporting a regime with an ideology that has supported mass murder and shows no sign of changing. On the other hand if they withdraw their support, they risk losing El Salvador to the so-called international communists. The army is reaching straining point. Forcibly recruiting from poor *barrios* like "October 10th" they inevitably end up with FMLN sympathizers within their barracks.

> If US aid were withdrawn, the FMLN would win in a matter of weeks.[24]
> *CRIPDES worker*

The Honduran army are now building a series of bases along the Salvadorean frontier. At the same time the US are funding a new airport in the Honduran town of Choluteca, strategically located between El Salvador and Nicaragua. It is as though they are preparing for the blockade of an El Salvador freed from the rule of the 14 families. For although the US managed to buy their brand of "democracy" for neighbouring Nicaragua, El Salvador is closer to ruling itself than ever before. Faced with foreign policy priorities in Panama, Mexico and Cuba, the Bush administration will be forced to recognize the failure of Reagan's strategy in El Salvador. As in Vietnam, all that remains is the impossible task of pulling out with dignity.[25]

In August 1989 the refugees at Colomoncagua made the dramatic decision to return to El Salvador, regardless of FMLN victory or a negotiated settlement to the war. Returning to their homelands in Morazan, they will be crucial to the rebuilding of their country.

> When we return, there will be 8,000 new teachers for our country.
> *Virgilio*
> What we are learning here, we can share with the people when we return. We can contribute to the organization of a peaceful El Salvador.
> *Mercedes*

At the start of the new decade, the returning refugees were planning a literacy programme for the inhabitants of Morazan. They believe that the organization that they have set up is the nucleus for a new kind of society in El Salvador. Some would call it socialist, others would say that it was a return to the communal lifestyle that existed before the arrival of the Spanish *conquistadors*. What is clear is that popular education has been at the heart of its development.

NOTES

1.   Introductory communication of PADECOES, the Organization for Communal Development in El Salvador, January 1989.

2.   A war apparently started by a World Cup qualifier between the countries. For more details see page 60.

3.   Cabarrus S J, Carlos R., "El Salvador: de Movimiento Campesino a Revolucion Popular", in *Movimientos Populares en Centroamerica* (San Jose: UNU/IISUNAM/FLACSO 1985).

4.   Cabarrus S J, Carlos R., op. cit.

5.   Camarda, Renato, *Traslado Forzado* (1987), p.13.

6. UNHCR figures: 500,000 to US, 400,000 internally displaced and 300,000 to other countries.

7. Account adapted from *Traslado Forzado*, op. cit.

8. UNHCR figures: 61 per cent aged 0–14, 31 per cent aged 15–54, 8 per cent older than 54.

9. The Spanish word *popular* is not equivalent to any English word. The closest translation is "of the people". Hence, popular movements, referring to those organizations of workers, peasants, women, indigenous groups; and popular education, referring to education "for the people".

10. By illiteracy, what is referred to is absolute illiteracy, the inability even to sign one's own name. The issue of what it means to be literate is explored throughout the book. For the purposes of this chapter, the self-definition of literate refugees was accepted, though in our opinion there is no clear line between literacy and illiteracy.

11. CEDOH, *Los Refugiados Salvadorenos en Honduras* (Tegucigalpa: CEDOH, 1987) p.18

12. *Traslado Forzado*, op. cit.

13. The Salvadoreans at Colomoncagua were a pawn in a much bigger counter-insurgency strategy being organized from Honduras. In the refugee camps on Honduras's southern border whole villages were displaced to make room for Nicaraguans fleeing the war on the Atlantic Coast. Not only were these refugees living off the land with no restrictions on their movements, they were also being encouraged to join US-backed guerrilla forces to destabilize the Nicaraguan government. These camps were supplying food, medical supplies and future fighters to the nearby Contra bases.

14. "The transmitter was thought to have been discovered once by the Salvadorean army. Top military were flown in to take the prized discovery back to the capital. On the plane home, the 'transmitter' blew up, a decoy to trap the military. Normal service on Radio Venceremos was resumed that evening." Francisco (CRS).

15. PADECOES (Society for Communal Development in El Salvador), introductory communication, January 1989.

16. PADECOES, ibid.

17. US aid to El Salvador 1981–9: $3,485 million. In 1987 alone: $572 million. (Source: "America's Watch" 13 July 1989, from USAID congressional presentation documents; USAID itself; Western Hemispheric Affairs Sub-Committee; and the Defence Security Assistance Agency).

18. CRIPDES is the committee for the repatriated refugees and the displaced, responsible for charting human rights violations. Two months after ARENA's victory in the March 1989 elections, 60 workers at CRIPDES were arrested during an army raid on the offices.

19. Figures from ANDES, the Salvadorean teachers' union.

20. Association of Salvadorean Women, and the Women's Institute.

21. Freire, Paulo, *The Politics of Education* (London: Macmillan 1985), Chapter 2.

22. Eligible voting population estimated at three million, not including those outside the country.

23. Archbishop Romero is the most important symbol of the struggle in El Salvador. As an outspoken critic of the regime, he was murdered while giving mass, an event which brought international attention to the brutality of the

repression in the country. Human rights groups throughout the world universally name D'Aubuisson as the man behind the murder. He was not brought to trial because his contacts with the army protected him.

24.   This happened in Nicaragua in 1979. President Somoza, as he was about to flee the country, blamed the international community for abandoning him by refusing him the military aid he needed to defeat the Sandinista guerrillas.

25.   See for example *Santa Fe 2*, a Republican Party think-tank document published in 1988 as a guideline to President Bush's foreign policy in Latin America.

2. Nicaragua, Lechecuagos: Literacy as a Political Crusade

German Pomares and I were training a group of peasants, teaching them
how to use a Garand, an M1 Carbine, an M3 machine gun and a 45 revolver,
when Carlos Fonseca came along and said . . . "And also teach them to
read".
Tomas Borge, Commandante of the Revolution

Literacy was an issue in Nicaragua long before the renowned National
Literacy Crusade of 1980. In their manifesto of 1969 the guerrillas of the
Sandinista National Liberation Front (FSLN) [1] promised that after the
revolution they would organise a "massive campaign to eradicate illiteracy
immediately". In their clandestine political work with *campesinos* in small
villages, improvised literacy classes played an important role. Anastasio
Somoza, the last in a 41-year family line of dictatorships, also found a use
for literacy. In 1977 he launched a "literacy programme" in the remote area
of Waslala which had become a stronghold for the Sandinista guerrillas.
However, the 108 literacy teachers who were sent to the region were really
security agents, who spent their time identifying guerrilla sympathizers. A
number of brutal *campesino* massacres ensued and unsurprisingly not a
single person is reported to have learnt to read and write.

In the words of the Nicaraguan nun and Sandinista literacy co-ordinator
Sister Josefina: "In the past the system supported and was supported by
illiteracy." Somoza, his family and friends owned the majority of the good
farming land in Nicaragua. For them widespread illiteracy was a positive
advantage.

Illiteracy in 1979 was not an educational fact so much as a political
fact, because the country's regime, the relations of production and the
socio-economic situation didn't require literate people.
Juan Bautista Arién[2]

For three months each year, the large *Somocista* farms needed an unskilled
labour force, which was poorly paid, hired and fired at will, and left
unemployed and landless for the remaining nine months. The written
word was unnecessary for the work. Literate *campesinos* were a threat to
the landowners because they would then be more likely to understand
their condition. Illiteracy was associated with a culture of silence and
a lack of protest. Education in Nicaragua was designed for the urban

middle-classes. Only six per cent of rural children finished primary school. Over 75 per cent of *campesinos* were illiterate.[3]

Conditions were typical in Lechecuagos, a dispersed rural area on the dusty volcanic plains of the Pacific coast (see map 1). Half the population owned small parcels of land but were dependent on the *Somocistas*, who owned most of the land, for credit to buy seeds and fertilizers. If their harvests failed they lost the little they owned. The other half of the population was already landless and was forced to seek work on the large cotton plantations of the *Somocistas*. Work was only available a few weeks each year, planting, weeding and harvesting, with no tools other than a machete. A few were given the job of spraying pesticides but with no advice on safety precautions and unable to read instructions for themselves, they often suffered serious illnesses. In the absence of any health centre their only – improvised – precaution was to save up to buy and drink a litre of milk before going spraying.

There were only three small ramshackle primary schools, little more than roofs, to serve the population of 10,000. These taught only up to fourth grade.[4]

> The school-books were all imported from the United States. They were
> in Spanish but they didn't make any sense to us.
> *Arnoldo, carpenter, Lechecuagos*

Teachers came from the city of Leon which was only 15 kilometres away, but transport was so poor along the dusty tracks that only horses or oxen and carts could find easy access. As a result teachers rarely appeared more than three days a week. When they did turn up they were not popular:

> In the past teachers were seen as punishers, outsiders, interferers.
> *Arnoldo*

Many parents could not send their children to school: once they were seven or eight years old they were needed to help with work in the fields and in the home. This suited local *Somocistas*. Without education the *campesinos* were divided. In Lechecuagos there was no social, political, community or trade union organization at all, except for an organization concerned with law and order run by Somoza's feared National Guard, who had a small barracks by the church.

Lechecuagos was strategically useful to the Sandinistas because it was near to Leon, which is Nicaragua's second city.

> In the late seventies the FSLN worked house to house in Lechecuagos
> getting sympathizers, collaborators and safe-houses.
> *Sister Josefina, Lechecuagos*

Most of the *campesinos* in Lechecuagos were not politically active at the time and had little understanding of the Sandinistas' struggle. They did, however, have weapons:

> People had guns to protect themselves. In practice the guns were more
> often used in macho behaviour at festivals or for solving family feuds. In 1978
> the Sandinistas went door to door and collected these arms, by force,
> saying that they were needed for the revolutionary struggle.
> *Arnoldo*

Campesinos resented losing their guns for a cause they did not understand
and the ill feelings grew when the National Guard started accusing them
of being guerrilla sympathizers. Several people were arrested. Matters came
to a head during June and July of 1979 when the National Guard sealed
off the only road, their life-line to the markets in Leon. As the only
available crop (cotton) was inedible, food supplies ran low very quickly.
People survived on wild fruits, particularly mangoes which according to
one resident, "lay so thick on the ground around people's houses that even
the pigs got sick of them".

Leon had been sealed off because the insurrection was in process.
Historically a liberal city in opposition to conservative Granada it was
the first city to be liberated by the guerrillas. Because of their isolation
the *campesinos* in Lechecuagos did not know what was happening until the
Sandinistas opened up the road and news of the victory spread. To these
people, who had played little or no part in the fight, the revolution was not
easily understood. Its main feature was the disappearance of the *Somocista*
landowners, who had fled the country. What would happen to their land,
and what other changes the revolution would bring, was by no means clear.

> There was a spirit of triumphalism and an atmosphere of confusion.
> *Arnoldo*

A SECOND REVOLUTION

> The Nicaraguan revolution is unique. From the start it was committed
> to political pluralism, unlike Mexico; a mixed economy, unlike Cuba; and
> religious freedom, unlike the Soviet Union.
> *Arnoldo*

While the Sandinistas had strong support in certain areas where Somoza's
dictatorship had been felt most harshly, they inherited a country with many
places like Lechecuagos, where there was only a minimal comprehension
of what had happened. The horizons of people's worlds often went little
beyond the boundaries of their village and their next meal. Having found
themselves unexpectedly in power (the revolution was a surprise: most
people expected the guerrillas in El Salvador to take power before the
FSLN in Nicaragua), the Sandinistas were faced with the urgent tasks
of communicating what the revolution meant and integrating people into
its process. They soon decided that a literacy campaign was the highest
priority – a second revolution, through which the huge energy that had
been generated could be channelled into consolidating a new Nicaragua.

Within two weeks of the triumph Fernando Cardenal was named co-ordinator of a National Literacy Crusade. As a Jesuit, he was one of three radical Christian priests prominent in the Sandinista leadership.

> When I started the literacy Crusade I had never taught anyone to read,
> nor had I ever received any course in literacy, not even a weekend course.
> *Fernando Cardenal*[5]

This was unimportant. The crusade was to be an experiment in popular education on the scale of a whole country. The priorities were clear from the start:

> This is not an educational event with political implications but a political
> event with educational implications.
> *Fernando Cardenal*[6]

The thinking behind the crusade started from a recognition of the political nature of literacy.

> There is no such thing as neutral education. Our people will learn
> to read by means of a process of conscientization and politicisation.
> *Fernando Cardenal*[7]

A strategy appropriate to the Nicaraguan reality was developed following investigation of past revolutionary experiences and the smaller-scale projects of popular education elsewhere in Latin America. Paulo Freire, whose work transformed the teaching of literacy on the continent, flew into the capital, Managua, for consultations with the Ministry of Education.

> One of the tragic mistakes of some Socialist societies is their failure
> to transcend in a profound sense the domesticating character of bourgeois
> education, an inheritance that amounts to Stalinism.
> *Paulo Freire*[8]

Freire's work challenged the idea that knowledge, whether of mathematical tables or the history of a revolution, can be taught as though it consists of packages to be fed to students who, by memorizing the information, magically acquire the attribute of being educated. For Freire this view of knowledge is responsible for transforming education into a business transaction:

> Education thus become an act of depositing, in which students are the
> depositaries and the teacher is the depositor. . . . This is the banking concept
> of education, in which the scope of action allowed to the students extends
> only as far as receiving, filing and storing the deposits.
> *Paulo Freire*

For Freire it is not enough to change the content of an education for it to be revolutionary, it is necessary to change the very structure of teaching. Popular education requires that the knowledge it produces is one developed *between* teacher and students, in relation to a lived reality.

A text or literacy primer based on the Nicaraguan revolution could not simply be a description of the new reality which students memorized. Nor could the process of learning to read be reduced to the rote learning of the alphabet. The aim of the crusade was not to dictate the aims of the revolution or to transfer the techniques of literacy. Rather, through a "problem-posing" text, the idea was to promote creative participation in the revolution via creative use of the written word. In adult literacy, mastering oral and written language constitutes one dimension of the process of being expressive. Another dimension involves enabling people to "read" their reality and "write" their own history.

> Rather than follow typical routines, the "reading classes" should be actual reading seminars with constant opportunity to establish the relation between a passage of text under discussion and various aspects of the world.
> *Paulo Freire*[9]

Central to the development of a truly problem-posing education is dialogue. The object of knowledge (the relevant part of the text and its relations to the world) is to be understood through dialogue between students and teachers. This, in turn, requires a text that problematizes reality. Any effective problematization must avoid being deliberately obtuse like a puzzle, or too explicit like a piece of propaganda, but rather ensure that knowledge is developed by both teacher and students in the process of de-coding the text.

A literacy primer was produced, called *El Amanacer del Pueblo* (The Dawn of the People). With this book the process of learning to read and write was to be linked to the development of dialogue through the use of images and "generative words". The images[10] were mostly photographs drawn from the recent revolutionary struggle and the daily realities of the Nicaraguan people. They could be easily recognized and used to stimulate an initial dialogue. Through a study of the images, and subsequently the words, and the relations of both to the reality of the learners, the educational and political dimensions of the crusade were fused. The words used were "generative" both in generating new words to be read and generating dialogue.

One lesson for example, has two photographs, one of a *campesino* ploughing a field with oxen, the other of a factory worker at a machine. The generative word is *TRABAJO* (work). By relating this word to the image, reflections on what it is to work and the relative status of urban and rural work can emerge. The discussion is then focused by placing the word within a phrase, in this case, "with our WORK we consolidate the revolution". Discussion is thus extended to include the role of all types of labour in the new Nicaraguan society. The next stage in this lesson involves breaking down the generative word into its component syllables. The regularity of Spanish, in which words are written largely as they are pronounced, means that through this process people can learn the building blocks of written language. So, the word *TRABAJO* is split into "TRA" "BA" and "JO". Each syllable is then presented with alternating vowels, for example "BA", "BE", "BI", "BO", "BU". In time the participants are able to create their own words and sentences out of different syllables. After only one lesson the participants can write their own words, like *BEBE* (baby), simply by recognizing the sounds and re-arranging the syllables that they have learnt.

> In our educational method, the word is not something static or disconnected from [people's] existential experience, but a dimension of their thought language about the world. That is why when they participate critically in analysing the first generative words linked with their existential experience, when they focus on the syllabic families that result from that analysis, when they perceive the mechanisms of the syllabic combinations of their language, the learners finally discover, in the various possibilities of combination, their own words. Little by little, as these possibilities multiply, the learners, through mastery of new generative words, expand both their vocabulary and their capacity for expression by the development of their creative imagination.
> *Paulo Freire*[11]

MOBILIZATION

When the mobilization began, these intricacies of method were probably the last thing on the minds of the 52,180 literacy *brigadistas*, who had joined the People's Literacy Army. They were joining a freedom struggle, a fight for cultural liberation. They had sworn pledges to take their "weapons" – pencils and books – to the remotest parts of the country, and so participate in the second revolution. A national literacy census (carried out house-to-house by Sandinista volunteers) had revealed an average of over 50 per cent illiteracy: the enemy was indeed everywhere. Echoes of the guerrilla struggle abounded. The brigades were organized into six fronts which reflected those used by the Sandinistas in the final insurrection. Each column of 120 *brigadistas* was divided into four squadrons of 30, all named after battles or martyrs of the revolution.

Most of the *brigadistas* were secondary-school students from the towns who were largely middle class and accustomed to some level of comfort. They had volunteered to leave their homes and families for the first time, to go and live in a rural area for five months where they would find no electricity, no running water, a very basic diet and a way of life that was completely unknown to them.

It is not the sort of sacrifice that can easily be imagined. Young people volunteered with enthusiasm on a wave of revolutionary euphoria. Television, radio and newspapers took up the cause and the spirit of the crusade and followed the mobilization each day in great detail.

> The training was chaotic. One moment we would be learning about first aid, the next, how to teach literacy; then we would be given a vaccination

2. Leamos la oración:

Con nuestro trabajo consciente consolidamos la Revolución.

3. Leamos la palabra:

trabajo

4. Leamos las silabas que forman la palabra:

tra **ba** jo

5. Leamos las silabas:

ba   bo   bu   be   bi

Ba   Bo   Bu   Be   Bi

6. Leamos:

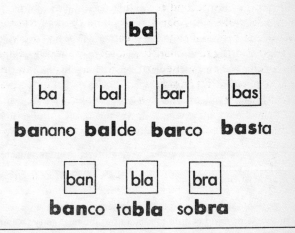

Figure 2.1: Trabajo ("work") – a page from a literacy primer, *The Dawn of the People*. Spanish is written as it sounds, so by learning syllables, people learn the building blocks of written language.

followed by advice on life in rural areas or suggestions for how to
start up a dialogue.
Brigadista Rosa

Preparing the literacy army was a vast task. The training specifically
for literacy was difficult in a country where only a handful of people
understood the new methods. The Ministry of Education started by
organizing a two-week course for 80 trainers who each took on the
training of a further seven people so that 560 people were familiar with
the new approach. These in turn taught others, who taught others, so
that by a multiplying effect almost 100,000 ended up with basic training
for the crusade. Beyond the literacy army for rural areas there were
also urban literacy "militias". All the *brigadistas* who received this short
course were also given a guide-book which was the key to consolidating
what they had learnt. As well as explaining the methodological steps the
guide elaborated on the themes contained in *The Dawn of the People*
primer so that *brigadistas* would be able to speak with some confidence and
accuracy.

THE CRUSADE IN LECHECUAGOS

On 24 March 1980 5,200 *brigadistas* were mobilised for the Leon region.
Thirty-six of them arrived in Lechecuagos – crammed into a single open-
backed truck and hanging off at all angles on the torturously slow and
bumpy journey. One by one they were deposited in basic wooden houses
with families whom they had never met before. Most of the *brigadistas*
were fourth or fifth grade secondary-school students (usually between
14 and 18 years old) from the college in Leon run by the Sisters of the
Ascension. There were also a few Cuban teachers who had volunteered
in solidarity. Because of their experience, they were allocated the most
inaccessible sectors of Lechecuagos where teaching was expected to be
more demanding.

It took a long time for most *brigadistas* to adjust to their new environment.
In the mornings they went out into the fields to help pick the last of the
cotton harvest, or clear the land to prepare it for planting yucca.

Within half an hour my hands were blistered from the machete, so
that for a couple of days it hurt even to hold a pen.
Brigadista Francisco

I tried to do everything that they did, but I couldn't. I was slow
in the fields and I couldn't even control the oxen to get water from the
well.
Brigadista Antonio

The *brigadistas* learnt very quickly that the *campesinos* were not ignorant.
In their own world the *campesinos* were highly educated . . . they were

experts . . . and in that world it was the *brigadistas* themselves who were
illiterate.
Co-ordinator Jorge

From 2 p.m. to 6 p.m. the situation was reversed. The *brigadistas*
co-ordinated the Collectives of Popular Education: groups of between
six and ten *campesinos*, usually composed of members from three or four
neighbouring families. They met sometimes in houses, but more often than
not beneath the shade of trees, sitting on logs or in the hot dust. It was not
easy:

> At first I felt ashamed in front of a group of adults . . . and they
> felt ashamed in front of me.
> *Brigadista Rosa*

> I was accustomed to timetables, but in the *campo* life was never that
> fixed. None of the *campesinos* had watches. They would turn up when they
> were ready, no earlier.
> *Brigadista Antonio*

The pressures of work were so great many *campesinos* turned up at lessons
exhausted, with little enthusiasm to learn. To avoid people dropping out
some classes were transferred to the early evening so lamps were necessary,
though it took a long time for them to arrive from Leon. But lamps brought
their own problems:

> The light would attract mosquitoes and children from all around, attracted by
> the unusual brightness; being bitten and having noisy games next to the class
> made it hard to concentrate.
> *Brigadista María*

Local resistance to schooling was a challenge to the *brigadistas*. *Campesinos*
who participated were sometimes labelled *fachento* (snob) by their
neighbours who retained their traditional suspicion of all outsiders.
Local myths also presented problems:

> Many *campesinos* insisted that reading from a cool piece of paper after
> working all day in the hot sun was bad for their eyes and would make them go
> blind.
> *Brigadista María*

Such a belief is perhaps rooted in the real problem that many *campesinos*
experienced with poor eyesight. It would sometimes take weeks for
brigadistas to identify this as the cause of a learner's difficulty and even
longer to find some spectacles which would help to remedy the situation.

One entrenched local myth asserted that it was unlucky for women to
read or write for three months after childbirth, so many women were
unable to join or had to drop out. Indeed, almost all women encountered
opposition from their husbands who could see little value in their wives
learning to read and write. Nevertheless women did participate and for

many it was the first time that they had been involved in any such collective activity outside the home. Those who did attend were often accompanied by their children whose demands made concentration on learning new skills considerably harder.

> The Collectives of Popular Education were completely unlike schools. They were never cut off from everyday life. We always had a baby crying or people wandering in and out.
> *Brigadista Rosa*

After the whirlwind of publicity in the town and the initial excitement of a new environment, many of the *brigadistas* felt abandoned and homesick. Shortages of supplies made the situation more difficult. The co-ordination which had worked so miraculously during the launch of the crusade was hard to sustain especially when the rains arrived in May and the dusty tracks became mudbaths. When they could, *brigadistas* visited their homes in Leon but this became increasingly difficult.

> Some of us nearly gave up in the first weeks, especially when it seemed that no-one was learning.
> *Brigadista Rosa*

The task of literacy teaching was not as easy as it had seemed during the brief training.

> Faced with actually being there we had to start all over again. I felt as if I knew nothing . . . At first I slipped into copying my own teachers, trying to force the *campesinos* to learn and getting impatient when they didn't understand something that seemed obvious to me.
> *Brigadista Antonio*

In response to this type of problem the squadron co-ordinator in Lechecuagos, Sister Josefina, organized workshops on Saturdays to review methods and share difficulties, so that the *brigadistas* had a forum to express themselves and could learn from each other. Similar developments were taking place throughout the country. New slogans appeared, such as "Don't just criticize, participate in the solution". However, it was time as much as training that brought change.

> I regained my confidence when the *campesinos* started to form their own words.
> *Brigadista Rosa*

> The hardest part had always been developing dialogue and getting them to participate, but as time passed and we came to themes like land and production or the church, they opened up.
> *Brigadista Antonio*

> Something magical happened – people started discovering a voice and finding their way around words.
> *Brigadista Mercedes*

Eventually it began to work. My students learnt how to write *machete*
and I learnt how to use one.
Brigadista Rodriguez

The interchange really happened. The *brigaditas* learnt and recorded the
history of the area. In the evenings the old people of Lechecuagos told
legends and tales beneath the stars. It was beautiful – a rich discovery of oral
culture.
Sister Josefina

Meanwhile the *campesinos* were also learning some history.

Before the crusade the *campesinos* thought Sandino was a bloodthirsty
criminal murderer . . . that was what they had been told by Somoza's
misinformation machine. The primer taught them a truer story.
Sister Josefina

It was not only the *brigadistas* who got a taste of rural life. Once they had
settled in, their parents, sisters and brothers would come to visit so that
by the end of the crusade there were links between whole families in
Lechecuagos and Leon. Historically, communication between town and
country had been minimal, based on ignorance and prejudice. Within only
five months, the crusade established substantial links, laying the basis for
a national identity which had never previously existed in Nicaragua.

By August 1980, over 150 *campesinos* had learnt to read and write in
Lechecuagos. Only a quarter of those who had started dropped out before
completing the primer, mainly from work pressures (at home or in the
fields) or eyesight problems. Only one *brigadista* left before the end of
the crusade: one of the Cubans, who had run into conflict with his host
family when he confessed to being an atheist. "They starved him out of
the house," recalls Sister Josefina, "You just could not and can not have
a revolution here without God."[12]

POPULAR EDUCATION FOR A WHOLE NATION

Nationally, 400,000 people learnt to read and write in the crusade and
Nicaragua's illiteracy rate fell to 13 per cent, one of the lowest in Latin
America. In recognition, Nicaragua was awarded the UNESCO Literacy
Prize. Internationally the statistics became Nicaragua's most widely quoted
achievement. Internally they were only one side of the story. It was the
richness of the experience itself that was most valued.

It was as if the young people had gone through a war; but a war
more purifying than the armed struggle.
Tomas Borge

Throughout the country people had studied subject matters that were
interwoven with the revolutionary process, they learnt about the different
programmes of the new government, in housing, health, the economy

and foreign policy, and they were introduced to the new institutions like
the Sandinista Defence Committees. The primer was like a manifesto of
change.
Jorge, literacy co-ordinator, Lechecuagos

However successful, a five-month campaign cannot create a literate
society. The crusade had to be the first stage of a much deeper
transformation of education.

> We must prepare the education of . . . newly-literate persons. This will
> be at least as difficult if not more difficult than the literacy crusade because it
> necessarily presupposes working at a time when the euphoria of the crusade is
> over, and without the 100,000 or more young people.
> *Fernando Cardenal*

The energy of the mobilization could not be sustained. For example, for
the five months of the crusade all schools had been suspended to enable
the students to leave without dropping behind in their own education. This
could not continue.

> The crusade gave us a vast experience and spawned a new methodology,
> but did not give us solid structures to build on. It created a mystique, a new
> praxis, but no organizational base.
> *Juan Bautista Arién, Director of Planning, MED*

What the crusade did leave behind was a new approach, the basis for
constructing a non-formal basic education. First, it spawned "a new
concept of knowledge."[13] In the crusade, knowledge was not seen as
a series of facts demarcated into subject areas. Rather, it was seen as
rooted in everyday life and consisting of socially-relevant awareness and
practical skills. The aim of the new curriculum was the socialization of
knowledge – not its accumulation. This was unlike the traditional approach
of western liberal-education where, in Freire's words, "the teacher talks
about reality as if it were motionless, static, compartmentalized and
predictable".[14] Reality was not to be compartmentalized, knowledge was
not to be segregated into self-enclosed subjects. This strategy was called
"globalizing".

Secondly, the crusade changed people's attitudes to teachers, establishing the notion of popular teachers, volunteers who had the basic
skills of reading and writing and were willing to co-ordinate the learning
process. The ideal at first was that the most advanced learners in each
of the groups from the crusade would take over the co-ordinating role
when the *brigadistas* left. Professional training was unimportant compared
to motivation and shared life-experiences with the learners.

A third component was a new idea of the school, the Collective of
Popular Education. This was the basic teaching unit, a highly flexible,
informal structure, consisting of a few people who would meet in whatever
available space and at whatever time they found mutually convenient.

These three inter-dependent factors were the basis of the new Popular Basic Education programme for adults. With four levels, this was built upon a Permanent Literacy Programme. In 1981 45,000 students signed up for literacy and 95,000 for the first level of the new Popular Basic Education. Over 15,000 Collectives of Popular Education were set up, with a roughly equivalent number of popular teachers.[15] In Lechecuagos almost all those who learnt in the Crusade joined in order to continue their studies and consolidate their skills.

Nine years on, in 1989, there were 106 Collectives of Popular Education for adults in Lechecuagos, with 219 young popular teachers (all local volunteers). The aim is now to eradicate illiteracy in the area. Most of the Collectives are small: between two and five adults, with two popular teachers who alternate responsibility. As before, the value of the work is not only measured in educational terms.

As in the crusade, for many of the popular teachers this is their first active role in the revolutionary process – so it is vital for their own political formation.
Luis Alemán[16]

There is now a clear recognition that the successful eradication of illiteracy depends on a two-pronged approach: active work with adults alongside the consolidation of the school system to prevent the creation of a new generation of illiterates. The point where these meet is with children who drop out of school early because of the economic difficulties faced by their parents who need them to work in the fields.[17] These children have now been made a priority group in Lechecuagos and a series of special classes has been set up specifically for nine-to thirteen-year-olds who have left school. Two hours each afternoon, these classes are run by the advanced students from new local schools, all of whom have had several years of experience in adult education. Their job is made easier because they know the children in question and the economic problems that they face.

Although illiteracy remains in some less accessible areas of Lechecuagos, the target of eradication is within range as illiteracy has already been eradicated from eight of its 20 sectors.

LECHECUAGOS 1989: THE IMPACT OF LITERACY

The success of a literacy campaign can only be fully evaluated in terms of its sustained impact. Too often people who pick up basic skills in well-publicized campaigns, lose those skills through disuse in the silent aftermath. Either no follow-up is available for consolidation, or the skills learnt find no application. In rural areas, people who have spent their lives without the written word find little value in the techniques of reading and writing unless other aspects of their lives change. But if literacy is sustained it can provide the tools for people to make these changes themselves.

Agriculture

> The literacy classes helped us to discuss the possibility of having our own
> land and enabled us to organize into a co-operative structure in order to obtain
> it.
> *José (co-operative member)*

The Agrarian Reform Law of 1980 offered the land deserted by the *Somocistas* to any organized groups of *campesinos* who wanted to set up co-operatives. Education has played an important role in the development of these co-operatives:

> Literacy has been essential for giving us confidence when we go to the bank
> and other institutions and for knowing amongst ourselves that everything
> is being done fairly.
> *Damasio (co-operative member)*

In Lechecuagos there are six co-operatives. Three of these involve collective ownership and collective working of the land, while the other three involve individual ownership of land but collective sources of finance and equipment.

> Before the crusade it would have been difficult for us to organize
> a co-operative because either we didn't have the basic skills necessary or we
> didn't have the belief that participating was worthwhile.
> *José*

The *campesino* union UNAG (*Unión National de Agricultores y Granaderos*) is now strong in Lechecuagos and has organized many training courses with newly-literate farmers. The land which was once dedicated to a monoculture of cotton, aimed largely at export, is now also being farmed for sugar, yucca, maize and some vegetables. Chemical fertilizers and pesticides are still being used but at least now *campesinos* can read the safety instructions. There is a greater openness to the introduction of alternative methods, including the use of viruses to control pests.

> Now we are able to go to a training centre in Leon to learn new
> agricultural methods. For example, we have just started to plant soya for the
> first time in this area, which we will be able to use for milk, oil and
> meat.
> *Damasio*

UNAG helps to run a "*campesino* shop" which sells machetes, spades, maize grinders, fertilizer, rope, beans, rice, soap, and other goods at subsidized prices. This was something that the *campesinos* had to fight for and which UNAG at first resisted, until a petition and a starting-up fund (with 250 donations amounting to $1,500) were collected house to house by the *campesinos* themselves. The shop is now run by a group of five elected representatives, two of whom have attended the Popular

Basic Education classes, particularly for assistance with mathematics to help them keep accounts.

> Those who are still illiterate tend to be landless labourers. Even though most areas now have schools and literacy collectives, such people do not have time to spend on what they consider to be luxuries, like education.
> *Arnoldo*

Despite the agrarian reforms about 30 per cent of *campesinos* in Lechecuagos still have no land. They have to survive by working at peak times on the co-operatives or in the fields of medium-sized landowners. Many are forced to migrate to the coffee harvests in Matagalpa or cotton harvests in Chinandega in the same way as they have done for decades. Another local survival strategy involves taking ox and cart up to the "Black Mountain" in order to chop down firewood for sale in Leon market. This is two-days labour for little profit. However in early 1989 over 30 individual cartloads of wood were confiscated by Sandinista police on the grounds that the practice was leading to deforestation. For these landless *campesinos* there was no effective organization to turn to in Lechecuagos.[18]

Health

> In the past, doctors were perceived in the same way as teachers and modern medicines were not trusted. The crusade made people more aware that there are some good things but it was only when the health centre was built and it was within their reach that the *campesinos* really changed their attitudes.
> *Arnoldo*

One of the priorities of the Sandinistas has been health care, particularly in rural areas which had been almost ignored in the past. Before 1979 the people of Lechecuagos had to travel to Leon to receive treatment and had to pay for everything. Many could not afford the fees and in most cases an uncomfortable hour-long journey was not practical. The *campesinos* had developed their own alternative as was discovered in the crusade.

> When a *brigadista* fell ill and the first-aid kit was of no use, the *campesinos* would help with the herbal cures that they had been forced to learn.
> *Sister Josefina*

Rather than simply rejecting traditional *campesino* cures the aim was to complement them with preventive campaigns, first aid and the option of modern medicines. In 1981 a health post was built at the back of the church in the centre of Lechecuagos. This provided basic medicines and vaccinations and trained volunteers for the Popular Health Brigades. These brigades worked to educate people about primary health care, with the focus always on prevention, especially of malaria, diarrhoea and respiratory illnesses that were all common in Lechecuagos. For a successful public health campaign of this nature reasonable levels of literacy were important so that posters, leaflets, pamphlets and of course instructions on medicines, could all be read.

> Once, in Somoza's time, a doctor gave me two packets of pills, one for my daughter and one for me, but the pills looked similar and I couldn't read the labels. It was very hot and I had a bad fever. In the truck on the way home I held the packet for my daughter in my left hand and my own in my right hand. But the road was so bumpy that I dropped them and when I picked them up I didn't know which was which. . . . My daughter had bad diarrhoea and the pills I gave her did nothing except make her feel dizzy. As for me . . . well . . . perhaps you can guess.
> *Angela*

Schools

Perhaps the most dramatic changes in Lechecuagos have been in education provision. In the past many people had rejected all forms of education as outside interference. The crusade provided a different image of the role that learning could play, even to those who had not been directly involved. Yearly since 1980 new schools have been built, partly under the influence of parental pressure, especially in remote parts of Lechecuagos. All of the schools form part of a Ministry of Education network, though some were built by parents, others with church money and a couple by international solidarity building-brigades. Where before there were three ramshackle classrooms there are now 17 schools, with 70 teachers, organized together into a decentralized structure known as a Nucleus of Rural Education (NER).[19] There are three Base Schools and 14 Satellite Schools. In the Satellites children can learn up to fourth or fifth grade of primary; if they then wish to continue they can attend the nearest Base School which will take them up to second or third grade of secondary. Within the next three years it is expected that complete secondary education will be available in at least one of the Base Schools.

Consultation Councils have been set up attached to each of the 17 schools in the Rural Education Nucleus, each with about ten members. About 150 parents are involved across Lechecuagos; and over 100 of these are people who learnt to read and write in the National Literacy Crusade. The majority of participants are women. These councils have helped to build and maintain schools, particularly the Satellites which often lack adequate facilities. With active parental participation, solutions are found even when material resources are lacking. The councils also act as pressure bodies, giving the local community a say in what goes on in schools. They are kept well informed of Ministry of Education policies and are familiar with the curriculum changes that take place, some of which they help to initiate or support. These curriculum changes also show the way that the thinking of the crusade has now filtered into many areas of formal-education practice. Involvement in practical work is encouraged. Students from the third grade upward engage in experimental agricultural work in surrounding fields. Fifth grade students participate in the health brigades, giving vaccinations. Most sixth grade students are involved as volunteer teachers in the Popular Basic Education programme for adults. Students at all levels are encouraged to engage in projects which draw together work from different subject areas and relate to their local community.

The consultation councils have become the most important form of community organization, holding regular meetings to discuss issues ranging from health to religion, culture to agriculture, sport to defence. Through concerted action the first electricity lines have been built in Lechecuagos. The parents pressured for the Leon road to be improved to ease transport of products to market. They also succeeded in a campaign to re-schedule buses so that teachers from Leon could arrive on time. Now, under watchful eyes, teachers (three-quarters of whom come from the city) attend almost unfailingly five days a week. However, many parents would prefer their children to be taught by local teachers in the same way that they as adults are taught by local students. This is a campaign for the future.

Much of the impact of the crusade in rural areas such as Lechecuagos has been a result of changes of *campesino* attitudes to their own lives. Whereas previously an educated *campesino* was someone who adopted urban ways of thinking, the new education offered the possibility of developing an educated *campesino* way of thinking. In the crusade, *campesinos* were encouraged to express themselves, to find their own voice. The revolution was not imposed by the crusade, it was learnt as something to be creatively defined by everyone.

> There is a new sense of pride in *campesinos*, a sense of self-worth,
> a feeling of belonging to and contributing to the country.
> *Arnoldo*

The word *campesino* itself has lost its old derogatory connotations. *Campesinos* are encouraged to perceive themselves as the backbone of the revolution, the people whose production will decide whether the revolution stands or falls. They are now demanding services for their own communities, confident in the knowledge of their own contribution to the building of a new Nicaragua.

NOTES

1. Frente Sandinista de Liberacion Nacional: named after Augusto Sandino, nationalist guerrilla leader of 1920s and 1930s, who forced US marines to leave the country. The FSLN was founded in his memory in 1961.
2. Juan Bautista Arién: Director of Planning, Ministry of Education (MED) and UNESCO representative. Quoted in an interview with the authors, May 1989.
3. Statistics from *Nicaragua: Politicas educativas de la Educacion Popular de Adultos* (Managua: Ministry of Education, August 1987.)
4. In most of Latin America the education system is divided into six grades/levels of primary education, followed by secondary education.

5.   Fernando Cardenal, Training document for literacy teachers, MED, February 1980.
6.   Brackley, Dean, "Who's Indoctrinating Whom? Education in Revolutionary Nicaragua", *Grail*, December 1985.
7.   Ibid.
8.   Freire, Paulo, *The Politics of Education* (London: Macmillan, 1985).
9.   Ibid.
10.   These images are based on the Freirian strategy of presenting reality in codifications which are then to be decoded in a dialogue. However, in many respects the images of the primer *The Dawn of the People* fall short of being codifications. They were not produced in consultation with the learning community and are often very direct and explicit in their content, thus requiring very little in the way of decodifying analysis. This point is explored in Chapter 3.
11.   Freire, op. cit.
12.   There are now five Sisters of the Ascension working in Lechecuagos. They are identified with the more radical "popular church" wing of the Catholic Church and influenced by what is known as liberation theology. The stories and imagery of the Bible, largely based on rural existence, are very evocative for Nicaragua's *campesinos*.
   The doctrines of liberation theology and the practices of the popular church in Nicaragua offer interesting parallels with popular (or "liberatory") education. Seeking to close the gap between priest and congregation, liberation theology is seeking a similar breakdown of relations to that pursued in popular education between teacher and students. Monologue from the pulpit is replaced by a dialogue which takes its starting point from the daily lives of the people. The church is no longer a fixed institution, no longer the only legitimate place of religious learning, for religious experience is everywhere, in the fields, under the trees and in the home. Like schools, churches are no longer in exclusive possession of knowledge and are no longer cut off from the community they serve. The aim of both popular education and popular theology is no longer the internalization of a series of concepts, no the achievement of a pure understanding that is detached and only finds value in another world. Instead, the aim of both is action, action to transform the world, and to make it more just.
13.   Eduardo Baez, Assistant Co-ordinator of Adult Education, MED, Managua, interview with authors, May 1986.
14.   Freire, Paulo, *Pedagogy of the Oppressed* (London: Penguin, 1972).
15.   Statistics from *Documentos: Primer Congreso Nacional de Educación Popular de Adultos* (Managua, June 1981).
16.   Luis Alemán, Sub-director of Adult Education, MED, one of the few members of the original MED team from the crusade who continues to this day. Interview with authors, April 1989.
17.   The economic factor is exacerbated by the fact that children have to buy their own school books and have to have some semblance of a uniform. "Ten per cent of parents have problems with this," comments Don Arnoldo, "but allowances are made – particularly for single parents – though not for children with alcoholic fathers."
18.   The organization which should represent these people's interests is the ATC

(*Asociación de Trabajadores del Campo*, the Rural Workers' Association), but this is not effective in Lechecuagos.

19.   There are now four other NERs in Leon and 34 in the whole country. It is a structure particularly appropriate for dispersed rural areas.

3. Nicaragua, Batahola:
The Paradox of Revolutionary Education

The Government of National Reconstruction took responsibility for giving all Nicaraguans the right to education. The expansion of primary education between 1979 and 1984 was dramatic. There are now 127 per cent more schools, 61 per cent more teachers and 55 per cent more children at primary school. With the organized participation of local people 1,404 new schools have been built.
Dianna Melrose[1]

Revolutionary education implies the constant transformation of reality. In Nicaragua, the Literacy Crusade set this process in motion, empowering people to transcend the limitations of their past. However, the difficulties really begin once the oppressive regime is forgotten, when the reality to be transformed is the product of the revolutionary state itself. If education is to continue to be transformative, it must challenge reality. How, then, is it possible for a revolutionary State to design educational programmes which to be revolutionary must challenge that state? Either the State dictates the content of a revolutionary education and silences criticism as counter-revolutionary, in which case the education system becomes as oppressive as its predecessor, or the State accepts the challenge and nurtures a continuing revolution in education, which might ovethrow the very structures that made it possible.

BATAHOLA NORTE, THE IDEAL

On the southern shore of Lake Managua lies the rural sprawl of a capital without a centre. Neighbourhoods of one-storey buildings look tiny next to the modern dual-carriageways that pass between them. In the absence of tower-blocks, a volcanic crater punctuates the skyline. From this crater radiates a series of unpredictable fault-lines. In 1972 downtown Managua – the commercial heart-land of the country – was 90 per cent devastated by an earthquake. Over 20,000 people died. The only buildings left standing were the Bank of America and the Inter-Continental Hotel. International aid for reconstruction ended up in private pockets more than in public hands, though the distinction was unclear at a time when the President personally owned most of the country's resources.

Somoza had a vision of a new capital. The skeletal remains of the old centre were allowed to crumble and become an overgrown pasture for grazing cattle. The new city was decentralized with suburbs built around shopping centres (owned of course by Somoza and his associates), united by new highways. It was modelled on US cities: perfectly structured for the modern car-owning family but very poorly designed for the vast majority of Nicaraguans who had no cars. Owing to lack of investment little planning of poor neighbourhoods (*barrios*)[2] took place and improvised housing sprung up throughout the city wherever there was space, and particularly along the open sewage lines. When the final insurrection was in full swing, Somoza found it hard to isolate the source of subversion and had to resort to almost indiscriminate aerial bombing of the city. But Somoza's bombing could not destroy Somoza's vision: Managua today retains a decentralized structure and a rural atmosphere. Except for occasional battered taxis, cars are rarely seen. Buses which bulge at the sides are the only regular transport holding the disparate city in shape. Over a million people, one-third of Nicaragua's population, inhabit the city, putting a considerable strain on resources.

After the Sandinistas took power in 1979 they faced a housing crisis in Managua. There was a large number of homeless people. The *barrios*, which had played a decisive role in the Sandinista victory, were seriously overcrowded. Building new *barrios* was a priority. A number were planned in the few relatively safe areas between the fault-lines. One of these was Batahola. Located between the US Embassy and the FSLN hill,[3] the area was a wasteland. This was cleared and solid one-storey houses were built, mostly with about three rooms. Electricity was connected, water supply provided and fixed drains put in. Conditions were considerably better than in most of the long-established *barrios* where struggles for basic services had rarely been won.

Lake Managua drains all the capital's sewage and until the revolution drained the waste – including oil, mercury, and DDT – from 35 industries. The water is murky and highly poisonous. In 1980, on the edge of the lake, where the smell of poison rises in the heat, huge sewage pipes were interspersed with the homes of the people of Acahualinca. This *barrio* suffered regular flooding and serious health problems. Most of the residents were *campesinos* who had recently migrated to the city. Batahola Norte was planned to provide housing for these people. In 1981, with half the new houses built, Acahualinca's residents moved in. However they had not been consulted over the design of the new houses and many found the area too cramped. It was an urban design and lacked the space to keep the pigs and hens that they brought with them. Moreover, they had been squatters on their old land but now they were expected to pay rent for their houses which put strains on their budget.

Within a year many of the houses were empty again as people returned to Acahualinca where they had more space. To fill Batahola Norte, details were sent out to people through unions and community organizations, through the Sandinista party itself and directly to factories and other workplaces. Batahola was rapidly populated by activists, people who were committed to the revolutionary process. During 1982/3, 1,800 families moved in, amounting to about 12,000 people. Most of the population was literate, many of them having been taught in the Literacy Crusade.

> The formation of the new person was not the monopoly of the education system.
> *Ernesto Vallecillo*[4]

New *barrios*, like Batahola, were an opportunity to create the ideal environment for developing a post-revolutionary society. While basic services for housing had been provided, communal services were not: there was no school, health centre or recreation facility. This was deliberate: the community itself was being given the opportunity to build the institutions that it wanted and had the responsibility of organizing collectively to do so. In the process, people from diverse backgrounds were being encouraged to forge a sense of community identity.

Adult education was to be the motor for developing the necessary organization while the state was to provide the material resources. The lessons of the crusade were to be consolidated in the same flexible and creative way that they had been initiated. Everything that was empowering – everything that involved collective action and reflection – became part of the new popular education that the crusade had launched.

> Popular education was everywhere . . . in the health brigades, in the work of the Defence Committees, in the communities, even in homes . . . people recognized that you don't need experts, that education is about people with experience, your mother, my aunt, sharing what they know. Popular education lives in the people: it is the revolutionary process.
> *Victoriano Artiaga, Director of Adult Education, 1989*

In Batahola, as in *barrios* throughout Managua, the focus for community participation and popular education was the Sandinista Defence Committee (CDS).[5] Through the CDS the community could define for itself, on a clean slate, what was needed. Schools, for example, were by no means taken for granted as the only legitimate means of organizing education. The crusade had shown an alternative and the work of the CDS itself showed that the Ministry of Education was not in exclusive possession of the right to educate or organize education. What was important was that the new generation was educated using the same principles that the crusade had established.

> Our revolution gave a vote of confidence in the capacity of our people to educate themselves . . . to be the subjects and agents of their own education.
> *Carlos Tunnerman, Minister of Education, 1982*

THE IDEAL IN PRACTICE

Concepts of education penetrate very deeply into the psyche of a population,

and reproduce themselves . . . no-one is exempt from this process.
Luis Alemán[6]

Contrary to expectations, the residents of Batahola did not spontaneously organize in response to their very urgent needs. The CDS did not become the focus of an active community.

> There was pressure on people to get involved . . . to participate in everything, but many were reluctant. They just wanted to lead their own lives.
> *Ernesto Guido, Batahola teacher*

Rapidly, the CDS became identified with a small group of activists who were seen to be more responsive to centralized CDS and Sandinista party directives than they were to the needs of the community.

One of the most urgent needs was education for children. During the first two years all that was available in Batahola was a few classes given in various houses, with no co-ordination between them. Many children were not receiving any form of education, creating the possibility of a future generation of illiterates. For those attending classes, conditions were difficult.

> We were all in one pre-fabricated wooden house with a muddy floor. There would be four different classes going on in one room with up to 500 students. It was known as the chicken coop.
> *Daisy, ex-student*

The CDS failed to respond to this problem either by strengthening what was available or developing an alternative. Into the vacuum left by this failure of community organization, the Church stepped. A Catholic chapel, set up by foreign priests, raised money from its networks in Spain and the US and brought in an international solidarity brigade to build a school. Named after Carlos Fonseca, co-founder of the FSLN, the well-constructed school now has 2,000 places. The revolutionary murals on its walls belie how little the local people were involved in building it.

The failure of the CDS reduced popular education in Batahola to the work of a few Collectives of Popular Education (these are described in chapter 2). Initially these met in people's houses, but they were poorly organized and it was not possible for the Ministry of Education to extend them in the absence of effective community networks. Here again the Catholic chapel stepped in, recognizing the need for more concerted adult education work. They encouraged a group of young Catholic catechists to take on the teaching and arranged for the Ministry of Education to give training and materials. At first there were problems.

> People were reluctant to participate and some were actively disruptive. Gangs of boys would make fun, throw stones, intimidate people and flirt with any girls who were learning.
> *Sister Margaret*

After the building of the school, all adult education took place at night in large classes in the schoolrooms. Perhaps this was a suitable image for adult popular education as a whole, which had become so detached from its reference points in daily life that it had to be separated from the reality outside by high walls and a caretaker with a rifle.

In Batahola, the Literacy Crusade had failed in its aim of making people active subjects of revolutionary change. People wanted the revolution to do things for them and if the revolution did not come up with the goods they were happy to receive them from the church. To transcend dependent attitudes such as this was a much greater task than anyone had imagined.

> Some students seem to find something comfortable in being passive. The trouble is that they are accustomed to being fed things and they do not feel that they are learning if they are not well fed.
> *Ernesto Guido*

Resistance to a more participatory role related to the learner's past experiences. For instance, dialogue – the central plank of the new educational methods – did not have a clear function in the eyes of many learners.

> If anything concerns us we discuss it through the day, when we are working. We don't need special lessons to learn how to talk to each other or discuss our problems.
> *Juana, learner*

> Most teachers just go straight to the syllables, because the political jargon of the generative words and sentences is unacceptable to most learners.
> *Isabel, popular teacher*

The textbooks that were produced for the crusade were still in use. Images and themes that may have been able to generate dialogue soon after the triumph, now lacked the immediacy that had made them work.

> People are not interested any more in hearing about Sandino, Fonseca and the struggle. On most themes there is nothing to say which hasn't been said or heard a hundred times before.
> *José, popular teacher*

People began to perceive the night classes as simply a 'poor substitute for real education' and, in the words of the National Assistant Director of Adult Education, Luis Alemán, "inferior in quality, a second-class education with amateur teachers".

UNDERLYING CONFLICTS

> Teachers, like the rich, will never give up power willingly.
> *Samuel Simpson*[7]

The Literacy Crusade brought into prominence a series of ideas and methods that were in contradiction to the established, formal education-system. Inherited institutional structures and professional teachers were seen as a burden by the new popular educators in the Ministry of Education. As Luis Alemán puts it "We used to be anti-school, real inquisitors! We wanted to eradicate all concept of school". The schools were associated with Somoza and the capitalist order. Teachers taught and were taught within that system. Their methods were traditional.

> Teachers take their own experiences of education as the most important basis for their own teaching methods. They have a suspiciously neutral attitude to social problems.
> *Samuel Simpson*

Formal education had to be changed so fundamentally if it was to be purged of the past, that some popular educators felt it should be forgotten altogether.

Unsurprisingly some professional teachers saw the development of popular education as a threat. Though many had participated in the crusade, the suggestion that anyone – regardless of training – could co-ordinate any learning process challenged their professional prowess. The crusade was an experiment from which they had learnt some new approaches but it couldn't be a comprehensive alternative to the schools. The exchange of experience between teacher and students characteristic of adult education was not seen as a realistic basis for the teaching of children.

> For professional teachers, the school vision structures all discussion of education. Informal methods struggle to be included. They have a different language and different values.
> *Luis Alemán*

Within the Ministry of Education, professional teachers lobbied for the Adult Education Programme to be made compatible with the formal system, using parallel grades and certificates. But the idea that the informal system should adopt the "hidden curriculum" of the school was anathema to popular educators.

> The hidden curriculum teaches all children that economically valuable knowledge is the result of professional teaching . . . . [it] transforms the explicit curriculum into a commodity and makes its acquisition the securest form of wealth. Knowledge certificates – unlike property rights, corporate stock, or family inheritance – are free from challenge . . . . They convert into guaranteed privilege.
> *Ivan Illich*[8]

Ironically, the popular educators in the Ministry were themselves by no means immune to the ideology of the school which they were so keen on destroying.

In the process of seeking an informal education, we ourselves formalized
things. We made calendars and fixed times, we set up rigid structures for our
supposedly flexible curriculum.
Luis Alemán

The very idea that they were somehow outside society and the bearers of
the authentic revolutionary method, untainted by the legacy of their own
educational past, was in retrospect recognized as absurd. Luis Alemán
acknowledges this problem by asking "Most educators simply reproduce
the past ideology; They need retraining . . . but by whom?"

At the grassroots level, the popular teachers and the co-ordinators who
worked in the Collectives of Popular Education failed to develop a clear
command of the new methods. Research in 1985, with 110 people in
23 CEPs in Managua, showed "a low or non-existent understanding . . .
despite training efforts stretching back to the crusade, which have focused
on the methodological question".[9] Clearly, the educators themselves
needed educating.

The end of popular education?
The formal education system was resilient. Learners, teachers and popular
educators, consciously or unconsciously, clung on to aspects of its ideology
and methods. Changing it involved changing the administration, teacher
training and curriculum, as well as student expectations, parental attitudes
and community relations. Popular education was much more vulnerable,
since, on its own terms, its theory ran counter to the idea of setting up any
permanent structures, promoting instead more flexible, student-centred
approaches.

Popular Basic Education for adults lost the struggle against formal-
ization. By 1984 it bore little resemblance to the crusade's follow-up.
From four levels (or grades) it was extended to six, to make it parallel to
the six grades of children's primary education, with associated monitoring
and assessment in order to create equivalents. The curriculum separated
the subject areas of social sciences and natural sciences, breaking with any
holistic approach to reality. As Eduardo Báez from the MED admits, "the
compartmentalizing of knowledge was reintroduced". Later, grades were
fused so that adult students could learn first and second grades in one year,
third and fourth the next, and within three years finish their whole primary
education. This encouraged students to look at their education as building
towards an end, rather than as an end in itself. The workbooks were no
longer starting points for self-discovery and collective understanding. They
were the keys to certificates and qualifications.

Collectives of Popular Education folded as many popular teachers
dropped out. Some were disillusioned, others were unable to cope. The
system required them to have specialized knowledge of subject areas and
pressured them to cover material quickly and get students through exams.

This was impossible for those educators who had only a basic level of formal education. As in Batahola, in many areas a centralized Adult Education Centre replaced the collectives. The large classes in these centres prevented active participation by learners. Reduced to mere techniques, literacy and basic education were taught in the same way as before the revolution.

Many learners dropped out because they had to travel too far to the new centres or the timetable of classes was incompatible with their work. Others disliked the increased pressure or feared "failure". Teachers had no time for individual problems. The whole experience had little in common with what they had started back in 1980. Dramatically, the rate of illiteracy increased to 25 per cent[10] as people lost their skills and the crusade became a distant memory.

DEVELOPING A NEW STRATEGY

Re-evaluating the Literacy Crusade

> In the historical moment of 1979 the slogans of the revolution were emblazoned everywhere and entered every discourse. Inevitably this new dialect, this new popular language spilled over into the texts, with the spirit of graffiti.
> *Juan Bautista Arién, Director of Planning, MED*

The crisis in popular education was traced by the Ministry of Education to the Literacy Crusade itself. The euphoria and enthusiasm that had powered the campaign had also blinded the organizers to its flaws. They had never resolved the contradiction inherent in organizing a national campaign based on the lived realities of the Nicaraguan people, when those realities were so diverse. How could themes be shared by a worker in the Victoria Brewery in Managua, and a subsistence farmer in the remote mountains of Nueva Segovia? In practice the themes concerned with the creation of a national identity often took precedence. Explaining the revolution, rather than exploring day-to-day problems, had been taken as the most important task. Since many of the people had no experience of the revolution prior to 1979, this could only be communicated down, from revolutionary vanguard via teachers to the people. In reality then, the crusade had been vertical, because it involved communicating a body of knowledge from teacher to student rather than sharing knowledge horizontally, between popular teachers and learners.

> We must distinguish "politicize" from "indoctrinate". If education is based on reality, it has to be political, but if it is outdated, one-sided and vertical then it can also be indoctrinating.
> *Veronica, popular teacher*

The guide-book for literacy teachers provides an example of how the crusade failed to live up to its own rhetoric. In this book there was a

short summary on each theme, which the popular teacher was supposed
to use as a guide to summing up a discussion.

> Most teachers just read out the discourse because that was the conclusion.
> People's contribution was devalued.
> *Rosa María Torres*[11]

> It was like giving us the answer, telling us what really happened or what
> we should think or say about something.
> *Silvia (learner, Batahola)*

The provision of such a political line on each debate was necessarily
intimidating and silenced many people, perhaps not because they dis-
agreed but because they were frightened of getting something wrong.
Often learners learnt little more than the slogans of the primer without
really making sense of their content.

> To substitute monologue, slogans and communiques for dialogue is to try
> to liberate the oppressed with the instruments of domestication.
> *Paulo Freire*[12]

The decentralization of politics

> We must move away from the conception of the Party and the state
> as inseparable and all-solving. Now we must start from the basis of peoples'
> experiences, stressing the need for their active participation rather than
> presenting the government as an omnipotent provider.
> *Pascual Ortiz, Assistant Director of Adult Education*

Since 1985, the Ministry of Education gradually implemented a series of
new strategies in response to their critique of the Literacy Crusade. First,
they decentralized their administration in an attempt to be more responsive
to local realities. Previously all regional and zonal offices awaited decisions
and commands from the central office. To change this dependency it
was no use issuing another command. People needed training to be
able to identify the problems and organize solutions for themselves. A
series of training workshops were set up, using participatory methods. By
introducing dialogue at this level it was hoped that such methods would
filter down to interactions between popular teachers and learners. The
Collectives of Popular Education were once again held up as the model
for teaching adults, in preference to the Centres of Adult Education.

Secondly, the Ministry decentralized the production of materials, as
the next stage in producing a completely restructured adult basic-
education programme. From 1990 the programme was to be based
on modules, already piloted in 300 communities. There were five main
areas: economics, political ideology, social problems, health and culture.
However, these were not subject areas as such, because, in Luis Alemán's
words, "we seek integration between them. We will follow the logic of
problems and will not let any subject build an internal, closed structure."

Some of the modules were to be used nationally such as one produced on the treatment of diarrhoea. Others were optional, for example, one on the farming of coffee will only be of value to learners in certain areas and not for the residents of Batahola. Each module was designed for 17 hours of teaching. The planners hoped that some would be produced by local offices to be relevant to their immediate environment. The modules would not only be of use in the Collectives of Popular Education. A module on vaccines or hygiene could be used by health brigades; a module on industrial production would be relevant to the Sandinista Workers Federation (CST). Many organizations[13] assisted in the production of the new materials, helping to ensure their relevance.

All the new materials produced by the Ministry of Education shared another common feature. To overcome the danger of political indoctrination that could reduce popular education to a series of empty slogans, the red and black flag of the Sandinistas is no longer seen alongside the blue and white national flag. References to the FSLN, the Frente or the Sandinistas do not appear. Modules were produced on the constitution and on the elections but their content did not include any party line. The Party has pulled out of education.

> In the running of education there must be no dogmas, no manuals, no strict rules – we must be flexible and work together, being led by each other and not by dogma.
> *Victoriano Artiaga*

A similar development took place within the Sandinista Defence Committees (CDSs). Many of these have already changed their names to Committees for Communal Development (CDCs), seeking to distance themselves from identification only with Sandinista-sympathizers. In Batahola, more people are now willing to join in the various activities which include clean-up campaigns, vaccination days, running a dispensary, preparing for the yearly floods, repairing roads, distributing materials and helping residents with legal papers.

> Problems inside each neighbourhood do not have a political colour. Mosquitoes and other agents of contagion and infection do not respect ideological creed.
> *Omar Cabezas[14]*

A Vision for the Future
Communities like Batahola were set up with ideals of participatory development which were rapidly lost. The belief that popular education was everywhere turned out to be an illusion. Decentralization and depoliticization are practical attempts to re-awaken these ideals and overcome the paradox of organizing ongoing popular education in a revolutionary State. The vision is of a Nicaragua composed of many different micro-societies within a national state which facilitates their

ability to transform their local environments. The new look CDCs together with the many organizations that have built strong links with the Ministry of Education in producing the new modules, will help to ensure that popular education is no longer simply the responsibility of the Ministry or to be found only within school walls.

The new approach sees the formal education system as part of the reality within which popular education functions.

> Informal education is complementary to the formal system and now serves to dynamize it and bring it up to date.
> *Juan Bautista Arién*

Confrontation has been replaced by a recognition of the differing roles of formal and popular education.

> We must maintain popular education until it is accepted by the people, because we must give the adult worker and *campesino* something real and useful and not just obsession with the memory of useless facts and the illusion of competing with middle-class children for university places.
> *Luis Alemán*

THE IMPACT OF WAR

> War is any revolutionary country's fundamental reality.
> *Pascual Ortiz*

Since 1982 Nicaragua has been paying a high price for the "low intensity" Contra war being waged from bases in Honduras and funded by Washington. By the end of 1988 over 29,000 people had been killed. Perceived as revolutionaries, teachers were picked out as targets by Contra soldiers. By 1984 over 100 popular teachers had been killed and 171 kidnapped. As a direct result of the war 840 Collectives of Popular Education were forced to close.[15]

The implications of the Contra war for Managua have been staggering. As defence spending soared to consume more than half the national budget, social expenditure plummeted. Samuel Simpson maintains that the capital was left with over 30 per cent of the country's population but only 3 per cent of its resources, and says "human and material resources have been sucked out of Managua to the war-zone. Managua has been the centre of sacrifice for the war effort." The problems have been amplified because many people have fled from the war-zones to the cities, setting up spontaneous settlements. Such refugees now make up ten per cent of the population in Managua.[16] One group of these displaced families settled on a piece of land next to Batahola Norte which had been set aside for building a recreation area. Rapidly, houses were put together out of scrap wood and metal printing-plates discarded by national newspapers. Electricity was obtained by illegally connecting wires to overhead power lines. Two communal taps provided the only water supply. Within a year there were 3,500 people living in the settlement which was named Dinamarca. The residents in neigbouring Batahola found their lights fading, their television flickering, their electricity bills higher, their water supply more erratic and their one piece of land for recreation completely occupied.

War inevitably erodes people's support for the revolution, as more people suffer personally. In Batahola, several hundred youths have been mobilized for military service, about ten per cent of them very reluctantly. Thirty-five have died. Several more have disappeared.[17] Popular education has been hit hard as most of the potential teachers are either fighting at the front or in hiding to avoid the draft. People in Dinamarca are less likely to be called up as there are no records of who lives there. The Sandinista Defence Committee, which was responsible for helping with recruitment in the *barrio*, lost the little trust that they had worked for. The change of name to Committees for Communal Development has not always improved their image. Often the same people are involved. In the absence of trust and with the lack of teachers it is difficult for "popular education to be everywhere".

Another impact of the war on education in Managua has been the need for increased industrial production. In 1984 unions won the right to have two hours of education each working day, at the workplace and with no deductions from pay. However, soon after this remarkable victory the state was forced by the war to introduce quotas and productivity bonuses to boost industrial production. Although the right still exists, few workers can now afford to take advantage of it because all hours worked mean more bonuses. More state factories are kept open 24 hours a day with shiftwork around which it is almost impossible to plan regular education courses.

However, the greatest impact of the war has been economic. More important than the diversion of resources to the front has been the effects of the US trade embargo. This has cut off Nicaragua from its major source of income: the sale of cash crops to the US. Worse, it leaves the economy disarticulated. Before the revolution, crops such as cotton were sold to the US and cloth was bought from them. There was no attempt to develop an internal agro-industry to give the country economic independence. The few industries in operation relied on US machines and spare parts. The embargo leaves Nicaragua's economy rather like a couple of cogs discarded by a car engine. Unable to buy spare parts or sell their agricultural products to traditional markets, they have been increasingly reliant on international solidarity. Inflation has become a huge problem over recent years. At its worst, towards the end of 1988, it rose to 20,000 per cent.

The people of Batahola Norte have been hit hard by the economic crisis. Most were wage-earners in the public sector, but the state could not afford to maintain their wages to keep pace with rocketing inflation. In 1989, the government implemented a survival economy, making massive cuts in state expenditure across the board in an attempt to stabilize the economy. Many state workers lost their jobs.

About 45 per cent of economically-active people in Managua now work in a parallel economy,[18] buying and selling on the streets, with no state regulation. Almost every family in Batahola is dependent on secondary incomes from this type of work. About 25 per cent of children in the *barrio* work during the day, shining shoes or selling newspapers, chewing gum, tortillas, fruit, or anything that is available. In such circumstances,

> it is hard for people to get a global vision of their problems. In the midst of economic crisis people think only of supply and survival . . . they inhabit micro-worlds.
> *Sister Josefina*

Meanwhile the Ministry of Education is itself trying to survive. In the 1989 government cuts, cutbacks in personnel were particularly harsh. The Managua Regional Office for Adult Education used to have 15 staff; it now has three. The Zonal Office which covers Batahola used to have 60 workers; now there are 15. Decentralization means very little when there is almost no budget to decentralize and virtually no workers to use it.

Despite the cuts, the Ministry cannot afford to pay the remaining teachers a decent wage. Teachers have found their wages losing value until they are working for considerably less than the cost of a basic basket of foods. A large number have dropped out and sought work in the *parallel* economy, joining the thousands on the streets. There is now, according to Samuel Simpson, a 70 per cent turnover of teachers each year in Managua. Although teachers are now held in better esteem in society than they were pre-revolution, "respect doesn't fill your stomach", in the words of Sister Josefina. Material resources are also a problem:

> At one time there was no paper in the whole of the Ministry of Education . . . not even toilet paper.
> *Victoriano Artiaga*

There are few resources for the printing of the new set of modules for adult education. Some funding may be available initially for the central production of modules, but sustained production and regional or local production is difficult to imagine. For the foreseeable future most areas are likely to continue to use the texts produced in 1980. There is a desparate need for international assistance in this respect, but Nicaragua suffered from its own success: after the crusade, funding sources for literacy dried up, because people thought that the problem had been solved.

Within Batahola, popular education continues to lose out to the formal system as family survival becomes a full-time occupation.

> People are more interested in eating than in building a new society.
> *Antonio*

The Ministry priority in the area has been to ensure that children who are forced by economic necessity to work during the day do not drop out of schooling altogether. They have been encouraged to attend adult education classes in the evenings. Other children are already forced to attend these evening classes because now the primary school does not have enough places to serve all the children in Batahola and neighbouring Dinamarca. In practice this has displaced most of the adults, who are reluctant to learn alongside children. Moreover, it means that the children are learning a curriculum designed for adults taught by teachers who are not trained to teach children. Popular education is being used as an overspill to make up for the cuts in the formal system.

The economic desperation caused by the war and the embargo is the most potent destroyer of popular education and collective action. People look at education in purely instrumental terms, only interested in learning something to the extent that it will qualify them for employment and money.

> Adults use Popular Basic Education pragmatically, as a stepping stone to reach sixth grade.
> *Juan Bautista Arién*

The new vision of the educators in the Ministry is incompatible with a war economy, which requires centralized control over human and material resources. Any revolutionary state faced with war and economic embargo has to make an extremely difficult choice. Either, in the interests of defending the revolution, the state centralizes power in order to survive (as in the USSR), or it decides that this kind of centralization contradicts the goals of the revolution, denying participation to the majority of the population. In this case an attempt is made to decentralize power, giving decision-making to the people. The Sandinistas chose this path and sought to use popular education to facilitate participation. In recognizing that they could not impose the revolution through education, the education became more revolutionary. However, they were left vulnerable, as the aims of popular education were destroyed by the economic crisis imposed on the country. Democracy cannot be achieved when people are hungry. Everything that the Sandinistas developed was undermined by the lack of resources. The culmination of this was UNOs win in the 1990 elections.

However, the loss of the elections does not signify the loss of the revolution. The vote (which gave the Sandinistas 40.8% and the United Nicaraguan Opposition 54.7%) was not one of uneducated, manipulated masses; that would have been a failure. Rather, it was an educated, pragmatic vote by people who understood the international arena enough to know that the crisis would not end while the Sandinistas were in power. It was the revolution which made this understanding possible. Any attempt by the new government to dismantle the democratic structures established by the revolution will be met by strong opposition from the same people who voted for UNO. On the other hand if a democratic path is followed then the revolution is far from over. The struggle for the survival of popular education mirrors the struggle for the survival of the revolution.

NOTES

1.   Melrose, Dianna, *The Threat of a Good Example* (Oxfam, 1985).
2.   The word "neighbourhood" only approximates to the meaning of the word *barrio* so on some occasions we use the Spanish term.
3.   Cerro Motastepe – which has "FSLN" written in huge white letters is somewhat reminiscent of Hollywood, or the Coca-Cola signs on hills above the cities in neighbouring Honduras.
4.   Ernesto Vallecillo, Vice-Minister of Adult Education, 1983, as quoted in Walker, Thomas, *Five Years of the Nicaraguan Revolution*.
5.   The Sandinista Defence Committees were first founded clandestinely before the revolutionary triumph; afterwards they rapidly became the organizational base of most *barrios*.
6.   Interview with authors, March 1989.
7.   Samuel Simpson, Director of Adult Education for Region 3 (which includes all of Managua), in an interview with the authors, April 1989.
8.   Illich, Ivan, *After Deschooling What?* (London: Writers and Readers Publishing Cooperative, 1974).
9.   Torres, Rosa María, *Los CEP: Education Popular y Democracia Participativa en Nicaragua* (Managua: Cuadernos de Pensamiento Propio No. 12, CRIES).
10.   This is an approximation as there are no detailed figures available. It is however a figure used widely by the national Ministry of Education workers.
11.   Rosa María Torres, crusade consultant and educational researcher with CRIES, now Pedagogical Director of Ecuador's National Literacy Campaign; interview with authors, Quito, Ecuador, June 1989 (see Chapter 5).
12.   Freire, Paulo, *Pedagogy of the Oppressed* (London: Penguin Education, 1972).
13.   These organizations and institutions include the Nicaraguan Womens' Association (AMNLAE), the Sandinista Youth (JS19J), the Campesino Union (UNAG), the Rural Workers Association (ATC), the Ministry of Health (MINSA), the Sandinista Workers Federation (CST), teachers' unions, university departments and of course the Defence/Development Committees (CDSs/CDCs). This mirrors the high level of inter-institutional co-operation and participation during the crusade. Some of these organizations were founded during the original crusade, but then separated from the Ministry of Education in order to develop their own work in their own spaces.
14.   Omar Cabezas, co-ordinator of CDSs/CDCs, quoted in *Nuevo Diario*, Managua, 30 May 1989.
15.   Statistics from Melrose, op. cit.; and from Daniel Ortega's year-end message 31 December 1988, quoted in *Envio*, vol. 8 No. 91, February 1989.
16.   Statistics on spontaneous settlements, of which there are 70 in Managua, from *Envio*, vol. 8 No. 91, February 1989.
17.   The war has also affected Lechecuagos where 170 youths have been mobilized. Thirty were recently recruited, five by force, having their houses surrounded at night. In the war three have died and two have returned severely wounded. There is a considerable resentment in the community, particularly over levels of training: "The only training my son had was hunting iguanas with a home-made catapult when he was a boy." Apart from the recruitment, the war seems very distant to the people in Lechecuagos who are far from the war-zones

in the north. The shortages felt in the towns are not felt in the same way in such rural areas, partly because they are accustomed to less and partly because rural areas have been prioritized by the Sandinistas.

18.   *Envio*, op. cit.

II

REFORM:
LITERACY AND
ORGANIZATION

4. Honduras, San Antonio de Jura: Co-operative Literacy

Honduras, the definitive banana republic, a self-confessed backyard of the United States – and long-serving military base – is a disjointed country.[1] The northern region, for decades little more than an oversized US banana plantation, is centred on San Pedro Sula, a modern city built from the profits of fruit export. A US rather than a Honduran flag flies from the new cultural centre, an imposing building in the middle of the city. Tegucigalpa, in the south, serves as the nominal capital. The letters of "C-o-c-a C-o-l-a" dominate the hillsides above both cities, reminiscent of the "H-o-l-l-y-w-o-o-d" lettering on Beverly Hills. The two are divided by a mountainous national park dominated by the spectacular Lake Yojoa. Until 1970, travellers between Tegucigalpa and San Pedro Sula, on what one would expect to be the main road in the country, had to cross the lake by ferry. This added a beautiful, though debilitating, two hours to their journey, and gave an indication of the country's lack of national unity.

Apart from a few large cattle farms on the banks of Lake Yojoa, the National Park, Azul Meambar, remained uninhabited until 1950 when El Salvadorean families began migrating in search of land. Coming from a country six times more densely populated than Honduras, and equally divided, they found in the wilderness their first ever opportunity to have land of their own. During the 1960s they were joined by Hondurans from the regions of Intibuca and Lempira, areas of poor land on the frontier with El Salvador. They first discovered the National Park en route to the coffee plantations where they worked as temporary migrant labourers. The long dry seasons and the shortage of land in their home regions finally persuaded these *campesinos* to move to the virgin territory of Azul Meambar and set up permanent homes.

In 1962, three Honduran families found a small valley by the River Jura, two hours' walk from Lake Yojoa through thickly wooded slopes, and decided to settle. Conditions were by no means easy. Clearing the huge trees and tangled undergrowth took many months during which time they survived on small fish caught in the river, and the bitter fruit of unknown trees. In the first year they planted their traditional crop of maize but found that it grew badly, and that the little that did grow was eaten before ripening by the numerous wild animals who inhabited the woods around them. Only through experience did they discover the ways of the land and the habits of the armadillos, racoons, coyotes and other creatures that shared their environment.

As the years passed more families arrived, following the rugged track that became thigh deep with mud in the wet season. One by one they built small shacks of wood and mud for their new homes. All learnt slowly, individually, as there was no organization in the community beyond an agreement to call the settlement San Antonio de Jura. To survive, many still depended on migrating to sugar and coffee harvests, or on renting land from the large cattle-farmers by the lakeside (to whom they would have to pay more than half the harvested crop). Of the land available for agriculture in Honduras, two-thirds is used for cattle farming, a source of beef for US burger companies and one of the main reasons why, in such an underpopulated country, *campesinos* were forced to chop down valuable wooded areas in a National Park to find small parcels of land from which to survive.

Having arrived earlier, the El Salvadorean settlers in Azul Meambar tended to have the more accessible and fertile land, a fact which the later Honduran settlers grew to resent. Within the park, the tensions that built up spilled over during the remarkable events of the Football War. In June 1969 Honduras and El Salvador were drawn to play each other in a two-legged World Cup qualifying match. The first leg, in Tegucigalpa, was won by the Hondurans, but the Salvadorean media claimed that their team had been deliberately food-poisoned before the game. When the Hondurans travelled to San Salvador for the return leg, their supporters were attacked with fireworks in the streets and their team lost the game. This provided the rather insubstantial excuse for expelling thousands of Salvadorean *campesino* settlers from their land in Honduras. The Salvadoreans sealed their borders, frightened as much as anything of the effect that so many returning *campesinos* would have on the shortage of land in their own country. The well-trained Salvadorean army intervened, crossing into Honduras to confront the relatively incompetent Honduran forces. After 100 hours of fighting, the Organization of American States intervened and the Salvadoreans were forced to withdraw under the threat of an economic boycott.

At the height of the war, the Hondurans in the park around Lake Yojoa saw their chance to claim more and better land. They called in the Honduran authorities. The few Salvadoreans who did not immediately flee were imprisoned and deported. But the land they left was not available for long. The large landowners from the lakeside cattle-farms acted swiftly, building fences and enclosing the abandoned land for themselves. Within days the situation was as bad as ever for the Honduran *campesinos*, if not worse, as the land was now concentrated in the hands of already powerful landowners.

The Football War, in spite of its title, had little to do with Honduran sentiments about their national team. Over 300,000 Salvadoreans had migrated to Honduras in the preceding years.[2] The tension between Honduran and Salvadorean *campesinos* was fuelled by the landowners who used the Salvadoreans as scapegoats. By claiming that they were to blame for the lack of land available to Honduran *campesinos*, the landowners diverted attention from the real cause of conflict, namely the unequal distribution of land. The war helped to raise the stakes and offered a quick and easy solution. The Salvadoreans could be removed and something resembling national identity could be asserted, a rather novel and even incongruous concept for a country that had spent so long at the whim of international capital, but a concept useful for quelling internal dissent. To show commitment to the idea of a sovereign state, the year after the war work started on the building of a road around the side of Lake Yojoa, to replace the ferry. This road became an appropriate symbol for the building of a national coherence, and at the same time undoubtedly helped the lakeside landowners to market their increased production.

CAMPESINO SPLITS

The lack of national unity in Honduras has historically been paralleled by a lack of unity in the *campesino* union movements. In the years after the 1954 Great Banana Strike (which mobilized 50,000 labourers against the US fruit companies) 16,000 people from the plantations were made redundant. Without an alternative they were forced to return to traditional *campesino* life as subsistence farmers, but they had no land. Inspiration from the Cuban revolution and their recent militant experiences in the strike taught them that direct action was the only option so they seized large areas of land. To help protect themselves from being dislodged from the land they formed the National Federation of Honduran Campesinos (FENACH), the first *campesino* union. Landowners throughout the country were frightened of the example this could set for other *campesinos*.

> The breaking of [the Great Banana] strike had successfully paved the way for a more sophisticated approach to controlling the labour movement than the mass killings and disappearances carried out by neighbouring governments and had set a clear pattern for Honduran labour relations.[3]

The liberal government's response to FENACH was to set up a parallel, anti-communist *campesino* grouping, the National Association of Honduran Campesinos (ANACH). This was formed by the same people whom the US had used to infiltrate and split the Central Strike Committee of the Great Banana Strike. In 1962, to give ANACH credibility, President Villeda Morales passed an Agrarian Reform Law which he presented to ANACH's first director. Believing ANACH to be the legitimate and most effective means to get land, *campesinos* flocked to join them. This successfully isolated FENACH, but the mild reforms were too radical for the landowning elite who orchestrated a nationalist military coup the following year. FENACH was outlawed and dissolved.

The 1962 Agrarian Reform Law made the work of claiming land into a long and legally complex process. Successful *campesino* leaders were little more than facilitators who could negotiate a way through the pedantic procedures and bureaucracy of the National Institute of Agrarian Reform (INA). Campesinos, who were largely illiterate, had no chance of coping with the paperwork themselves, so literate *campesino* leaders were a small intermediary class who could easily be bribed and co-opted by landowners and the government. Contacts and corruption were often more important than the legitimacy of a particular case.

It was not until 1968 that a more radical *campesino* tradition re-emerged, with the support of the Catholic church, who formed the National Union of Campesinos (UNC). ANACH also began to adopt a combative approach, under the influence of ex-FENACH members who had joined its ranks. Land seizures became common, a way of forcing the early settlement of claims to unused land. Landowners and the local military responded with massacres of those who had taken the land. By the early 1970s the UNC was launching national demonstrations in response to this brutality. Aiming to defuse the movement, a reformist military government implemented a law which legalized the occupation of land that the INA was in the process of reviewing. Settlement of cases speeded up dramatically: in 1974 almost 10,000 families obtained land, whereas previous to 1968 the largest number of families to benefit in a single year was 250.[4]

Once again, the big landowners and conservative wings of the military found the reforms unacceptably threatening. Reformist leaders of both the government and INA were forced out by more hard-line figures who sought to give landowners control over the land-reform process. Massacres became more common again, frightening the Church out of an active role and causing disputes within the *campesino* organizations about the best strategy for the new conditions. Both ANACH and the UNC developed splinter groups. Infiltration and the buying off of leaders speeded up the disintegration. By the early 1980s, there were 14 fragments of a previously united movement. Land reform slowed to a quarter of its pace as isolated groupings were unable to challenge the concerted forces of landowners and the military.

The repression of the *campesino* movement reached a peak in the 1980s as the US took a greater strategic interest in the country. Unrest in Guatemala, the threat of revolution in El Salvador and the reality of revolution in Nicaragua made Honduras a vital regional base for the US, because of its frontiers with all of these countries. Between 1982 and 1986, 14 new US military sites (airstrips, military bases, naval bases and surveillance sites) were constructed on Honduran soil. During this time Honduras was effectively ruled by a triumvirate of President Suazo Córdova, General Alvarez of the armed forces, and US Ambassador Briggs. In order to forestall any resistance to what was a gross violation of national sovereignty, they passed a number of decrees aimed at suppressing the popular movements.[5] For example, in 1982, they passed Decree 33 which made the taking of land by *campesinos* into a terrorist act. This gave legal backing to what had been the practice of landowners for many years, namely bringing in police, security forces and the army to dislodge any *campesinos* invading their land.

EARLY ORGANIZATION IN SAN ANTONIO DE JURA

San Antonio de Jura developed in isolation, having no contact with the *campesino* movements. The people had learnt that rather than growing maize, it was safer to plant a root crop like yucca (which could not be devoured by wild animals), or coffee (which was not to the animals' taste). Ironically coffee, which had always been the crop of the large plantations (which usually occupied fertile lands ideal for growing basic grains), was found to be suited to the thin soil of the slopes, so the *campesinos* grew it in order to earn money to buy the food crops that they couldn't grow. At first there were problems. Although the *campesinos* had been harvesting coffee for decades, they had never before had the chance to grow it, so they did not know where to start. Moreover, selling their harvest was hard as they had no effective transport and no knowledge of the processes involved. As a result, they were forced to sell their harvests to intermediaries, who would only give them half the market value and who thus acquired the locally poignant name of "coyotes".

In the early years the only organizing force in San Antonio de Jura was the Catholic Church. The progressive ideas of liberation theology had flourished in the areas of Intibuca and Lempira, and reached the village of San Antonio de Jura with new migrants in the late 1960s. A small church was built, and with the help of a migrant teacher a school was set up which received Ministry of Education recognition (signifying nothing beyond a wage for the teacher). Nearly all the adults in the community were illiterate, as they had never had a chance to learn in their old villages. Recognizing this, during the 1970s the church set up groups to listen to radio literacy programmes, broadcast and organized by the UNC and Catholic Church.[6]

> Most people found the programmes difficult to follow and so dropped out, but a few of us kept on, seeing that we needed to learn in order to deal with the problems we faced here.
> *Pedro*

People dropped out for many reasons. Without watches or clocks or rigid schedules, it was hard to organize a group around the fixed times of radio broadcasts. There were few radios in the community. To repair them if they broke down, and to buy batteries (as there was no electricity), involved a long journey and considerable expense. The lack of face-to-face teaching limited the programme's success. Advanced learners tended to get frustrated and slower ones were left behind.

The small group of learners who continued with the UNC Catholic radio schools helped to found a co-operative in 1981, with 12 members, each making a small financial contribution to get it under way. At this time any form of organization, particularly a co-operative, attracted attention and suspicion. Rumours spread in neighbouring villages of the National Park that they had received funding from Cuba and that they had plans to develop an armed struggle. In practice, their goals were more modest. By pooling their produce they could sell it in larger quantities and get better prices, particularly as they were not forced to sell everything at the height of the harvest season. However, without transport they were still dependent on the "coyotes", so one of their first goals was to build a road from the village to the lakeside, to link up with the main highway between Tegucigalpa and San Pedro Sula. They rallied support within the community and during three months of 1983 a rough road was hacked out of the hills through the collective effort of dozens of people. For the first time a sense of unity was felt within the village.

A NEW UNION

In 1985, against the current of fragmentation in the popular movement, a new national *campesino* grouping emerged, the product of convergence as opposed to division. Five of the 14 strands of the movement united, abandoning their past identities and gathering together all their base groups to form the National Rural Workers Congress (CNTC). The CNTC was different right from the start. Leaders were not to be like patrons simply seeking to guide *campesinos* through the maze of land reform law. Instead the laws themselves were to be challenged, by encouraging direct action in the take-over of land. The ultimate aim was the eradication of all unjust forms of land ownership. Most importantly, unlike the previously bureaucratic, leadership-centred unions, the CNTC was to build from the base upwards.

The CNTC faced one major obstacle to its ideal of empowering its local groups. Over 75 per cent of its members were illiterate, making it difficult for them to participate in all aspects of union business. So, in 1986 Luciano Barrera – a man whose personal history characterized the ideals embodied in the strategy – was appointed to co-ordinate the planning of a suitable literacy programme. Luciano had no access to education throughout his childhood or youth and remained illiterate up until 1972 when he was a member of a *campesino* group that joined the radio schools literacy programme. He learnt rapidly. As he says, "after six months I became a promoter which meant that I co-ordinated the class whilst also studying in it." A few months later Luciano became a supervisor, assisting other local groups as well as his own. Soon afterwards he was made a regional adviser, and began to have a say over the content of the programmes from which he was learning. Eventually the national council of the radio schools asked him to join them to help decide policy and run training programmes.

Following this role model the CNTC hoped to use the literacy programme to strengthen its base groups as well as generate new local, regional and national leaders. Meanwhile, the personal ascent of Luciano Barrera continued. In 1987, he was elected as General Secretary of the CNTC. With this election Luciano was able to ensure that the literacy programme was made the central plank of the CNTC's work.

A technical team was appointed whose task was to develop a literacy programme in line with the CNTC's ideals. Rather than producing pre-packaged materials in a Tegucigalpa office, the team initiated an extensive investigation with *campesinos* in 25 base groups, in order to decide which themes they themselves wanted in their literacy programme. After a number of meetings the comments and ideas of different groups were systematized by the technical team. A pilot programme experimented with the results of this investigation using the literacy primer which it had produced. Groups met for two hours every day, co-ordinated by promoters who received training but who were also often learners themselves. All were volunteers.

The primer used powerful photographs, and generative words such as Child, Family, Women, School, Work, *Campesino*, Rural Community, Co-operative, Meeting, and CNTC. Every day classes started with a half-hour discussion, prompted by an image on a poster relating to the week's theme. By the end of the week the *campesinos* had spent two and a half hours reflecting on this theme, and exchanging opinions.

The images that are used in the CNTC primer are good examples of codifications.[7] That is, the images are not so explicit in their meaning as to be propagandist, nor at the same time are they puzzles which are open to any interpretation. They are instead images that embody problems or contradictions of *campesino* reality, which require analysis and reflection to de-code. For example (see Figure 4.1), one generative word is *Reunión* (meeting), associated with a photograph of a room with about 30 people in it, including a group of women (two with babies). Some people are voting, others are distracted. The photograph can stimulate discussion about many things: perhaps about women's participation, perhaps about democracy, perhaps about the running of a meeting or how people feel in meetings. The image is evocative, and of immediate relevance to the learners in any CNTC base group. By being faced so directly with their own way of life the learners are for the first time able to discuss aspects of their lives which before they had only lived. The codification achieves this by creating the necessary distance between *campesinos* and their actions. Rather than being in a meeting they are forced to think about what they do in meetings. This is likely to lead to discussion about how to change the structure and running of meetings. The CNTC team felt that everything discussed in the classes would find concrete application in the work of their base groups.

After the primer was piloted, meetings were held with all the different groups in order to evaluate the success of the different themes and to consider what follow-up materials should be produced. This respect for, and responsiveness to, the ideas of the base groups has been central to the development of effective materials and the creation of a programme which

Figure 4.1: Reunión ("meeting") – a photo of a CNTC union meeting used as a codification in the CNTC literacy primer.

campesinos feel to be their own. A revised primer was introduced to 209 base groups of the CNTC in 1987. These groups were given the same powers as those in the pilot programme to participate in future revisions and in the development of further materials.

Since 1987 the technical team, in permanent consultation with base groups, has produced a range of high quality educational materials for three levels. For the CNTC the second and third level materials are as important, if not more important, than the literacy primer. There is no clear line when literacy is achieved. Indeed, the key to success is, simply, to continue doing it. Relevant materials which keep up the learners' interest are thus essential. For the second level the CNTC have produced two books. *We Struggle for our Health* is a remarkably practical introduction to health issues, precisely adapted to Honduran *campesino* reality. It deals with everything from the prevention of diarrhoea to the personal diagnosis of breast cancer, and gives details of how to obtain, prepare and take both traditional and modern remedies. The other second level book, *Organized and United We Strengthen the CNTC*, is a guide to the building and running of an organization, from the grassroots upwards, providing a history of the *campesino* movement, details of the CNTC statutes and suggestions for efficient ways of working.

For level three, the CNTC has produced a further two books. *Our Campesino Reality* studies and compares different regions of the country from the viewpoint of the *campesinos* who live there. In each chapter it builds from the geography of a department to an examination of the socio-economic problems that *campesinos* face and the solutions they have found. The study of other regions helps learners to see their own conditions more clearly and acts as a basis for them to prepare an examination of their own area. Finally, *The Rural Adviser* analyses the agricultural situation of Honduras and gives details of soil conservation methods (practical advice on terracing and crop rotation), common pests (with vivid pictures to help in their identification), different fertilizers (both organic and chemical) and the techniques for growing, harvesting and storing the most common crops (including coffee, bananas, basic grains and vegetables).

For all three levels of the CNTC's literacy programme there are mathematics books which have a highly practical focus, never losing sight of how the *campesinos* themselves will use the skills. However, despite the enormous applicability of all these books, the CNTC publication which has proved most popular by far is *The Shaggy Dog Tales of Teofilito*. These short stories were written by the first ever General Secretary of the CNTC, Teofilo Trejo. In them he uses traditional *campesino* language, including many words that have never before been used in written form. The stories have been used to lighten the literacy programme both at the training level and in the classes themselves.

CO-OPERATIVE LITERACY

> After the radio-schools declined there was no adult education here. No other
> union seemed to think literacy was important. Only once, a political party
> tried to start something, just before the elections, but after the elections we
> never saw them again.
> *Pedro, co-operative member*

In 1986 a representative arrived in San Antonio de Jura to give details
of the newly formed CNTC. The small co-operative, which until then
had remained independent of any national grouping, decided to affiliate.
The main reason for their decision was the CNTC's strong emphasis on
education, as the majority of *campesinos* in the village were still illiterate.

By early 1989 a group of 35 people in San Antonio de Jura had
completed all three levels of the CNTC's literacy programme and were
eagerly awaiting a fourth level. Over three years it has of course given
people literacy skills, but through those skills it has also opened up many
new areas of knowledge and understanding.

The co-operative

The impact of the CNTC programme on the co-operative has been
substantial. The San Antonio de Jura co-operative meetings are now
attended by almost all members, whereas in the past an attendance of
half was considered good. Those who do not turn up usually send written
apologies. People arrive more punctually and work through a clear agenda.

> Now most of us in the co-operative can read and write, so we can do
> things that were unimaginable before.
> *Juan*

Reports from sub-groups are read out and detailed minutes are taken.
Good accounts are maintained. The level of participation in discussions
has increased beyond recognition.

> If someone thinks something, they know when and how to say it. In the
> past we were mostly silent.
> *Bernardo*

Problems are now resolved in a systematic way. For example, the co-
operative pooled funding to buy a truck for selling their coffee and buying
food. In this way they completely bypassed the "coyotes". A storehouse
has been built and a shop opened which stocks basic goods for the whole
community, including batteries, food, matches, cigarettes and soft drinks.

> Through the book on organization we learnt about the vices that people can
> have which damage good organization, vices like individualism, immobilism,
> and radicalism. We've been able to identify these and counteract them.
> *Carlos*

One member of the co-operative had to be forcibly removed. After several years in the army he had returned unexpectedly to the community, for no apparent reason. Two co-operative members had been alert and succeeded in identifying him as an infiltrator planted by the specialist army Batallón 316, which has been linked to death-squad killings.

> He had joined to spy on us and give information to the authorities. Some time after we threw him out he died in a gunfight here in the village. That could have brought serious repression down on all of us but his parents defended us and agreed that his death was an accident.
>
> *Anonymous*

This experience tested the unity of the co-operative. In earlier days many people might have dropped out for fear of reprisals. However, the new-found discipline and a clear sense of their own rights meant that on this occasion members held together.

The literacy programme in San Antonio de Jura has been important as a means of developing links between the local co-operative and the regional and national offices of the CNTC. Members are committed to belonging – and contributing – to a national organization. One of the first promoters in the village, Nestor, has followed in the footsteps of Luciano Barrera. After working at local and regional levels, he became a consultant on the CNTC's national literacy team. One of the newer promoters, Bernardo, was recently chosen to represent the CNTC at an adult education conference in Mexico, where he gave an account of the literacy programme at the grass roots, and then received a month's training with international experts. For the first time, the people of San Antonio de Jura have a clear idea of what is happening in the *campesino* movement, both internationally and in other parts of their own country. The CNTC produces a monthly publication, *Cumbo and Machete*,[8] which gives updates on land-invasions and other relevant developments in Honduras.

The co-operative acts as a living example for the whole community of the benefits of collective work. Members now get better prices for their coffee. Improved agricultural techniques, learnt from *The Rural Adviser*, augur well for the future. The use of nurseries to grow coffee seedlings, before transplanting them to permanent locations, has produced stronger plants. The threat of soil erosion on some slopes has been reduced through terracing and laying down tree-trunks. With improved productivity, fewer people are now dependent on migrating to sugar and coffee harvests. People now have time to enjoy listening to the co-operative music group – with traditional double bass, fiddle and guitars – who have taken to writing their own songs about life in San Antonio de Jura.

The community
The CNTC programme was open to everyone in San Antonio de Jura, not just to members of the co-operative.

For the first time people are seeing beyond their immediate lives and
beyond their need to get money. There is a mentality of self and collective
improvement.
Bernardo (literacy promoter)

The health books have proved particularly useful. The number of cases of
diarrhoea – especially amongst children – has been reduced as awareness
of hygiene has spread. Fewer hens are now seen pecking in the kitchen
dust, spreading bacterial infections.

We are no longer bringing up our children scrambled up with pigs and dogs.
Dora

Where before the river and the trees had served as toilets, now concrete
latrines are used, built by co-operative members. The date of their
construction is often scratched in the concrete, evidence that most
appeared soon after the topic was studied (and step-by-step directions
given) in the health book. Malnutrition is less common as people know
more about the nutritional values of different foods. In the absence of
any health centre increased competence in first aid has proved invaluable.
The use of lemon, garlic, onions, camomile and eucalyptus for common
ailments has reduced unnecessary suffering and saved money.

In comparison with the school education available in San Antonio de
Jura, the CNTC programme is popular, even amongst the younger
generation. There is no library or secondary education in the village.
The nearest secondary school is two hours away, but it is private and too
expensive for anyone from the village. As a result, several primary-school
leavers have joined the CNTC literacy programme to extend their studies.
For them, the CNTC programme is a new type of education. Their school
books tended to be imported, teaching about things which made little sense
to the children.

We learnt about cars and planes and flying to the moon and going on
picnics, and shopping in supermarkets. It wasn't very useful.
Maria (aged 14)

In the circumstances, the new Ministry of Education plan to produce a
series of textbooks called *My Honduras* would seem promising. However,
Honduran teachers, of whom 15,000 are unemployed, were not allowed
any part in producing the materials as all the work was given to a team
of "experts" from USAID. The books were printed in Costa Rica. Their
contents are perhaps predictable, full of patriotic symbols like national
trees, national flowers and flags. Meanwhile, the Ministry of Education
budget continues to be cut.

Less than ten per cent of our national budget goes on education. Primary
schools get very little of that. Some goes to the universities and some goes to
the Ministry of Sport, but a lot more goes to the institutes and schools run

by the Ministry of Defence. They hide the figures but a lot of army training comes out of the education budget.
Raul Mejía, COLPROSUMAH

In the absence of an effective state provision of rural education, the role that the CNTC plays – particularly in remote communities like San Antonio de Jura – is critical.

FROM WORDS TO ACTION

Many of the people from San Antonio de Jura who were not members of the co-operative, but joined the CNTC literacy programme, have now decided to join the co-operative itself. From the original 12, the co-operative has grown to a membership of 40. Such an inspiring example has spread beyond the village, and led to the setting up of another co-operative, an hour's walk away in Buena Vista, which was founded with the support of the one in San Antonio de Jura and immediately chose to join the CNTC literacy programme.

In Buena Vista's literacy classes, early discussions based on codifications and generative words returned again and again to the theme of land. Many members were landless. Several of them had spent five years in negotiations with the Agrarian Reform Institute (INA) trying to get rights to 150 *manzanas* of land (one *manzana* equals .43 hectares) which stretched from Buena Vista down to Lake Yojoa, and which had been idle for a long time. The land had originally been owned by some Salvadoreans. When they had abandoned it in 1969, following the Football War, one of the lakeside landowners (who already owned 750 *manzanas*) claimed the land for himself. There were no legal papers for the land, partly because it was in a national park and should not have belonged to anyone. The landowner had no intention of farming the land himself, but hoped to hire it out, at exorbitant rates, to the local *campesinos*. The land was left idle, because none of the *campesinos* could afford the rent. They found that their polite and formal requests to be allowed to take over the land and farm it for themselves were making little impact on the INA. As history taught them that land had only ever been secured as a result of direct action, discussions in the literacy classes became increasingly explicit.

The discontent in Buena Vista was echoed nationally. INA was dragging its feet every application and spent most of its time seeking to play off the different unions against each other. However, the unifying example of the CNTC began to spread. Meetings were held between all of the *campesino* groupings in the country. To test the possibilities of unity, it was decided that a collective action of land-seizure would be organized on a national scale. The date was set for 20 May 1987. Local co-operatives who had submitted applications to the INA went ahead and claimed the land, marking it out with improvised fencing, clearing it and planting a few symbolic crops. At the same time the regional and national offices of the INA were occupied by aggrieved *campesinos*, seeking recognition of their rights and resolution of their demands. A series of other demands were also made, including the removal of the Institute's director, the release of political prisoners and the revision of systems of credit for *campesinos*.

The government was thrown into confusion. At first they sought to use traditional divide and rule tactics, but all organizations (except for the now right-wing UNC) stood firm. The army was keen to respond with violence but the government of President Azcona was concerned about international publicity, especially at a time when the US wanted to isolate Nicaragua diplomatically by stressing the apparent democracy of its neighbours. The unions were claiming that they accepted the law, and that they had only been driven to action by the INA's incompetence. It was a finely pitched line. President Azcona decided to defuse the situation by setting up a new commission to investigate all the claims.

The 18 members of the Buena Vista co-operative took their chance. On 20 May they occupied the land that they had been applying for, announced their reclamation to the INA, and marked out the land with fences. The literacy classes became a key forum for discussing policy in the following weeks and also for developing the skills necessary to develop the land.

> We saw the literacy process and the reclamation of land as inseparable.
> Neither would really be effective without the other.
> *Carlos, member of Buena Vista*

As a small group, the Buena Vista co-operative could not take advantage of all the land. They planted six *manzanas* of yucca and informed other local *campesinos* of the availability of land, confident that many would flock to join their new co-operative now that they had something to show for themselves.

These hopes were dealt a serious blow in July 1987, two months after the reclamation. Despite President Azcona's national "conciliation" and the fact that he had set up a commission to bypass the INA and speed up settlements, the INA intervened, calling in the feared Public Security Forces (FUSEP) who forcibly dislodged the Buena Vista members from the land. Immediately the co-operative decided to re-occupy the land and continue their plans to develop it but the event left a mark on the community. Other *campesinos* became hesitant to join the co-operative because they feared reprisals. The Pentecostal pastor in Buena Vista, an influential figure, fuelled these fears. He spoke out against the co-operative, denouncing it as subversive and their literacy classes as indoctrination.

A year later the lakeside landowner decided to try to resolve the affair. He spoke to his nephew who worked in the INA and placed a few bribes in the right hands to persuade the San Pedro Sula military police to get involved. Technically Buena Vista was not part of their territory, but the bribes persuaded them to get involved. In violent exchanges 16 of the co-operative members were arrested. In later tribunals only one was found guilty – and was imprisoned for fifty days – though the nature of the charges was never made clear. The rest walked free and re-occupied the land, but the action produced one desired effect for the landowner. Within a few weeks, attendance at the literacy classes dwindled to only five people. Eventually even the promoter himself dropped out, fearing that as a prominent figure he was a major target. The literacy classes have been abandoned but the remaining handful of co-operative members cling to their land in the defiant hope that some time in the future their fortunes will pick up.

The experience of Buena Vista was not isolated. Although nationally 14,000 *manzanas* were reclaimed on 20 May (as much as had been gained in 18 months of negotiations), most of it was soon lost through either local legal actions or not-so-legal military actions. In the process 470 *campesinos* were arrested and four were killed. Since then, the CNTC has come under increasing pressure, with the literacy programme a particular target. Classes have been forced to close (particularly near the US army bases in Yoro and Colon). Activists have been threatened and detained. A couple have disappeared. In Santa Barbara one literacy promoter has been murdered.

The CNTC response to threats against its literacy workers has been to be open about its work and seek official recognition. In 1988 it initiated a network of all the non-governmental groups who work on literacy in Honduras. This has helped in co-ordination between groups, avoiding the overlapping of work and facilitating the sharing of skills. Following the strategy of the United Nations – similar to that developed in El Salvador – this group then approached the Ministry of Education to seek support for their work. The director of literacy was sympathetic and agreed to set up a system of identity cards giving acknowledgement of the Ministry of Education to the work of all the groups. CNTC literacy workers can now carry a card which offers them a measure of protection against anyone who accuses them of subversion. It may also help to exempt them from forced military recruitment. There is only one serious limitation, for, as Rosa Lila Rodriguez (a member of the CNTC technical team) points out, "Most of the soldiers are illiterate so they won't make any sense of the cards"!

WOMEN AND THE UNION

A big problem within the CNTC is the domination of the union by men. In the San Pedro Sula regional council (which covers San Antonio de Jura) there is only one woman out of nine representatives. In the national co-ordinating committee there is only one woman out of a total of 14. In both cases these women only seem to have been elected because their posts deal specifically with women's affairs. However, the four co-ordinators of the national technical team for the literacy programme are all women.

> We face a paradox. At times it seems we must start by educating the men
> so that the women are allowed more space, and yet we are adamant that it
> should not be up to the men to decide whether the women participate.
> *Doris Hernández, head of technical team*

The co-ordinators are responsible for producing all the literacy
materials. In the primer there are two powerful images of women. In
the first they are seen hard at work in the fields. In the second they are
seen bearing food and serving drink to the men who are working in the
fields. Over five days of discussions the double labour of women and their
double exploitation is likely to be explored in some depth.

The men may openly discuss women's roles and their exploitation in
the literacy classes, but they seem reluctant to address the same issues so
freely when it comes to daily practice. In San Antonio de Jura few women
participated in the literacy programme. Only six out of the 35 participants
in the original literacy group in San Antonio de Jura were women. The
pressures of domestic duties and the level of *machismo* in the community
prevented many other women from joining.

> The men think that they alone are capable, so we are left with a mountain
> of children in the poverty of our homes, whilst they go and learn or drink
> themselves silly.
> *Helena (aged 35)*

Many men, who are now third-level learners, still refuse to let their wives
or daughters join, either because of entrenched beliefs about roles, or for
fear that their wives may do better than them! Even the wife of one of the
promoters has remained illiterate. Deprived of education the women have
little chance to be involved in community affairs. Both co-operative and
local-council meetings are male-dominated. However, the women who
participated in the literacy programme have started to challenge their roles:

> Some of us have begun to see the possibilities and are refusing to be treated
> as objects any longer.

In the San Antonio de Jura co-operative a women's sub-group has started
meeting regularly and they have plans to set up a women's group in the
community as a whole, but as yet this group has little power and the few
women involved are mocked by men in the co-operative meetings.

> When women speak, the men start talking among themselves. If we raise
> the issue of women's participation, they start joking.

The national technical team is acutely aware of the difficulties faced by
women who do participate. They were at first cautious about producing
materials just for women or about encouraging women-only classes,
wanting to avoid accusations of separatism which might antagonize
relations with men and end up further marginalizing the few women

who do get involved. However, recent experience has shown them that providing space and materials specifically for women might be effective. A women-only group was set up in Comayagua. Sixty women enrolled, which made it one of the biggest groups in the country and gave a clear sign that a women-only group can generate the momentum to challenge *machismo* effectively, thus enabling women to participate. The national technical team now have provisional plans to produce a book specifically for women. As with all their publications, consultation will take place:

> The contents will depend on dialogues with women in the process of producing the book, but it is likely to include details of women's rights and aspects of relations with men.
> *Doris Hernández*

CONCLUSIONS

Participatory investigation is the centrepiece of the CNTC literacy strategy, helping to ensure that despite working on a national scale, the starting point of all the materials is the regional and local realities of the learners. There have been regular local forums in San Antonio de Jura, at the beginning and end of each course, where learners have been able to give their opinions, air their criticisms and offer their recommendations to literacy workers from the regional office in San Pedro Sula. Moreover, every member of the CNTC national technical team has visited the village to discuss proposals and listen to viewpoints. The *campesinos* of San Antonio de Jura feel very strongly that the literacy programme is their own.

> In the past we always thought that education was something that came from outside, brought by other people. When we started with the CNTC, I didn't think it was real education, because it was about things I already know about. But now I can see my own life in a different way and I can do things with my life that I never thought were possible.
> *Pedro*

From participatory investigations, the national technical team have produced the codifications that fill the literacy primer, which the learners in the first level of the course decode. If the materials effectively grasp the contradictions of the learners' reality then this decoding becomes more than the study of a workbook. In decoding the image the learners are confronted for the first time with their lived reality in a manner which enables them to reflect on it. Rather than being submerged by the never-ending flow of demands on their time, they are able to step outside and see their lives in a new light. They can see their relations to the world and the world's relations to them; they can see how they are formed by the world and how they too can form it. This process is called conscientization. It is not consciousness raising, nor politicization, which too often is simply another form of imposition. It is a more comprehensive emergence from dependency, from passivity, from the "blindness" associated with a culture of silence. It gives people the opportunity and the ability to identify their own agenda in the knowledge that the world no longer has to be an imposed, static reality.

> One of the important points in conscientization is to provoke recognition of the world, not as a "given" world, but as a world dynamically "in the making".
> *Paulo Freire*[9]

Conscientization is not a process completed in the moment of realization. It is intimately linked to subsequent action. Through the continuing evaluations the CNTC gives Honduran *campesinos* their first possible taste of the power of such action. Their voice is heard, and this helps to determine the future contents of what they learn. The second and third levels thus become part of their own actions. They begin to see that it is possible to change the world, that illnesses can be reduced, that yields can be improved, that land can be occupied and used. The *campesinos* begin to see the power of their actions: the power not only to make individual changes, but to change their whole community. Conscientization cannot just be personal; it is the awakening of a whole community, inseparable from organization. Conceived and executed in this way, literacy can be the basis for changing whole nations.

NOTES

1.   President Sauzo in 1981 declared with apparent pride that his country was a "backyard" of the United States. Its history as a military base stretches back to 1954 when it was used as a US base for the overthrow of the Arbenz government in neighbouring Guatemala. Presently host to the Contras, it is expected to become an important base to contain a possible El Salvadorean revolution.
2.   Lapper, Richard, *Honduras: State for Sale* (London: Latin America Bureau, 1985)
3.   Ibid.
4.   Aspects of the history of the *campesino* movement in Honduras based on (a) Centro de Documentación de Honduras (CEDOH), Especial no. 34, March 1988, *25 Anos de Reforma Agraria*, and (b) Instituto Hondureno de Desarollo Rural (IHDER), *Honduras Agraria*, no. 3, January 1988.
5.   One of the most important groups in the popular movement was the teachers' union, COLPROSUMAH. The manner in which this union was infiltrated and divided was classic. A small paid-off group splintered from the Union's Congress, accusing the leadership of being undemocratic and communist. Selling themselves as a (so-called) demographic splinter of COLPROSUMAH they immediately got recognition from the Supreme Court. The Ministry of Education sequestrated the real Union's pension funds (made up of teachers contributions!) and the army occupied and dismantled the Union's offices. The split between the so-called Democratic COLPROSUMAH (which is small but rich) and the Authentic

COLPROSUMAH (which is large but starved of funds and recognition) continues to this day.

6.   The UNC set up the Suyapa Radio Schools.

7.   See Freire, Paulo, *Cultural Action for Freedom* (London: Penguin, 1973). The concept of codification is introduced here as the CNTC work gives better examples than that in Nicaragua. The images in the Nicaraguan primers, although clearly based on these ideas, were centrally produced for urban and rural realities, involving no participatory investigation to identify themes and ended up opening fewer channels for discussion, perhaps even channelling people into certain analyses. It should be noted that codifications are by no means always photographs. They may be sketches or even pieces of theatre.

8.   The *cumbo* and *machete* are the symbols of the CNTC: the *cumbo* being a hollowed container used by *campesinos* to carry water in the fields, and the *machete* being their all-purpose tool.

9.   Freire, Paulo, *Politics of Education* (London: Macmillan, 1985).

5. Ecuador, Santa Lucia: Literacy and Human Rights

> If we remain on the margins of the state, we only have marginal possibilities
> of making marginal change . . . we are left working on a small scale.
> *Rosa María Torres*[1]

The CNTC programme in Honduras illustrates how literacy can further
organizational aims in struggles for social justice. Another way of working
is through or within a government, which has more resources than any
individual non-governmental organization and thus the chance to make a
greater national impact. In Honduras, the nature of the regime makes this
kind of work impossible. In Ecuador, a new social-democratic government
has opened up channels through which progressive groups could work,
using the structure of a government programme to strengthen the popular
movement. A historical precedent for this exists in Latin America: in Chile
in the 1960s, progressive organizations used the government literacy
programme (co-ordinated by Paulo Freire) to raise demands to which
the Frei government could not respond, helping to create the necessary
support for Allende's Popular Front and more radical social policies.

President Borja came to power in Ecuador at the head of a social-
democratic coalition in 1988. He replaced the authoritarian government of
Léon Febrés Cordero, characterized by Ronald Reagan as "an articulate
champion of free enterprise",[2] whose commitment to monetarism and
debt repayment had left a legacy of rising poverty and human rights
violations. The presence of Fidel Castro and Daniel Ortega at the new
President's inauguration was one sign of a government heralding change.
His programme involved prioritizing the paying back of the "social-debt"
accumulated by governments to the detriment of their voters.

BORJA'S CAMPAIGN

On International Literacy Day 1988, the President announced that there
would be a three-month National Literacy Campaign the following year
as a major part of the repayment of the "social debt". The campaign
was named after Monsignor Leonidas Proaño, a liberation theologist who
worked with poor indigenous *campesinos* in the Andean Sierra, defending
their rights and doing literacy work. In 1976, he was arrested by a military
government that found his work subversive.

All that which means change needs an element of risk and, for that reason,
needs courage to run that risk.
Monsignor Proaño (campaign slogan)

Two weeks after the President's announcement in 1988, a planning
conference for the Proaño campaign was held. Representatives from
government ministries and a wide range of non-governmental groups
were invited, including trade unions, women's organizations, indigenous
groups, and organizations involved in literacy work and social-science
research within Ecuador. It was decided to leave the planning and
execution of a programme in indigenous languages to CONAIE, the
Ecuadorean confederation of indigenous peoples. Spanish speakers were
to learn through the government campaign.

> This is clearly a government campaign but not a party one. The aim is
> to use the campaign for popular interests, not political ones.
> *R.M. Torres*

Ideology
The campaign had three stated objectives:

1) to involve in the world of written communication all those sectors of
   our country who, forced by circumstances and the need to survive,
   could not participate in this fundamental form of expression;
2) to stimulate in the whole of Ecuadorean society the need for improved
   understanding of national reality, its geography, history, linguistic and
   cultural diversity, its socio-economic problematic and its relations to
   Latin America and the rest of the world;
3) to re-activate the spirit and feeling of democratic life, generating
   social participation, dialogue, critical reflection and an open and
   pluralist discussion of the democratic task itself.[3]

Rosa María Torres was appointed head of the pedagogical team in charge
of preparing the campaign materials. Her involvement with the campaign
was a matter of much dispute. She worked for five years in Nicaragua and
was involved in the planning and evaluation of the Nicaraguan Literacy
Crusade. Accused of being a communist by the right-wing press, she
was attacked by the left for importing models from abroad. Neither is an
accurate assessment.

> We can't import models because conditions are different in each country
> *R.M. Torres*

Neither was the campaign introducing revolutionary materials. Rather, the
primer was based on the democratization of the United Nations Charter of
Human Rights. The generative themes of the lessons were human-rights
issues, conceived not as abstract declarations but as concrete practices.
For example "You and I have the right to work" is accompanied by a

codification of work involving four photographs: those of a lathe worker, a seamstress, a teacher and rural-co-operative workers. Dialogue was to be based on the nature of different forms of labour and how the work experiences of the learners related to Article 23 of the UN/Charter and relevant articles in Ecuador's political constitution. It was hoped that the dialogue would create a basis for participation in democratic organizations at grass-roots levels, which would ensure the fulfilment of human rights throughout society.

Educational methods

> In the 60s and 70s, popular education generated a series of revolutionary ideas. But now, there's a stagnation. . . . In the last few years, there's been no development of theory. The orthodoxy that literacy is not just a technique has tended to generate a discussion exclusively linked to social change and a neglect of the didactic and educational aspects which have remained traditional . . . we've ended up with backward methods and inapplicable ideals.
> R.M. Torres

The structures of literacy campaigns and programmes since the 1970s have often been based on a number of principles which have been taught rigidly, and passively accepted by many educators as the new orthodoxies. Freire's work was an attack on purely technical approaches to education, yet all over Latin America it has itself been translated into techniques just as mechanical as those of the system it was trying to replace. Even in Nicaragua, for example, where dialogue and the critical analysis of reality were at the heart of the educational philosophy, in practice this often meant a group of students being explained a political line on an issue in just as mechanical a way as that employed by the traditional formal-education system it was supposed to replace.

> Dialogue occurs between equals but a power relation exists between educator and learner. If this is denied, the relation will remain because the resistance to change comes as much from learners as teachers. To construct dialogue, teachers must first understand why it's difficult to generate it.
> R.M. Torres

It is the responsibility of the teacher to recognize and work towards overcoming a relationship which inhibits dialogue. Therefore the training of literacy teachers had to be at the heart of the structuring of the campaign. A workshop on techniques – on generative words and syllabic families for instance – was not sufficient. Training required the education of teachers to be at least as wide-ranging as the literacy classes. A number of different methods were used. As well as the guidebook for each lesson, a series of workshops were organized in the five months before the campaign, using videos to ensure that the methodological principles were not lost (as they had been in Nicaragua) on the journey from the national office through the regional and local offices to the workshops for literacy teachers themselves. In addition, training at a distance operated through a series of work documents, pamphlets published every week for eight months and distributed to everyone involved, from administrators to literacy teachers.

> The guide is the recipe book. The work documents contain the wider vision.
> *R.M. Torres*

There were five groups of documents: *Information on the campaign; Proaño's thought; History of literacy teaching in Ecuador; The educational dimension of literacy teaching;* and *The social dimension of literacy teaching,* a series covering themes such as human rights, housing and land reform. This last series of documents were produced by different non-governmental organizations, a concrete way in which it was possible for groups to use the structure of the campaign to raise the profile of political issues.[4]

Mobilization

> States achieving success in campaigns have had the political commitment, motivation and power to be able to organize an effective mobilization of all available human, institutional and material resources needed.[5]

The campaign drew some of its inspiration from other mass campaigns, specifically Nicaragua's. The plan was to mobilize secondary-school students to organize groups for teaching literacy in a similar manner.[6] Unlike in Nicaragua, where the initial wave of revolutionary euphoria was sufficient to promote voluntary involvement and where it was possible to suspend schools for five months, in Ecuador, participation had to be compulsory. 70,000 sixth grade secondary-school students (16–18 year olds) were mobilized in this way as literacy teachers. However, because of parental resistance, the students stayed in their own area, travelling short distances daily to teach. There was little of the town and country interchange that characterized the Nicaraguan crusade.

To create the public profile that would generate the necessary enthusiasm in different social sectors, the whole range of the media was used, from weekly television puppet-shows involving humorous fables on the consequences of illiteracy, to murals, posters and radio discussion-panels on issues raised by the campaign. Perhaps the biggest impact was made by the work documents themselves. Each week 200,000 copies of the new document were printed and distributed, one for every 50 inhabitants. These reached well beyond those immediately involved in the campaign, to teachers in schools and within the universities, to unions, politicians, popular organizations, and through literacy teachers to their families and friends.

THE CAMPAIGN IN PRACTICE

Santa Lucía: Rural and urban life

Ecuador is a small country yet in its environment, culture and politics, it can be divided into three quite distinct areas:

1) In the Andean Sierra, most of the inhabitants are Quichuan Amerindians, descendants of the Incas. These mountains contain the capital Quito, but much of the area is farmed by villagers on cold, rocky, steep land.

2) On the eastern side of the mountains the sparsely populated Amazonian region is part of a vast tropical rain-forest. Numerous groups of indigenous peoples are attempting to preserve their ways of life here in the face of deforestation caused, in Ecuador, by exploration and drilling for oil.

3) The Pacific coastal strip, with a mostly *mestizo* population (i.e. of mixed Spanish and Indian descent), is largely flat farming country on the equator. It is the centre of class politics and contains Guayaquil, Ecuador's second city.

Going to Guayaquil . . . it's so different that for me it's difficult!
Ruth Moya, Quito[7]

Guayaquil is very regionalist: people are not interested in the Sierra, in the indigenous people. This regionalism was sharpened by León Febrés Cordero who used it for political gain.
Angel Nieto[8]

In order to focus on the Spanish campaign, we chose to work in a province of the coast where the majority of learners are Spanish-speaking *mestizos*. The province of Guayas is named after the last chief of the Huancavilca people, one of a number of tribes which settled at different times on the Ecuadorean seaboard. His wife, Quill, gave her name to the provincial capital, Guayaquil, a busy smog-filled port and trading centre where the industrial elite and the parties of the political right have their stronghold. Rich farming land – the source of its trading wealth – surrounds Guayaquil.

Santa Lucía is a municipality or canton of Guayas, an hour's drive up a good road from Guayaquil. It is a rural rice-growing area with many small villages (*recintos*). While the major road exists, much of the transport is still river-based. Flowing leisurely through the canton is the broad River Daule. Pumps take water from it at regular intervals to irrigate the paddy fields. Locally, the river was called *Estero Loco*, the mad estuary, because of its unpredictable flooding during the rainy season. Now, although there are still occasional drownings when swimmers neglect the force of the current, a dam to the north has tamed the extremes of its behaviour.

The unjust distribution of land is a problem that dates back to the colonial

era. The Spanish conquerors deprived the indigenous peoples of their land and took control of them. But, in addition, they forced the Indians to work for them, submitting them to slavery and forced labour.
Work document 32: *The Problem of Land in Ecuador*

There is a long history of popular organization among the *campesinos* of Guayas. The first violent mobilizations took the form of protests – fostered by the newly-formed Socialist Party – against landlord abuses during the economic crisis of the 1920s.

> The struggle on the coast almost always goes violently beyond the narrow boundaries of the law and necessitates retrospective legislation.[9]

The first agrarian reform law (1964), forced by illegal mobilizations and land take-overs, had little effect: clauses protected large landowners and, as in Honduras, *campesino* organizations were not represented in the reform's administrative agency. A demonstration in Guayaquil on May Day 1966 was seen as the signal of the law's failure in Guayas. Land occupations and struggles with landowners continued. The evictions of rice farmers from occupied farms were so frequent that, in 1970, a national government had to issue a special decree (Decree 1001) to stem the growing incidence of violence on the rice plantations. Under the decree, some land was shared, encouraging the formation of a large number of co-operatives. With names such as Che Guevara, Salvador Allende and Struggle for Progress, they broadcast the euphoria of their victory.

There are still 30 rice-growing co-operatives in Santa Lucia alone. But the practice bears little relation to the names.

> The co-op system failed here . . . because the co-op leaders exploited the *campesinos* . . . the most educated took over. . . .
> *Eduardo Moreno*[10]

While disparities in education were not the only factor, illiteracy certainly contributed to the demise of the rice co-ops and the failure of land reform in the Daule valley. A co-op elite has ended up reproducing the same form of exploitation of landless *campesinos* and migrants from the Sierra that the landowners made use of before the co-ops existed: that is, cheap, temporary wage-labour. In addition, many landowners avoided agrarian reform by dividing their land into parcels and giving it nominally to the *campesinos* who were really only the labourers on the land. Papers were signed by barely-literate *campesinos* and life went on as before.

During the 1970s the pressures of recession in the international markets for rice hit the co-ops hard. Unable to afford repayments on credits, they were at a disadvantage in relation to the larger landowners who had enough capital to make more profit by lending money to small co-ops and who also had a monopoly control of the rice-processing industry and distribution for export. This new breed of landowners was a capitalist business elite based in Guayaquil.

> The coast constitutes the principal area for the capitalist development of agriculture in the country.... The land is being concentrated in the hands of a capitalist business sector.
> Work Document 32

If the co-ops were to survive, they needed intervention from the state. In 1980, after years of military rule, the return to democracy put Jaime Roldos in power on a wave of popular support. To promote the rights of *campesinos*, his government set up FODERUMA, an aid agency providing credit and the technology needed to compete on the rice markets. In Santa Lucía, the *campesinos* founded a co-ordinating committee (CCC) to help the co-operatives make the most of the new agency.

> There was no consultation about what we needed ... we had to accept what FODERUMA offered and at first it seemed good: they were offering drinking water, electrification, and technology for rice dryers and husk removers. There was a foreign worker who came to teach us to use the technology. He helped us organize to use it for our own interests. But he was then called a revolutionary and forced to leave the country. They didn't want people to take control of the technology, they wanted people to be dependent on it. FODERUMA then withdrew the money.
> *Armando Vega, ex-head of CCC*

During the time of Febrés Cordero, FODERUMA loans were offered at preferential rates to *campesinos* who left the co-ops and set up as individual farmers. In the absence of any collective use of credit, the money was often dissipated wastefully, leaving *campesinos* in more debt to state institutions and forcing them to sell their land to the new generation of agricultural businessmen. The CCC was dismantled leaving all the co-ops working in competition with each other as well as with the large landowners. Many are still in debt to FODERUMA from that time.

> In this way, lands that had passed into the hands of co-operatives as a result of the *campesino* struggle, today have returned into the hands of businessmen.
> Work Document 32

The loss of land and homes (confiscated to pay debts) has forced many *campesinos* into the central town of Santa Lucía. They are now either landless labourers on surrounding farms, working for pitifully low wages, or scraping a living from new forms of work. The town (population 18, 600) is a small trading centre receiving all the commercial goods that pass on the road to Guayaquil.

> A few years ago, Santa Lucía wasn't much more than a village. Now, with the road and the links with Guayaquil, the place is growing ... there's a big class of traders and salesmen now.
> *José Cruzati (school caretaker, Santa Lucía)*

Moving to the town has brought its own problems. The local authorities have proved unable to deal with the rising population of the town.

> Four out of every ten new houses [in Ecuador] are illegal constructions.
> Work Document 15: *Housing in Ecuador*

For a period in the 1970s, Ecuador was the most rapidly urbanizing country in Latin America. The cities and towns acted as a safety valve, absorbing landless *campesinos* and seasonal rural workers. Guayas is now the most densely populated province in the country.

From a brief survey, then, the impact of illiteracy in Santa Lucía is clear. It facilitates the exploitation of rural workers by landowners, leaving unorganized *campesinos* vulnerable to deception. Within popular organizations such as the co-ops, illiteracy promotes dependency on strong leaders and ultimately leads to the reproduction of relations of domination. The campaign should provide an opportunity to challenge this oppression. An assessment of the literacy campaign on its own terms must also be an assessment of what it contributes to fulfilling two fundamental human rights in the UN/Charter: the right to work and decent working conditions (Article 23), and the right to housing and adequate living conditions (Article 25). These are the rights most relevant to the people of Santa Lucía.

The campaign in Santa Lucía

> In the rural areas of Guayas we've had less problems because we've been working there for eight years.
> *Angel Nieto*

We were in Santa Lucía early in the campaign. The brunt of the teaching was being carried by 74 student teachers. Their work was complemented by the so-called *bonificados*, experienced literacy teachers who receive a small allowance from the state – a great deal less than a wage – for what is effectively voluntary work in the villages. They had been working in the area since 1980, the legacy of a programme of the Roldos government. The student teachers, organized from the town's secondary school into six brigades, were all sixth-formers fulfilling a state obligation to teach literacy:

> The campaign obliges students to make people literate. I think this is positive. . . . Our students are very *memorista* so it's a good experience for them . . . linking knowledge with reality.
> *Angel Nieto*

Two-thirds of the students were working in the villages where they lived or in the central town. The rest were working in other villages because there were no students living there. Teaching took place every afternoon, the students taking the motorboat up the river to the village where their classes were held in small primary schools or houses.

> The first lesson was very exciting because for some people it was the first time they'd sat behind a desk.
> *Alexandra, student teacher*

In the town, classes took place in schoolrooms at night, with mosquitoes for company as the electric light attracted every flying insect in the vicinity.

> People are motivated to learn. We don't have to go and search for them . . . they come.
> *Lisa, student teacher*

Training continued throughout the campaign. Every morning, an hour of school was set aside for discussion with "animators" about work documents, the guide and specific practical problems. These animators were school-teachers responsible for monitoring the students.

> When there are problems which can't be resolved easily in the class the animators come to the communities with us.
> *Alexandra, student teacher*

The work documents were certainly having some impact:

> Document number 5 (On the Declaration of Human Rights) was the most useful because now we know our rights.
> *Luis, student teacher*

> Document number 7 on Leonidas Proaño was important because it gave us a model to follow . . . the campaign is only three months of teaching but he dedicated his whole life to it.
> *Lisa, student teacher*

However, not everything was running smoothly. In the first week of the campaign, the Guayaquil television station, owned by business interests and Guayas landowners, had put out a programme condemning the campaign and accusing the government of using it to gain political credits for the next election.

> There are people who oppose this type of programme, saying it is a government introducing communism to the people.
> *Santiago, Vice-director, adult education, Santa Lucía*

Part of the problem was the association of Bishop Proaño with liberation theology, regarded as subversive in many circles.

> Liberation theology [should be understood as] a political doctrine disguised as religious belief with an anti-papal and anti-free enterprise significance.[11]

This opposition was being felt locally. Transport services had refused to adapt to the demands of the campaign so some student teachers were unable to reach their classes or had to leave early. The rector of the

Santa Lucía secondary school was not in favour of the campaign yet he had been named president of the campaign executive committee by the Guayas campaign director, another right-wing political appointee.

> The students plan to remove him from the college after the campaign.
> The animators are also against the rector. He gives no orientation or teaching
> . . . it's negligence more than active opposition.
> *Eduardo Moreno*

Throughout the administration of the campaign, there were similar appointments as vested interests attempted to subvert its effectiveness.

Attacks from the political right suggest that the campaign was fulfilling its objectives, and that it had the potential to pose a threat to entrenched interests of the landowning elite and the industrial class in Guayaquil. But to evaluate that threat, the campaign must be considered in terms of its contribution to the two major social processes at work in Santa Lucía, namely agrarian reform and urbanization.

The Right to Work

> In Santa Lucía, 90 per cent of the work available is work on the land.
> *Jaime, campesino*

The right to work in Santa Lucía is essentially the right to work the land. The literacy classes could provide a forum for discussing land reform. However, given the current balance of forces in Guayas, which are tilted so heavily towards large scale agro-industry, the classes would have to be associated with government provision of land or the dispensation of resources required to fulfil the demands arising from them. In Nicaragua, the Literacy Crusade was able to act as the foundation for change in rural areas because land had been made available through the departure of the *Somocistas*, and resources were provided by the revolutionary government for the development of necessary infrastructure.

> The end of a campaign should not be just literacy, but the basis of
> community development.
> *Carlos Poveda, Director of Ecuador's 1980 literacy programme*

In 1980 the literacy programme of the Roldos government attempted such a strategy of integrated development. It was linked to a full-scale adult-education programme as well as to the building of schools in remote rural areas (many of the village schools used for the campaign in 1989 were built by literacy groups during the 1980–84 programme). FODERUMA was an agency set up to provide the link between literacy and land reform by making resources available to *campesinos*. Yet even such a developed programme with such strong links to the communities proved vulnerable to the economic cuts of the following government (of Febrés Cordero). There can be no guarantees of continuity in Ecuador as there seemed to be in Nicaragua.

In the 1980–84 programme, we had a network of promoters and community teachers. The students were part of the network and not at the centre. But when Febrés Cordero came to power, the only social programmes to receive funding were pragmatic economic ones. Adult education was completely cut. . . . What's to prevent this from happening again?
Carlos Poveda

In Santa Lucía, the painstaking work of using literacy to develop organizations able to fight the Guayaquil elite was reversed. Where necessary, strong-arm tactics were used:

When people organized to fight, the leaders were detained . . . six people disappeared in Santa Lucía. This wasn't reported on TV or in the press. They were killed for organizing labourers with small bits of land into effective co-operatives.
Eduardo Moreno

Literacy teachers promoting *campesino* movements had their work undermined:

They took away all our transport and fares to the community. . . . In El Palme, Cordero sent a letter to the chief saying "get Moreno out of there", so they sent me to an area where I knew no one. . . . Literacy is successful only when you know the reality of an area.
Eduardo Moreno

Clearly, to talk about the right to land is one thing, but to be able to enforce that right is another, requiring the backing of the state against entrenched interests over a sustained period. The 1989 campaign in Ecuador is not linked to any substantial new agrarian reform. Neither is it directly linked to community development in rural areas.

How can you talk about human rights when economic conditions are so bad? Literacy has to be in the context of economic resources to fulfil the demands that it throws up.
Carlos Poveda

In Santa Lucía, another way of making a contribution to the right to work campaign would be if the literacy classes were linked, as in Honduras, to the popular organizations that are fighting for more land (i.e. the co-operatives). By strengthening the co-ops the campaign could help the *campesinos* to reverse the tide of land-loss to the Guayaquil elite.

The *campesinos* don't need to be told that they are oppressed. They already know that. What they lack is the power to change their reality.
Eduardo Moreno

The government of Febrés Cordero left a legacy of fear of organization amongst the *campesinos*. To overcome this, the campaign would have to be very explicit about the need for organization. However,

> The campaign is not in direct language . . . it doesn't give real priority
> to radical action.
> *Eduardo Moreno*

In the primer, the right to work is presented predominantly in an urban
context and is not linked to either union organization or co-operatives.

The right to housing

> In the province of Guayas, 47 per cent of the population have no running
> water, 21 per cent lack toilets, 20 per cent have no electricity and 35 per
> cent lack drainage.[12]

As *campesinos* have been forced off their land through the exploitation of
economic crisis by big business, a related crisis has been created in the
urban areas. The towns do not have the capacity to house the new migrants
and the land available for building houses is controlled by corrupt local
councils and unscrupulous private landowners.

> The vast majority of the country's population, with low incomes and unstable
> employment, do not have access to the formal housing market, that is to say, to
> registered, authorized constructions which are supervised by the local councils.
> Work Document 15: *Housing in Ecuador*

Success of the campaign strategy in the towns depended on strong links
between the literacy classes and popular organizations at national and local
level. The democratization of human rights has little concrete meaning if
it is not associated with the organizations in civil society attempting to
ensure that those rights are practised. Literacy teaching isolated from
the mechanisms of social change becomes charity, a way of giving those
"poor illiterates on the margins of society" an opportunity to integrate
into modern society.

For example, a discussion of the right to housing could involve analysing
why there are people without homes: in Santa Lucía, who owns the
land where houses could be built and the policies of the canton's local
government would be relevant factors. If linked to an organization, a
literacy group amongst homeless or inadequately-housed migrants could
become part of the struggle for housing. If there is no link made, such
people are likely to blame their own ignorance for their conditions, in
which case it is a small step for them to believe that literacy skills are a
way of correcting the deficiency that makes them unable to find a home.
The belief thus gains currency that a learner has to change to meet the
needs of society rather than the other way round, and that the campaign
provides the cure.

Near the centre of Santa Lucía is a housing co-operative. Patria Libre
is one of four new co-ops that have been created in the last two years with
the aid of the Popular Democratic Movement (MPD), one of the major
political parties of the left. A symptom of urbanization without a housing

policy, it consists of a collection of about 50 ramshackle wooden houses on stilts by the side of the main road on flooded land. Most of the members are landless *campesinos* who work as day labourers on surrounding rice farms. Conditions are harsh: the paddy fields are infested with snakes and mosquitoes carrying malaria and dengue fever. Every year people die from snake bites.

> The canton wanted to build a stadium on this land because the football pitch was flooded. We were arguing about it. On 3 April [1988] we occupied the land and spent a month working here constructing houses and guarding it day and night.
> *María, co-op member*

A month later 200 police arrived at 5 a.m. and the inhabitants were thrown off the land. They fled and many of the new houses were destroyed by tractors and fires.

> It was a town councilor who signed the order to remove us. We had a meeting and we decided to block the road as a protest against the aggression . . . it was a Tuesday . . . for four hours we stopped the traffic . . . the soldiers came . . . attacked the whole village with tear gas . . . 50 were arrested and 2 were shot dead with rifles.
> *María*

Condemnation in the media of the state's actions was organized by the co-operative with the help of MPD members. Prisoners were released after three days and the residents returned to the land, building new homes from the wreckage.

> It took time for us to rebuild . . . many lost everything when we were forced off the land. Now we are looking for legalization of our right to be here and we are struggling to get light, water and drains. The local council wants to know nothing . . . they say there is no money.
> *José*

> This happened when León [Cordero] was president. But it would have been the same with Borja: the landowners haven't changed, the police are the same . . . there's the same possibility of bribery to get them to throw us off.
> *María*

Fourteen people from the co-operative were going to the literacy classes in the secondary school every evening:

> The campaign's good. The materials are practical.
> *Juan, learner*

But:

> In the classes, we never have the opportunity to talk about our problems here in the co-op . . . we're just learning our letters.
> *Rosa, learner*

"Is there any discussion of organization?"
"Yes, we're going to organize a little party to celebrate the end of the campaign."
"Do you ever talk about action on human rights abuses?"
"But that would be communist."
Lisa, student teacher

In classes where members of the housing co-op were learning, we observed mechanical teaching by students who clearly didn't have much idea of literacy as anything beyond the technical knowledge of the alphabet. No attempt was made to even begin to discuss the human rights that the generative words announced.

I'm not going to join the course if it teaches me no more than reading and writing.
Helena, worker in village bar

One reason for this failure of the campaign methodology in practice was the lack of interest by the students who were teaching. With involvement obligatory many were doing the work purely to fulfil requirements to gain their own qualifications for higher education.

As a brigade leader, it's my job to motivate other student teachers. This is hard. Most of them do the bare minimum of work, refusing to turn up at special meetings or visit the homes of adults who drop out.
Miguel

With minimal motivation, it was unlikely that students would go out of their way to make contacts with popular organizations or prepare their classes adequately to ensure their relevance to the learners.

The failure of the campaign to make contacts with local organizations has marginalized it. Rather than promoting collective action to combat the housing problem in Santa Lucía, the campaign leaves learners having to adapt to the housing conditions as they are. Many see themselves as acquiring the necessary skills to fit the needs of the job market in Guayaquil. They want to migrate again in the hope of finding an income that will put decent housing within their grasp.

When I finish the course, I'll be able to work in the markets in the city.
Juan

But in the city, economic and educational problems remain. The new arrivals will, more likely than not, find themselves blamed once again for not being able to secure a good job and adequate living conditions.

In Guayaquil, there are 300,000 marginal workers who need special education.
Carlos Poveda

So the literacy campaign, far from promoting a democratization of society in Santa Lucía has, at best, helped to maintain a status quo and, at worst, divided communities by promoting migration to the city.

The failure of the campaign to connect with the popular organizations attempting to fulfil human rights can be seen at national level too.

> Where's the spirit of the campaign? Fifteen days ago, there was a teachers' strike in the middle of training of student teachers.
> *Carlos Poveda*

The teachers' union, UNE, is also affiliated to the MPD. A strike by the teachers is not the sign of a campaign offering opportunities to the popular movements. The problem is its identification with the government.

What is recuperable?

It will be a few years before the campaign can be fully evaluated. There are two main reasons. First, the effect of the dissemination of the work documents is one that needs a lot of time to show itself. If the campaign could raise the profile of social and civil rights amongst a whole generation of 17-year-olds that could have a very far-reaching effect. Already, the work documents have created a national debate on a number of sensitive social issues. Information which before the campaign was only available in a few specialized research institutes in Quito was suddenly everywhere. The documents on teaching methods are now in the home of every single educator in the country. This can only contribute to a genuine democratization of Ecuadorean civil society. There is, however, a proviso: the documents are not read by the adult learners. Just as the Nicaraguan crusade had more of an educational impact on the students living in rural areas for the first time, the Ecuadorean campaign will leave its strongest mark on secondary-school students and other people who read the work documents, rather than the *campesinos* and workers who participated as learners.

Secondly, a great deal depends on the follow-up. A three months campaign with a lot of publicity which leaves no permanent structures behind it can have little impact.

> Three months is not long enough to teach anyone to read and write . . . there is some enthusiasm about the campaign but everyone knows that it's not going to last.
> *Lisa, student teacher*

What matters is whether any momentum generated by the campaign is used to create some form of permanent basic education for adults. The follow-up will not depend on the students who, having completed their three-month obligation, will return to their full-time education. It is the *bonificados*, the permanent literacy teachers in the countryside, who will be responsible for its success or failure.

The state has the duty to offer not only literacy, but its continuation, because to know how to read and write is scarcely a tool for something; if people are only given the tool and not the something, if there are no possibilities of using reading and writing productively and creatively, they are left with a knowledge like knowing how to dance which does not really serve them in developing their lives.
R.M. Torres

Of course, the problem here is that the state is as vulnerable to political overturn as was the government of Roldos. Following his death in a plane crash in 1981 (in suspicious circumstances) the materials of the adult education programme changed to focus more on party political issues than community development. After the election of Febrés Cordero, almost everything was dismantled. With the political right in ascendancy again, under the populist leader Abdala Bucaram, and Borja's government tied by international economic restraint, there are certainly possibilities of a repetition of history.

CONCLUSIONS

The United States . . . should establish programmes to support democracy in permanent institutions including the military and in political culture.
Santa Fe 2

The literacy campaign has been accused of being a social palliative, a way of appearing to be a government of the people while not making any significant socio-economic changes. Certainly, Borja's government seems a paradigm case of the social-democratic movement being promoted by US policy-makers in the region. In Argentina, Uruguay, Brazil and now Chile, authoritarian governments have been replaced by democracy. But this democracy can do nothing about the fundamental economic problems of Latin America, especially the foreign debt. Stable democracy did nothing to prevent the riots in Venezuela after the International Monetary Fund imposed a harsh austerity package on the Peres government in February 1989. Borja's government in Ecuador could do nothing about Citibank taking $80 million from government accounts – for the payment of interest on debts – while blocking the computer information system so that the Central Bank of Ecuador couldn't discover any information immediately afterwards.

As the literacy campaign started, Ecuador's foreign debt was running at around $11.5 billion. Borja is not in a position to commit government funds to social programmes or to fundamentally change economic policy because of the level of international economic pressure. In such circumstances, the literacy campaign will fail because of the inability to link it with the fulfilment of social demands generated by it. Even if the campaign were sufficiently involved with the popular organizations the response to its demands would almost inevitably be a repressive one:

> Ecuador declared a national state of emergency today and ordered troops to take control of oil installations during a strike by Texaco workers.
> The Independent, *29 September 1989.*

Teargassing of demonstrations in the capital is commonplace. Political students appear to have been behind many recent protests. Twelve high schools were indefinitely closed in 1989, allegedly responsible for street incidents. Thirteen students were tried for sedition and one was shot dead by the army. Given this type of restricted democracy, with repressive measures always an option if the interests of international capital are threatened, a government campaign that sets out to democratize human rights rapidly falls into contradiction. On the one hand it is politicizing a generation of young people while on the other hand it can be used to domesticate the language of human rights and democracy.

> The US should . . . differentiate those human rights groups that maintain the democratic regime from those that support statism.
> *Santa Fe 2*

Any attempt to ensure that "statist" social rights such as those of employment and housing are satisfied will be met ultimately by violations of civil rights by the military in the interest of national security. The literacy campaign does not challenge this. It is significant that while campaign work documents have been produced on the problem of the land, indigenous peoples, women, health, education and the environment, there was no document on the foreign debt. The language of social change in Latin America has to move on from that of human rights and democracy, because of the appropriation (and de-reading) of that vocabulary by those interested in maintaining the status quo. Therefore, key areas for popular education are now the debt crisis and practical organization. It is precisely in these respects that the campaign in Ecuador has been found to be lacking.

NOTES

1. Pedagogical Director of Literacy Campaign, at conference for "Literacy, Popular Education and Democracy", Quito, June 1989.
2. Corkill and Cubitt, *Fragile Democracy* (London: Latin American Bureau, 1988).
3. *Nueva*, March 1989, Quito.
4. A number of non-governmental organizations were involved, for instance, Centro Andino de Acción Popular, CEDIME, CIRE, Central University Quito, Organización Panamericana de la Salud, Consejo Nacional de Desarollo, CIUDAD.
5. Johnston, Lind, *Adult Literacy in the Third World: A review of objectives and*

strategies (SIDA, 1986).

6.   The groups, named Popular Literacy Circles (CAPs), each consisted of one or two teachers and one to ten learners in what is a very similar structure to the CEPs in Nicaragua (see Chapter 2).

7.   Director of CEDIME, a non-governmental organization based in Quito and working largely to promote indigenous languages and culture.

8.   Co-ordinator of literacy and adult education, Guayas Province (interview with authors, June 1989).

9.   Iturralde, Diego, "Notas para una historia politica del campesinado ecuatoriano (1900–80)", in P.G.Casanova (ed.), *Historia Politica de los Campesinos Latinoamericanos* (Quito: CEDIME).

10.   Campaign co-ordinator for canton Santa Lucía (interview with authors, June 1989).

11.   *Santa Fe 2* (in translation from Spanish). This is a US think-tank document prepared for the Bush administration.

12.   *Boletin Socio-Demografico Guayas* (Quito: CEPAR, 1986).

6. Mexico, San Miguel Teotongo: Reading and De-reading, Literacy and Debt

The United States makes the demented claim that tiny Nicaragua, with three million people and an economy in shreds because of the protracted Contra War and other hostile US actions, is a threat to national security. How would the US like it if Mexico, under intolerable pressure from its citizens, became a far more left-wing, or right-wing, anti-American country? Eighty million angry people and a common frontier from California to Texas sounds like a rather more credible threat.[1]

Tenochtitlan, the capital city of the Aztec Empire, was founded following the fulfilment of a prophecy: a city should be built when an eagle was seen, perched on a cactus, with a serpent in its beak. The location, however, had its drawbacks. It was in the middle of a shallow lake, and looming over it was Tetlalmanche ("the hill that throws rocks"). As history unfolded it was not a volcanic eruption, but the equally violent Spanish *conquistadors*, who destroyed the Aztec city. Nevertheless the volcano remained in place to oversee the Spaniards as they drained the lake and established Mexico City in the large valley, cooled by mountain air.

Four hundred years later Mexico erupted in revolution. In the south large sugar-plantation owners were taking over the ancestral lands of many *campesinos*, forcing them to work in conditions akin to slavery. Without an alternative, the *campesinos* united into a guerrilla army, led by Emiliano Zapata. They rode north to the centre of power, demanding land and liberty, bearing rifles and religious flags, with symbols of the Virgin stamped on their sombreros.[2] In 1914 they converged to threaten Mexico City, strategically gathering on the volcano that looks over the whole valley. Faced with other peasant armies further north and an agitated working-class within the city, the government collapsed. The first revolution in the continent had succeeded. Most of the *Zapatistas*, however, were interested in land rather than administration, and found urban life alien. Rather than wait for laws to be passed, most returned to the south to seize land for themselves directly.

Sixty years later many descendants of the *Zapatistas* returned to Mexico City, this time without unity and without arms, forced to migrate from the increasingly impoverished rural south. For these *campesinos* the Mexican Revolution brought no sustained change; since 1929 the aptly named Institutional Revolutionary Party (PRI) had been in power and had failed to ease inequalities that left *campesinos* living on little more than *tortillas* and chilli, while hundreds of millionaires flaunted their wealth in the cities. Throughout the 1970s more than three per cent of Mexico's rural population migrated to the cities each year, transforming the country.[3] These people became known as *paracaidistas* (parachutists) arriving, as if from the air, with little or nothing to their name, desperately looking for a place to live and work.

Mexico City is now the largest city in the world. Up until 1970 the volcano of Tetlalmanche had been used only for quarrying, mining or growing maize and beans. Building was prohibited because of fears of subsidence or eruption. But as demand for land in the city grew, landowners saw their chance and divided up the land on Tetlalmanche, to sell it in small parcels, just big enough for houses. Unaware of the legal position or the dangers, and unconcerned about the physical difficulties of building on the slopes, desperate *paracaidistas* bought or rented the land. The first settlers on Tetlalmanche came from the villages of San Miguel and Teotongo in Oaxaca, so they named their new community San Miguel Teotongo. The local government responded to illegal settlement by refusing land titles to anyone building a house. Inconsistently, they turned a blind eye to the landowners who were selling the land. As in Santa Lucía (see Chapter 5) the new residents faced regular police harassment. Houses were destroyed, but no attempt was ever made to offer the parachutists an alternative site, so they simply waited for the police to withdraw, and then started building again.

The new residents arrived with high expectations of city life, but without any legal status they found that they were deprived of even the most basic services. They organized a union in 1975 and stopped all payments to the landowners. With no power beyond the strength of numbers they demanded water, electricity, drainage and waste disposal, as well as education and health care. By 1989 the *barrio*[4] had more than 80,000 residents (larger than Zapata's army of 1914), and so should have become a significant voice, challenging the authorities of Mexico City. But the government in the valley below has become increasingly distant from them, obscured as much as anything by a thickening smog that deprives Tetlalmanche of its once threatening stature.

The institutional inheritance of the Mexican Revolution has long forgotten its roots in popular uprising.

> The PRI are like a monarchy. They only hold elections as a grandiose display
> for the world, but they are an illegitimate government, elected by fraud
> and propped up by force.
> *Roberto, resident of San Miguel Teotongo*

The 1988 elections in Mexico were widely seen as fraudulent. The PRI made the electoral rules. Pro-PRI soldiers were often the only witnesses at vote counts. Announcement of results was delayed for days in some areas, while figures were fixed. Many opposition voters failed to receive electoral cards, which were kept in PRI offices for use on election day. Ballot boxes of opposition votes appeared in rivers and on rubbish dumps. A popular saying sums it all up. "In Mexico even the dead vote, and they all vote for the PRI."

The PRI of course won the election with an absolute majority, but even they confessed that it was by the slimmest margin in their history.

THE DEBT CRISIS

> The financial plague is wreaking greater and greater havoc throughout the world. As in medieval times it is scourging country after country. It is transmitted by rats and its consequences are unemployment and poverty, industrial bankruptcy and speculative enrichment. The remedy of the witch doctors is to deprive the patient of food and subject him to compulsory rest.
> *President López Portillo*[5]

Throughout the 1980s the residents of San Miguel Teotongo and similar *barrios* have seen their conditions of life deteriorate. This is the direct product of the Mexican government's inability to pay back its debt to foreign banks. The debt has its origins in the money invested in the country in the 1970s. The huge profits (known as petrodollars) generated through the quadrupling of oil prices by the newly-formed OPEC (Organization of Petroleum Exporting Countries) ended up in Western banks and needed to be recycled (i.e. spent on something). Further money was available after the US treasury detached the dollar from the gold standard in 1971. New money could then be printed much more freely. The banks decided that the best way to use this abundance of money was to invest it in the Third World on the assumption that governments could not go bankrupt. Huge loans were offered to countries with little regard as to where the money ended up.

Mexico was seen as a safe bet. Oil deposits seemed to ensure a secure economic future for the country. Money was invested in building up the industry which would provide a guaranteed source of oil for the US, and help to avert any future threat of being held to ransom by the new powers in the Middle East. Other large-scale projects were undertaken, of little immediate value to the majority of Mexican people, including the investment of $10 billion for a single project: the construction of the Sicartsa Steel Mill. Much of the money invested in the country was never spent on the projects for which it was allocated. Taken by corrupt officials put in charge of a bonanza, it left Mexico almost as soon as it had arrived. Between 1980 and 1982 $40 billion was transferred abroad from Mexico to secret bank accounts and luxury apartments, often in Miami.

In 1979 interest rates began to rise, doubling from 10 per cent to 20 per cent within two years. President Reagan kept the rates high in an attempt to hold down inflation and attract capital to the US to pay for tax cuts and high military spending. Mexico, along with other countries who had

Learning to read in Colomoncagua (Chapter 1)

Popular education in practice: pottery workshop, Colomoncagua
(Chapter 1)

Don Arnoldo, literacy teacher and community activist, Lechecuagos
(Chapter 2)

Campesino meeting in San Antonio de Jura (Chapter 4)

Patria Libre housing co-operative, Santa Lucia (Chapter 5)

A view over Mexico City from San Miguel Teotongo (Chapter 6)

The Wild West – horseman on market day in Cabrican (Chapter 8)

Learning to read: an outdoor class in El Alto (Chapter 9)

Comandante Hercules, a Miskitu fighter in Karata (Chapter 10)

borrowed during the 1970s, suffered. A drop in commodity prices during the 1970s left them receiving less income from their exports. Now they were also faced with rapidly rising bills for repayment of the interest on their loans. Even if the borrowed money had been properly invested, which it had not been, it would have been difficult to pay. By 1982 Mexico's foreign debt was $80 billion. The interest payments were completely unrealistic.

> We said we had a major problem with a capital P. We didn't say the problem was a particular debt [but] the whole international financial structure. We said it was everybody's problem.[6]

In August 1982 Mexico declared itself unable to pay, thus sparking off the debt crisis. The fear was that other countries who had similar debts would follow suit. Shock spread throughout the world. All the banks depended on guaranteed future repayments on past loans to balance their books. If investors lost confidence in Mexico's (and other countries') ability or willingness to pay, then the banks would have to write off the loans and their books would go deep into the red. Two Midwest banks collapsed. There was an international scurry of activity to avert damage to major financial institutions. In the space of a few days, the banks, the US Treasury and the International Monetary Fund cobbled together $8.3 billion as a new loan,[7] but it was only given subject to a series of conditions. Mexico had to prove its commitment to making future payments by removing subsidies on basic goods, reducing wages, increasing exports whilst decreasing imports, and cutting government spending, especially on health and education. This was the first of the famous IMF Structural Adjustment Programmes (popularly, or unpopularly, known as austerity programmes) and it became a model for dealing with other debtors. Since then over 50 countries have followed Mexico in announcing their inability to meet debt repayments, but the human cost of doing so has become increasingly high.

The new loan that Mexico received did little more than cover the costs of repaying the earlier loans. With no new investment many of the large-scale projects ground to a halt. The Sicartsa Steel Mill was left incomplete and, without new money, remains worthless and unused.

> Bankers deal with governments and are concerned with balance sheets, not with the millions whose bad luck it is to be subject to those governments.[8]

The impact of the austerity measures on Mexico's people is startling. Malnutrition has doubled from 17 million to 33 million people (one-third of the population). Wages have halved and unemployment has doubled (40 per cent of Mexicans are now unemployed or seriously under-employed).[9] With a $10 billion annual interest bill, over 50 per cent of Mexico's export earnings need to be spent just on paying the interest on the debt, amounting to $27 million every day.

WHO PAYS THE BILLS?

Effectively Mexico's poor are paying the bill for the incompetence of international banks and the corruption of their government. The slopes of Tetlalmanche are exposed to strong winds that whip up blinding dust clouds around the concrete, breeze-block, scrap-wood, card-board and plastic-sheet houses that make up San Miguel Teotongo. Everything looks unfinished. Iron poles rise through concrete walls to enable future extensions; the only space for most people to build is upwards, but as yet no one has the money to do so. Cramped families share their space with dogs, hens and pigs. In the absence of organized waste-disposal in most of San Miguel Teotongo rubbish piles up in improvised dumps behind houses, ideal breeding grounds for vermin and disease. With no proper drainage, the streets operate as open sewers. In the rainy season water often gathers two or three feet deep at the bottom of the volcano making it almost impossible to enter or leave the *barrio*. There is virtually no piped water supply so people have to depend on occasional water trucks that give each household a ration of water.

Despite all this some outsiders have visited San Miguel Teotongo and have taken away an impression that it cannot be really poor. Most houses have television aerials which is seen as a sign of affluence. This is a serious misreading. For a community like San Miguel Teotongo it is much easier to connect electricity (which can be done cheaply and illegally, so there are no bills) than a water supply (which would require substantial investment in pumping the water up the volcano's slopes). Moreover, a television costs nothing to maintain. Even the most destitute of families may be seen gathered in a dimly lit room watching a flickering old television at night.

New families are arriving constantly. The 1985 earthquake was felt only lightly in San Miguel Teotongo, but afterwards thousands sought refuge here from other poor neighbourhoods like Morelos, Obrero and Guerero, where badly constructed housing had collapsed. Other people have arrived in San Miguel Teotongo because it is the first community they see when coming by bus on the motorway from Puebla. Integration is hard. There is a remarkable mix of cultures and backgrounds, but

> on arriving people forget their past. Once they settle here they have no choice but to forget their roots and get on with survival.
> *Jaime, resident of San Miguel Teotongo*

With overpopulation the settlement is rising higher and higher up the slopes of the volcano. At higher altitudes the winds blow stronger and the temperature drops lower at night. Severe respiratory disorders are common; malnutrition is widespread. Yet there is only one health centre for the 80,000 people of the *barrio*.

> You have to be very lucky to find the health centre open and very rich
> to afford the medicines.
> *Elena, resident*

San Miguel Teotongo is located 15 kilometres to the south of the centre of
Mexico City. Most of the work is in factories to the north of the city. The
state buses do not run to San Miguel Teotongo so those residents who
are lucky enough to have a job often have to travel for up to three hours
through the city to get to it, and three hours to return. It is scarcely worth
it. Those who know their rights might get the minimum wage but austerity
programmes have ensured that it will provide for less than half of their
basic needs, and in practice many workers receive less than the minimum
wage. The majority have no "proper" work at all and simply improvise
a living from scraps, doing odd-jobs, maybe selling something on the
streets, perhaps resorting to crime. In these circumstances parents often
have to depend on their children to help out with earning a subsistence.
Education seems irrelevant.

> Education is a cost . . . you need money . . . and it is a waste of money.
> If the only end of education is to get a job then why not take a job and money
> whenever it is available?
> *Francisco, resident*

This philosophy is remarkably similar to that of the government and the
IMF. Technically education is free and available for everyone. In practice
parents have to buy books, uniforms and pens for their children. The
schools are crowded and under-resourced.

> Only about 60 per cent of children finish primary school here and only
> 25 per cent of them join secondary schools. Teachers are badly paid and so
> badly motivated and there is an 80 per cent shortage of basic textbooks.
> *Father Antonio, headmaster, San Miguel Teotongo*

With very little to look forward to and very little in the way of alternative
entertainment, many children even at the age of 12 years old resort to
alcohol and drugs. The inhalation of solvents is the most popular form
of abuse as it is cheap and blindingly effective.

GOVERNMENT READING

There are no firm estimates of illiteracy in San Miguel Teotongo but it
is widely agreed by residents and outsiders who work in the *barrio* that
more than half of the adult population is unable to read and write. The
state organization responsible for literacy is the National Institute of Adult
Education (INEA). INEA has 16 area offices to cover the twenty million
residents of Mexico City. One of these is the Ixtapalapa Sur office, which
co-ordinates literacy work in San Miguel Teotongo and 40 neighbouring
barrios. A workforce of 22 people in this office was scarcely adequate, but
since 50 per cent cuts in 1987 the remaining 11 workers are faced with

an awesome task. Only one of the 11 has any substantial training in education, and that one is Lucia Gómez, who is (fortunately) the training officer. However,

> very few people can survive in this city with only one job so most of the staff here and in other INEA offices have at least one other occupation, usually selling things on the streets.
> *Lucia Gómez*

The literacy teaching is always done by unwaged workers called promoters. They are usually referred to as volunteers though this is often misleading as most are doing the work as part of a compulsory social service. In the past university students did the literacy teaching, but

> from 1980 onwards, with the economic crisis, the university students refused to co-operate because conditions were too difficult. In response to this INEA made literacy teaching part of obligatory social service for secondary-school students.
> *Lucia Gómez*

This switch of strategy has presented problems.

> The promoters now are too young and inexperienced, and have almost no motivation. In the training half my time is spent on improving their hand-writing and spelling.
> *Lucia Gómez*

In the eyes of the INEA workers, San Miguel Teotongo has a population of aggressive thugs, illegal immigrants, Colombian drug dealers, El Salvadorean guerrillas, Guatemalan refugees, Cuban *provocateurs*, Russian military advisers, political fanatics with stockpiles of weapons and criminals who will cut off your fingers to get rings. Such an image is not the best basis for organizing a literacy programme in the *barrio*.

It is perhaps suprising that there are officially 15 INEA literacy promoters operating in San Miguel Teotongo, a mixture of reluctant secondary-school students and a few women, some of whom do it for the few *pesos* that INEA offer as a supposed reward for motivated volunteers,

> The money is supposed to be just a token, an incentive, it amounts to very little, but with the economy as it is some women have started to see it as an alternative form of income.
> *Lucia Gómez*

The promoters have problems recruiting for classes. Owing to economic pressures most adults have very little time to learn. Moreover, in Mexico City people are assumed to be literate and if they are not they are often keen to hide the fact.

> People are ashamed, and fear that they will be laughed at if other people find out, so they avoid going to classes.
> *Consuelo, promoter*

If people are brave enough to attend a class, they have certain expectations, for example that they will be given a book which they can keep. Since the 50 per cent expenditure cuts in 1987 this is not always met. If books arrive they often do so late, and often there are not enough to go round. Some end up being sold on the streets. In 1989 the promoters in San Miguel Teotongo were forced to ask learners from the previous year to hand back their books at the end of the course, and yet this was usually the only means that past learners had to consolidate their year's learning. There are few other books available that can be used appropriately. The only written materials widely seen in the *barrio* are the popular *historiettas*, comics for the semi-literate with escapist stories usually based on soft porn or violence.

In the absence of books INEA workers in Ixtapalapa developed another strategy for recruiting adults: linking up with the local branch of the Social Security System which hands out subsidised *tortillas*. It was arranged that only people who were literate, or who were attending literacy classes, would get *tortillas*. This, however, caused such an outrage that it had to be stopped. INEA promoters in San Miguel Teotongo have developed more acceptable ways of involving people.

> When there are no books we have to find strategies to keep people
> entertained.
> *Angelica, promoter*

So literacy classes are now linked to anything from aerobics to origami, from cookery classes to karate. The problem is that the associated activities have tended to overshadow the literacy teaching itself.

For many promoters it is no problem if they fail to teach literacy. Those who are doing obligatory social service often just pass their time in the easiest possible way, and then leave. This causes problems.

> The adult learners often leave when their promoter does, because they don't
> want to have a new promoter and they don't see why they should continue if
> the promoter doesn't.
> *Lucia Gómez*

To fulfil their social service, the only requirement that the promoters face is that of filling in occasional forms. Roberto, a promoter in San Miguel Teotongo in 1986, recalls the process well:

> We were forced to lie. If we did not have 12 people enrolled and an 80
> per cent pass rate then we were threatened with failing our social service. So
> we lied to make it easier for ourselves and INEA workers would never come
> to check up, because they wanted to believe our lies: it looked good for them.
> It was deceit from bottom to top.

More recently the situation has deteriorated further.

> Since our budget was cut we have lost the person who used to check
> and analyse the statistics.
> *Lucia Gómez*

The national literacy statistics which INEA produces in abundance are
essentially based on these lies. The official rate of illiteracy is just 6.1 per
cent, and falling. Moreover, in 1986, INEA could proudly declare that they
had taught 1,200,609 people. However, even by their own statistics, these
achievements can begin to look fragile. In 1987 only 18 per cent of those
who finished the literacy programme enrolled in any follow-up, meaning
that 82 per cent were very likely to lose the few skills that they had picked
up.

Dr Millan, the national director of literacy for INEA, is confident and
reassuring, but is clearly unfamiliar with Ixtapalapa and San Miguel
Teotongo:

> Literacy has been a priority for this government, so the budget for the
> literacy programme has not been affected by the economic crisis.

According to Dr Millan illiteracy barely exists in the city, and the priority
now is in rural areas and with indigenous peoples. The key to success
has been the application of the ideas of Paulo Freire, whose method
of generative words was brought to Mexico by an Argentinian in the
1970s. Fourteen generative words are used in the Mexican primer, with
between 30 and 40 pages of mechanical exercises based on each one. A
mere 15 minutes (out of about eight hours) is allocated for discussion of
each word. Even then,

> Relations in our classes are very vertical. . . . I am convinced there is no
> discussion.
> *Dr Millan*

According to promoters in San Miguel Teotongo,

> political, social and economic affairs don't interest people here.
> *Angelica*

> I avoid politics because it creates divisions and makes the work hard.
> *Rosalia*

Dialogue with Dr Millan is also revealing:

> We use aspects of Freire, first by ensuring the contents are socially relevant
> and second by using the method of generative words.
> – But is there dialogue?
> No, I'm sure there is no discussion . . . it is difficult between young
> promoters and adults.
> – So it can't be a generative word . . . if it does not generate discussion?
> Yes.
> – So it is not a generative word?

No, no, you are right.
– So?
Frankly we do not apply the methods of Paulo Freire even though we
are in agreement with them.

There is a bizarre belief verging on mysticism (shared by most people in
INEA, from national workers to people in regional offices, and amongst
the promoters themselves), that generative words have magical properties
and that through them some miracle will take place, whereby illiterate
people will become well-motivated and enabled to learn. In practice,
however, few of the people who use the phrase "generative words" are
using it in the same way as Paulo Freire, who first coined it. The same
applies to other Freirean concepts like codification and conscientization.

There is nothing in itself wrong in changing the meaning of words:
all language necessarily evolves through usage. No text should be strait
jacketed by a supposedly authoritative reading. But it is objectionable to
find the language associated with education for liberation used as a tool
for gaining control of people's lives, for domestication.

> By adapting Freire's terminology pseudo-Freireans turn his codes of unem-
> ployment, hunger, oppression and liberation into developmentalist modules
> of family planning, nutrition, sanitation. . . . Pseudo-Freirean pedagogy con-
> verts dialogue into a form of "discovery learning". . . . In this conversion
> dialogue becomes a search for the "right" answers, pre-determined by the
> programme planner and provided to the teacher. . . .[10]

Pseudo-Freireanism is sometimes the product of a misreading or mis-
understanding of Freire's work, but sometimes it appears as a deliberate
attempt to hijack a set of radical ideas and methods. In both cases the
effect is the same, giving reactionary literacy programmes a progressive
gloss, and taming the methods themselves by inoculating people against
Freirean language. This process is an example of "de-reading": the
appropriation of progressive language by the people who are threatened
by it.[11]

Pseudo-Freire for a Pseudo-Revolution

In the 1970s literacy was accepted as an international devlopment priority.
To attract investment a literate labour force was considered necessary, so
even the most reluctant of governments planned large-scale programmes
aiming at functional literacy. Today – with the debt crisis – the situation
is in danger of changing. To attract investment involves making cuts
in public spending, and therefore cuts in education and literacy work.
Literacy no longer seems a priority for governments who have large
numbers of unemployed workers. Indeed, training the unemployed may be
considered foolish as this could present a threat to stability. The apparatus
of the Mexican INEA has to stay in place – because international concern
requires it – but the literacy statistics are now of only nominal importance

to the state.

This is certainly the way that residents of San Miguel Teotongo feel about INEA.

> At root INEA is just another institution aimed at keeping people down,
> at stopping them from protesting.
> *Reina, resident*

> Their education programmes are really manipulation programmes because
> they deliberately avoid giving people a conscience.
> *Father Antonio*

> The government is only interested in instruction, not education, because
> they fear that if people know more they will like the government less.
> *Roberto, ex-promoter*

> When people discuss things they start to learn, they start seeing things
> . . . and they start uniting and becoming a threat. That is why there is no
> discussion in the INEA classes. The state is frightened that people here are
> waking up.
> *Maria Elena, resident*

One of INEA's promoters in San Miguel Teotongo has a full-time job as a "propaganda eliminator". This involves travelling around Mexico City tearing down political posters and erasing political graffiti, in order to "keep the city clean".

In the absence of any serious intent to educate people the role of INEA, according to the people of San Miguel Teotongo, is as "a bureaucratic number-crunching machine" in pursuit of international prestige.

> INEA is a fantasy . . . an apparatus to be used by those who are employed
> in it . . . because they alone profit from it.
> *Father Antonio*

Most importantly INEA is identified as an arm of the Institutional Revolutionary Party (Dr Millan, for example, is a party-political appointee). For many people it is this, more than anything, that damns INEA.

> INEA workers are government workers, so they are just as likely to try
> to throw us off our lands, in one way or another, as the PRI themselves.
> *Reina*

> INEA is like other institutions that are arms of the government. They all
> give superficial remedies to deep problems . . . it is like giving headache
> tablets for a broken leg. It is only done to give the president something to fill
> his speeches with. There are hundreds of institutions like this . . . full
> of administrators appointed by nepotism who have no experience or ability.
> Together they all prop each other up.
> *Father Antonio*

In the same way that the language of education for liberation flows easily, but meaninglessly, from the lips of Dr Millan, the rhetoric of revolution is still used as a tactic by the PRI 80 years on from a long-forgotten revolution. INEA's pseudo-Freirianism falls neatly into place next to the PRI's pseudo-revolution.

INEA's identification with the PRI has always caused problems in San Miguel Teotongo, but at the time of the 1988 elections the situation was particularly bad. During a period of special tension, an INEA adviser from the Ixtapalapa office visited the *barrio*. He received a cold welcome and was later assaulted and driven out by a hail of stones. For several months all salaried workers from INEA were frightened to go near the area, regarding it as a zone of conflict. The myths of San Miguel Teotongo as a place where even the police fear to patrol became entrenched and were embellished. Any understanding by INEA workers of daily life for the people of the *barrio* was completely lost beneath prejudice and legend.

> What is clear is that you can't implement a literacy programme, or indeed any other social programme, without understanding the community and without its support.
> *Silvia, popular health worker*

THE ALTERNATIVES

With problems in the formal education system, an economic crisis felt in every home, and the rejection of state literacy initiatives, the teaching of adult literacy may seem to be low on the agenda of priorities, even indeed an absurd idea. But on the contrary,

> most of us want to learn to read and write, if we can do it in a way that is relevant to our lives.
> *Elisa, resident*

The people of San Miguel Teotongo want a different kind of literacy:

> You can't plan literacy on a national level because it becomes an imposition. It is no use just giving people techniques. People must be made aware of their class through literacy. It must be part of the struggle, and the struggle is against the government, against the system, so an effective literacy programme can never be organized and run by the government.
> *Maria Elena, resident*

In 1983, a group of families settled high up on the steep slopes of Tetlalmanche volcano. The police tried to move them immediately, not because the area was dangerous or subsiding, but because it had recently been declared an ecological reserve.

> There was nothing here, no sign of wildlife and no plants. It was a ridiculous excuse.
> *Julieta, resident*

The families resisted and settled the area, calling their particular sector of San Miguel Teotongo, "Francisco Villa". Soon after they had settled, various landowners turned up demanding rent from the families, showing documents which they claimed were their rights to the land. Several illiterate families started paying, seeing no alternative. Only when a neighbourhood meeting was called did it become clear that these landowners were con-artists and their land-rights were forged. The experience drew the families together to resist similar actions in the future.

Today there are 52 families in Francisco Villa and they have organized as a branch of the original union which was set up by the founders of San Miguel Teotongo. For them the union is central.

The community is the union and the union is the community.
Elisa, resident

Everything in the neighbourhood is now collectively organized.

Struggle is not part-time for us, not a luxury or leisure activity. It is the heart of our lives: to resist, organize and change.
Miguel, resident

The entire neighbourhood has been planned and laid-out by the residents themselves, and making space for a school, recreation areas, the building of a community house and the setting up of workshops, laying water pipes, levelling roads, digging drainage channels. All the services are the product of a vociferous and persistent fight with authorities.

A series of committees is organized by the families to deal with running what has become a remarkable experiment in holistic democracy. A technical committee works on building, maintenance, plumbing and electricity supply, while a health committee concentrates on hygiene, for example organizing clean-up campaigns (even to the extent of washing pigs!). The supply committee runs a small shop receiving fresh, cheap goods direct from rural co-operatives. A justice committee helps to steward marches, sorts out any arguments between residents and gives advice to anyone involved in legal conflicts outside the community. With incidents of domestic violence it censures husbands and liaises with the women's committee, which also works on distributing social security breakfasts. A finance committee keeps budgets for the other committees and various accounts, for example of the contributions made by residents to collective building programmes. A press committee prints leaflets, publicizes campaigns and works to counteract media misrepresentation. Finally there is an education committee which helps to train people for the workshops (for example, in carpentry and building), sets up political debates and organizes a literacy programme.

As in Colomoncagua (see Chapter 1) the success of this democratic structure depends on literacy, while at the same time the success of literacy depends on the democracy that makes the skills relevant and gives people the chance to employ them.

> We need literate people to work in the committees; the positions must rotate
> every year otherwise a small elite may begin to dominate and corruption may
> set in.
> *Miguel*

The learners in the literacy programme are mostly women. Most of the
men have to go to work, leaving the community for more than 12 hours
each day. In their absence it is the women who do most of the committee
work and who are left having to face the authorities and pressurize for
change.

> It is vital that we women learn to stop our organizations being dominated
> by men as they have been in the past.
> *Julieta*

The literacy classes are run by residents themselves and are always open.
Anyone who wishes to learn can go at any time to the community house
or find a teacher, who is one of their neighbours. Paradoxically one of the
most active teachers is a man, Miguel, who is always at home. He makes
a living repairing radios and televisions that lie in fragments around his
one-roomed house.

> Some people argue that because of the economic crisis, literacy must be
> linked to productivity so that it will help people get work and thus money.
> But why do the people want money? So they can spend it on improving the
> conditions of their lives. We have found that the most basic conditions can be
> best improved by collective work and collective struggle. By teaching literacy
> as conscientization we can thus reach the desired end much quicker.
> *Miguel*

Remarkably the people of Francisco Villa have decided to use the INEA
primer as a basis for their work (though they do not regard themselves
as part of INEA). The materials were obtained by persistent demand
involving regular visits to the Ixtapalapa office.

> The materials are free and it is our right to have them. We don't have
> the resources to produce our own.
> *Julieta*

However, the materials are not taken at face value: they are used "on our
terms, in our way". The words on the page may not generate discussion
in INEA classes, but here they do.

> We can make the materials relevant. "Spade" may not seem like a political
> word, but it can be if we talk about having to dig our own drains. "Rubbish"
> could be treated without mention of political struggle but for us, here,
> it is a highly sensitive issue. The materials themselves don't matter, it is
> how you use them.
> *Miguel*

In the eyes of the teachers in Francisco Villa, discussion is central to the learning process – but not just any discussion.

> If politics is ever mentioned in the INEA materials it is dry and theoretical. People only discuss what is in the books, not what is in their lives. What we do is make links so that the words are not just words on the page but become words in action.
> *Miguel*

Transforming words into actions means many things in Francisco Villa. It means negotiating with bureaucrats, taking notes at meetings with officials, lobbying people, producing leaflets, making banners, writing graffiti. It means learners writing their first words on placards demanding "we want water" or "no to the fraud", and feeling the power of those words as they carry them on demonstrations. It means reading about their rights, understanding the constitution.

> Freire talks of a magical or submerged consciousness, one in which people are fatalistic. He is talking really of rural areas, but here it is the same, people are submerged beneath the modern state, beneath television soap-operas, they are paralysed, made apathetic. Our literacy programme is not for helping people to read comic books, because that would be to remain submerged. We work to lift the veil . . . to help people see the country in which they are living and fight for their rights.
> *Miguel*

What is unusual about the work in Francisco Villa is the use of explicitly rejected government materials to further an anti-government struggle.[12] This may suggest that the materials are in fact good, in which case INEA's failure is in using them badly or not making enough contact with community networks. But the materials, as they are designed and laid out, do stifle discussion beneath endless technical exercises. The success of the Francisco Villa programme points to another conclusion: that literacy materials are much less relevant in evaluating the potential impact of a programme than any reading of Freire's work would suggest. In themselves codifications mean very little. What matters is who is using them and how they are used.

THE UNION OF SAN MIGUEL TEOTONGO

The people of Francisco Villa and other sectors work together in the Union of San Miguel Teotongo. This has large assemblies every Saturday, recognizing that some services need to be demanded by the whole *barrio*. Since its modest beginnings this union has many achievements to its name. Collective pressure on the social security offices forced them to provide a *lecheria* (milk distribution point) in the *barrio*. Pickets of local government offices made them build a library (though as yet it is supplied with very few books). Lobbying the city dustmen, at dawn every day for a week, made them agree to clear the rubbish from some areas of the *barrio*. Collective work was used to construct a popular health centre, supplied with committed and trained volunteers. Negotiations with the bus companies mean that one or two routes now run through the *barrio*, though the steep slope and unstable roads make this difficult. Protest marches have stopped the police from building a barracks on one of the community's green areas, which is reserved for recreational space. Likewise, the invasion of another green area by PRI workers (who built a branch office for their Party, defended by barbed wire, dogs and rifles) was eventually ended by successful legal action, using the constitution against the very people who wrote it. The office was dismantled.

The union recognizes that the source of the deprivation that they have been suffering is in national and international politics. They are active members of the National Popular Urban Movement (CONAMUP). Founded in 1981, CONAMUP traces the present unemployment, lack of services and high cost of living to the foreign debt and subsequent austerity measures. Although the government's unjust budget (which gives more to the police than to education) is important, it is the injustice of the debt itself that is at the centre of CONAMUP's campaigning work. It demands that the government cease debt payments immediately. There are demonstrations almost every week though few are as large as the one in 1986 when 100,000 people gathered in the central square of Mexico City. In this struggle, although the PRI are seen as guilty collaborators, the prime enemy is the United States.

> PRI are just pawns in the international game.
> *Reina*

> The US want to use the economic crisis, which is of their making, for political manipulation. They want to dismantle what remains of the revo-lution by selling off our state industries, giving private businesses complete control.
> *Miguel*

The US Republican Party foreign-policy think-tank document, Santa Fe No. 2, estimates that 85 per cent of the Mexican economy is state controlled and recommends that 'the US must support whatever efforts are made to sell off state enterprises . . . to pay off the debt'. The latest US government proposal for dealing with the debt, the Brady Plan, promises Mexico a 35 per cent reduction in its debt. But this means in practice that Mexico will have to guarantee payment on the remaining 65 per cent, and sell its assets to do so. Austerity will continue as the PRI follow the rules of the international game. They have substantially eased investment restrictions. According to the *Sunday Times* "[there is] a planned sale of more than 200 state owned enterprises over the next two years" (27 August 1989).

Perhaps this is the price of US acceptance of the blatant fraud behind PRI's last election victory. The implications are, however, disturbing. Selling off state industries may not seem to be a bad idea when the state is so corrupt, but,

> They are stealing our future. Soon there will be nothing left even if we remove PRI. Everything will be run for profit and not for people.
> *Miguel*

Meanwhile, damage to the environment of Mexico City is reaching catastrophic proportions. Rather than put regulations on industry, the PRI announced in December 1988 that school holidays were to be re-scheduled and that children should avoid doing sport in the mornings – in order to minimize the threat of brain damage from excessive inhalation of polluted air!

Mexico has been comparatively good at playing the international financial games, threatening to pull the plug on the world banking system at regular intervals and juggling with the IMF and US to get new loans. But the IMF holds the strongest hand because of their refusal to deal with the debt of different countries except on an individual basis. In this way, they divide and rule. While Mexico remains isolated its people will continue to lose. The new President, Carlos Salinas de Gortari, was architect of the austerity plans under his predecessor, so there is no likelihood of a change in government policy in the immediate future.

The residents of San Miguel Teotongo and hundreds of similar *barrios* simply will not take another long period of austerity. Unless a solution is found to the debt crisis (such as cancelling debts on loans which were never really invested and pursuing the money through secret international bank accounts, as well as redistributing the wealth that is within the country), the violent scenes witnessed in Venezuela after austerity measures were announced in 1989 will be repeated a hundred times over in Mexico. The people of San Miguel Teotongo will be at the centre of any such conflict. The future of the *barrio* is uncertain. Two years ago a crack appeared in the volcanic slopes of Tetlalmanche. History will decide which form of activity will lead to what sort of eruption.

NOTES

1. George, Susan, *A Fate Worse Than Debt* (London: Penguin, 1988).
2. The Virgin of Guadelupe: a vision of a brown virgin that has become central to Mexican nationalist history.
3. de Janvry, Alain, Elisabeth Sadoulet, Linda Wilcox, "Rural Labour in Latin America" World Employment Programme Research Working Paper (ILO, 1986).
4. We use the word *barrio* for the sake of consistency throughout the book, though in fact the word used in Mexico is *colonia* and San Miguel Teotongo is known as a *colonia popular*.

5.   Speaking on 31 August 1982 after declaring Mexico's inability to pay its debt, and rejecting International Monetary Fund advice by nationalizing the banks. This strong stance did not last long. He handed over presidency to Miguel de la Madrid and then left the country to go to Rome, taking with him $1 billion! (according to James Henry in the *New Republic* as quoted in Susan George, op. cit.).

6.   Susan George, op. cit.

7.   The US Treasury exerted considerable pressure on banks to come up with the money. Loans by the IMF are now generally regarded as a green light to banks – signifying that it is safe to invest in the country because the country has agreed to adjustment (i.e. austerity) programmes.

8.   Susan George, op. cit.

9.   War on Want, "Debt Crisis Newsletter No. 4", November 1987.

10.   See "Co-opting the Ideas of Paulo Freire" by Krishna Kumar and Ross Kidd, in *Political and Economic Weekly*, Bombay, vol. XVI, no. 1 & 2, January 1981.

11.   Throughout Latin America this can be found: for example US attempts to use the language of "democracy" in El Salvador and Honduras, the appropriation of the language of "human rights" in Ecuador, and the use of "freedom" by monetarists in Chile.

12.   Women in other sectors of San Miguel Teotongo have criticized Francisco Villa because their literacy group, although predominantly made up of women, includes some men. One group, the Women's Solidarity Action Group (Equipo Mujeres en Acción Solidaria: EMAS) have started their own classes in other sectors. They argue that it is necessary to use materials aimed specifically at women and to have women only classes: 'how can women be liberated when their oppressors are in the same room, watching over them?" (*Juana*, EMAS).

EMAS have produced a primer which provides good backing for their argument, using themes and images that are directly related to the position of women in urban *barrios* like San Miguel Teotongo. Themes include the injustice of housework, the need for crèche facilities, contraception, pregnancy, the female body, vaginal diseases, domestic violence, rape and types of women's organizations. More general themes include the inequalities of wealth distribution, drug addiction, malnourishment and inflation. Most of the women who join EMAS groups are activists already who need to develop their literacy skills. "The themes are very explicit in their political content. Non-activists tend to reject them." *Reina* (EMAS)

7. Chile, Santiago: Breaking the Culture of Silence

History is ours, for it is made by the people.
Salvador Allende, Chilean President, 11 September 1973, while the National Palace was being bombed by Chilean air force bombers.
In the culture of silence the masses are "mute", that is, they are prohibited from creatively taking part in the transformations of their society . . .
Paulo Freire[1]

In 1973, the Chilean military, under the leadership of General Augusto Pinochet, seized power from the first democratically-elected Marxist government in the world: the Socialist Popular Unity government of Salvador Allende. The generals declared a state of siege, dissolving Congress, destroying the electoral register and suspending the Constitution. Sympathizers of Allende were killed, tortured, imprisoned or exiled. Between 1973 and 1977 an estimated 30,000 people were killed, 2,500 disappeared and tens of thousands passed through the prisons and concentration camps. The silencing of a people took other forms beyond immediate brutality. Popular organizations – political parties, unions, student bodies and neighbourhood committees – were either banned or their leaders replaced by military personnel. Newspapers were closed, with many journalists arrested or blacklisted.

Control of the mass media was critical to suppressing the voices of dissent. For example, in 1973 there were four Chilean television channels: a national network and three university channels. Under the socialist government, there was a large element of social influence over their output mediated through various bodies including a national television council on which government and workers' representatives sat with the university rectors. The military *junta* moved quickly, eliminating workers and parliamentary representatives from the council and appointing new rectors for the universities, all of them military men. The Directorate of National Television was replaced by a Director-General appointed directly by the government. All powers of the university television corporations were vested in the new rectors. In summary, all social administration of Chilean television was lost and replaced by direct military control.

A climate of fear combined with a rigid control of information to create a society where the working classes had been effectively silenced. This allowed the state to implement a strict monetarist economic strategy without popular resistance:

> The Chilean economic experience is very similar to what we are developing here, although in the case of Chile it was possible to impose a policy and regulate its implementation.
> *Cecil Parkinson*[2]

The results were a consumer boom in the late 1970s and recession from 1981 onwards.

> Many factories have closed because production has been oriented to the world market and not to our needs.[3]

Unemployment, five per cent in 1973, had risen to 25 per cent by 1982. The official figures hid the full extent of poverty. Government schemes such as the minimum employment scheme (PEM), provided wages significantly below the minimum wage in order to take people off the unemployment lists. In 1980, 4.5 per cent of the population were on PEM receiving a wage that was a quarter of the legal minimum.

A NEW MOVEMENT

> Women have been the most dynamic sector of the population since 1973.
> *Herman Mondaca*[4]

Before the coup, few women were involved in the popular organizations. The systematic destruction of these, coupled with unemployment and poverty, forced women into a more active role. An example comes from the experience of a group of 14 women in Lo Hermida, a *barrio* of Santiago, Chile's capital, that houses 60,000 people. As in all the popular *barrios*, standards of housing and services are basic. One woman we met had recently constructed an extension to her house out of mud and wire meshing found on a tip.

> During the period of Popular Unity, there was money and work . . . we had what we needed in the house. Our husbands were working . . . we'd go hungry . . . but it was hunger of one day, not like now, when we pass several days without eating.[5]

Unemployment challenged traditional family roles. With the loss of work opportunities for men in the formal economy, new ways of making an income were required and it was women who were forced to develop these alternatives. Despairing husbands were left to look after the children while women abandoned what they saw as the protected space of the home to search for ways of feeding their families. For many women, this involved overcoming both the fear of a largely unknown and inhospitable world as well as the resistance of husbands ashamed of their wives leaving the home.

> We have many conflicts with our husbands: they created a lot of problems for us, especially at the beginning because the woman became the man of the house.

> Our husbands are very egotistical . . . they get angry when we leave the house but not when we return with money.

The first step for the women of Lo Hermida was setting up a canteen for children. Food was supplied by Catholic aid agencies and the Church provided a location for the cooking. The canteen fed the children but did nothing for the adults. A meeting was held to see what the alternatives were.

> I had never been to a meeting. . . . Everything was unknown, I'd never been part of an organization.

The women decided to set up a laundry as a source of income. A site was found and the Church supplied the necessary materials. From there they had to decide on norms of working, find clients through house-visits and by using local radio as publicity, do accounts and set up an organized structure to supervise and direct the work itself. The whole process was a learning one. Work was shared and profits divided equally.

What started as a way of surviving economic hardship became a means to understanding why that hardship came about. In the years immediately following the *coup d'etat*, the Church was the only institution allowed to function with some degree of independence. It operated as an umbrella, the only shelter available for the work of semi-clandestine organizations. Through individual clients as well as through Church organizations that the laundry worked for, the women in the laundry came across many people who had been involved in Popular Unity and others who had suffered from the violence.

> We saw that our problems are not individual but collective and that we had to unite to deal with them.

First working with groups of the unemployed, then groups of relatives of the "disappeared",[6] they began to involve themselves in the wider struggle against the regime. In 1978, they organized a hunger strike for the detained and a candle-lit march on which people were arrested by the army and teargas was used to "restore order".

> Far from frightening us, it did the opposite . . . we continued in a more dedicated way.

Literacy
In 1984, the Cultural Action Workshop (TAC), an independent non-governmental organization, started working with the laundry workers.

They wanted to help them recover the history of their experiences, in the form of a book to be written by the women. To help the research, the team distributed written summaries of previous meetings. They were surprised to discover that over a third of them had serious reading difficulties – this in a country with official literacy rates of 91 per cent.[7]

> No one knew that I was illiterate, not even my husband, and no one in the laundry despite six years of working together.
> *Rosita, member of the Laundry Workshop*

> This alerted us to the fact that in the majority of popular organizations, the post of Secretary, or any that required knowledge of reading and writing, were life-posts.
> *Maria Eugenia*[8]

TAC decided to set up literacy classes – along Freirian lines – in Lo Hermida, as a strategic task to overcome the obstacles that put a brake on participation in popular organizations. They began with nine people, mostly members of popular organizations, using improvised materials and teaching in the church. At the end of the year, certificates were given at a party to the two women from the laundry who had participated. The following year the TAC developed a primer with the people who had

MIEDO

Figure 7.1: Miedo ("fear") – an image from the TAC primer *Learning Together*

learnt to read and write in the first workshop. The themes were chosen to reflect the reality of the population, and the codifications were drawn by a local artist. Themes included tea (sugared tea is a major part of the diet), the taking of land for housing, fear (see Figure 7.1), unemployment, games, and hospital.

TAC's work has contributed to participation in *barrio* organizations. It has also given a boost to the expression of local culture. Alongside the literacy work, short story competitions have been held on specific themes including literacy itself and life in Lo Hermida. Some of these have been published. In addition, they have now set up a team of local teachers to multiply the work and set up groups in different parts of Lo Hermida. The team has four groups operating in the different sectors of the *barrio*. One of the most active members is Rosita, who learnt to read and write with the laundry and who is now teaching others to lose their fear of ignorance. The teaching team has recently written a guide in order to be able to extend the experience beyond Lo Hermida to other *barrios* of Santiago and other urban populations in Chile.

Literacy's relevance

> When the "soaps" are on TV, no one will turn up to classes.
> *Rosita*

For all its successes, TAC's use of literacy work to recover culture and strengthen organization faces the serious problem of lack of motivation to learn by many of the people they are trying to reach. Literacy is no longer the exclusive means of access to the outside world and the importance of the written word is on the decline.

> It is not a part of the culture to read papers, magazines and books. It seems to be only part of school.
> *Raoul, literacy teacher, Lo Hermida*

The written word doesn't play a big role in urban daily life because other forms of communication have displaced it. In *barrios* like Lo Hermida, television is everywhere. While only half the homes have a sink for washing dishes, four in every five households own a television. Average television viewing in Santiago is 28 hours a week.[9] It is at first a shock to see, even in the poorest homes, a television usually in the dominant position in the house, providing a constant stream of censored news, soap operas[10] and game shows interspersed with a mountain of publicity (up to 40 minutes an hour) for consumer goods and foodstuffs that are far beyond the budgets of any of Lo Hermida's viewers.

In the 1960s, a strong critique of the mass media developed in Latin America which assumed that the institutions were part of the ideological apparatus

of domination and instruments of US imperialism . . . it was easy to put TV and the school together as instruments of domination. So much of the effort of popular education was reactive, trying to develop an alternative to TV. We think this is a defensive position and it ideologically condemns TV, and so doesn't use its possibilities.
Valerio Fuenzalida, director of CENECA

Popular education groups perceive television as a threat. For many, it presents a world view at odds with any critical perception of reality, and one which promotes passivity in the face of hardship. News programmes present demonstrations as the work of terrorists threatening the peaceful order of the Chilean state. Soap heroines don't achieve their goals by organizing workshops. The woman of the popular *barrio* is notable by her complete absence from the screen. Yet the screen has a profound emotional influence on these women, "to the point that women who only own a black and white TV describe some programmes in colours".[11] The position taken by popular educators, of rejecting outright a medium which is so influential on the people they are teaching, is bound to marginalize their role. If education is to start from people's reality, this is an example of reality being ignored.

A NEW LITERACY

Read . . . to apprehend mentally the meaning of written or other characters.
Oxford English Dictionary

The printed text is important but it is consistently losing its monopoly and is being challenged by alternative means of communication and record-keeping.
Raff Carmen, lecturer, Manchester University

Television demonstrates the power of visual images as a form of communication. Literacy teaching recognizes this on one level: the codification of the literacy primer is a visual image. The dialogue generated by the decoding of the image is associated with the word. For Freire, reading the word is ultimately about reading the world. The codification, then, is a recognition of the need for the visual image as a representation of that world. What theories of literacy have not recognized is that visual images have their own language, and that "visual literacy" is assuming a greater significance in a country like Chile where 90 per cent of homes have a television and where video is set to become a mass medium.

If today, the problem of reading occupies the forefront of science, it is because of this suspense between two ages of writing. Because we are beginning to write, to write differently, we must re-read differently.
Jacques Derrida[12]

At first, the idea that visual images can be read or written seems absurd. After all, everyone can watch (or "read") television so the concept of the visual illiterate seems untenable. But this is also true of alphabetic reading:

> Of course, illiterates can read . . . can recognize the shapes and colours
> of words on buses so that they don't get lost . . . this means that an illiterate
> can "read" because she can recognize the key words in her daily life . . . but
> illiteracy limits the ability to analyse and create new words, new experiences.
> *Raoul*

Reading is not a technique, but a way of analysing experience critically in order to be able to participate in a wider society. If the word offers less access to communication than the image then visual literacy attains greater importance. To "write differently", then, is to produce visual images using film and video. This makes it necessary for us to learn to "re-read differently" – to analyse those images in an active, interpretative manner rather than passively accepting their intended content.

> Writing in the narrow sense – and phonetic writing above all – is rooted
> in a past of nonlinear writing.
> *Derrida*, Of Grammatology

The Incas were traditionally thought to have run an empire without writing. There were no manuscripts found by the *conquistadors* and the empire was thought to have been run on the basis of accounts which were kept by means of the special arrangement of knots on coloured pieces of rope. However, these knots, as encoded information, were a form of writing with their own language and grammatical rules. Computer analysis of the designs on Inca ceramic materials suggests that these images conceal further remains of a written Inca history. Information is encoded on the basis of the spatial arrangement of shapes and colours. To restrict the concept of writing to linear, alphabetic writing is to fail to understand different ways of thinking, some of which are becoming relevant again as images become the dominant way in which our thoughts are structured. It is conceivable that what we now think of as writing is merely a short historical interlude in the modes of representation and communication of human thought.

As yet, there are no literacy groups in Chile that have taken on board the idea of a new literacy. However, in the work of other groups elements of what might make up a teaching programme for the new literacy are highly developed.

Literacy Materials

> In 1982–3, there was no video work in Chile. We did an investigation
> and found that young people had very clear images of the government
> and the opposition . . . they identified the regime as authoritarian/dictatorial,
> but in relation to images . . . colourful and happy, while audiovisually, the
> opposition were perceived as morose, serious and in black and white.
> *Herman Mondaca, PROCESO*

PROCESO made their first video documentary in 1982 with minimal technology: a borrowed camera and a tape recorder. The aim was "to rescue the memory" of the inhabitants of marginal *barrios*, a memory that had been systematically silenced by the regime's censorship of all media. They had showings in the *barrios* and among the students of Santiago.

> Our support came from the new social movements emerging at that time
> . . . women's groups, groups of the unemployed.
> *Herman Mondaca*

The next video was a thirty minute piece on human rights involving the testimony of different people and some discussion.

> With the second video, we saw that we were doing something different
> . . . we removed the narrator or commentator . . . we wanted to give a voice
> to the participants.
> *Herman Mondaca*

The video was effectively a codification: it encoded the contradictions and complexities of the reality of the people who watched it – and it generated dialogue:

> We showed it in Lo Hermida . . . 350 people came to see it and it
> generated a big discussion . . . two human rights committees were set up
> afterwards, overcoming traditional political divisions among the people. The
> video didn't say "organize!". It just showed the reality . . . people saw it and
> spontaneously reacted.
> *Herman Mondaca*

In 1983 the opposition movement became more vociferous in its demands. Popular organizations such as the women's movement were operating more openly though still subject to police repression. PROCESO decided to use the opportunity to make more videos which went deeper into specific themes: women, the young, human rights. They decided that the popular sectors of society should be the source of all information and commentary in the videos, which were also to be used to make a contribution to popular education among those sectors. The videos were distributed through other organizations, students, women's groups and the Church. Echoing the work of popular-education groups like the CNTC in Honduras, PROCESO set up a distribution and feedback department so that the viewers could have a voice, giving their criticisms, responses and ideas for new videos.

> We saw that our work must be socially useful. Our role was to receive
> views and return them to people in a structured way.
> *Herman Mondaca*

Reading

After the coup, many university departments were transformed. Study of media and communications was heavily attacked because of its association with left-wing politics. For example, there was one course at the Catholic University which was gradually closed by the government, first losing its courses on television, then having its cinema-studies cut, until eventually it was based purely on theatre. As a response, in 1977 a group of academics set up a research body (CENECA) to continue monitoring and evaluating the media, independently of the university system. Their work involved studying the transformations in communication and culture since the coup: monitoring censorship as well as analysing new laws and their impact.

> We investigated how people saw TV and we found it confirmed that people don't watch TV passively . . . . People see their TV from the perspective of their material conditions, and their educational, social and political position . . . there was an active reading and we had to strengthen that in order to make it more so.
> *Valerio Fuenzalida*

To complement the research side of their work they set up a number of programmes of "social and cultural animation", designed to spread the experience and insights of the research. One active reception course was organized with 60 women from the urban women's movement (MOMUPO) and unions of domestic employees. It aimed to "stimulate creativity, critical understanding of reality and validate solidarity and social participation". In the medium term, it hopes to "create a social actor capable of actively demanding an orientation in the programming of TV, adequate to her interests, needs and motivations". The course used the different types of programme – soaps, news, game shows – in order to develop the active reading of television.

The way in which any television is watched and the effects that it has are dependent on a complex of social factors. For example, soap operas are usually considered a form of escapism, a way of living in fantasy what is impossible in reality. A study of the viewing habits of women residents of popular *barrios* revealed a more complex reason. The women preferred the Chilean soaps to Mexican or US imports, in spite of the greater opulence and potential for escapism in the latter. This suggested that the identification of the women with soap heroines was rooted in something more than a desire to forget their own problems. The conflicts on which the dramatic structure of soaps are based are ones which are not far removed from their own lives: abandoned children, incestuous fathers, single parents, barriers to love and so on. While the material way of life of soap heroines creates a distance from the viewers, these conflicts form the basis for a strong emotional identification with the heroine. It is this rather than the type of dress the heroine is wearing that spontaneously generates topics of conversation amongst the urban women on the subject of their favourite soaps.

For CENECA, this is the basis for active reading/reception. In a class of women, a discussion of reasons for liking soaps can lead to a consideration of why certain heroines are admired, and to think about why family conflicts are presented in soaps whereas economic ones are not. Ultimately, the women are in a position to think about the kind of conflicts that they would use if they were writing a soap themselves.

> Previously, people were passive and credulous . . . and they became selective and demanding.
> *María-Elena Hermosilla, CENECA*

Women began to read the contents of their favourite programmes more critically. Just as in Mexico, the materials used for literacy were almost irrelevant: what mattered was how they were used. Even the television of Pinochet's Chile can be a codification of life in urban popular *barrios* if read in a critical, active manner.

Writing

> Official TV arrives at our communities and we are simple adornments of the propaganda of the mayor or state functionary who opens a public toilet; foreign TV arrives or sometimes alternative TV and it only shows the misery or the poverty. But we want neither, we want to show the beauty as well, the beauty of our lives.
> *Video workshop of the urban women's movement*

At a meeting in 1985, members of PROCESO and the women's movement MOMUPO decided to make a documentary. The difference from previous work was that the women themselves were to make it. It would be about their view of the history of popular women's organizations during the dictatorship.

> We were familiarized with the machines and the basic techniques. It took us a long time to learn these things: sound, lighting, editing and ways of presenting things to the camera. We had to learn the language of video and television.
> *Coty Silva, MOMUPO*

PROCESO's only role was in teaching the techniques and doing the camera work itself. Each of the women involved was an activist in a different *barrio* of Santiago. Every meeting was recorded over the following months by the PROCESO workers as the women discussed the nature of women's organizations developing out of specific conflicts. The women took on the role of investigative reporters of the realities in their own areas. Over a year, more than 50 hours of recording were made. Four years later, the edited video (*Gestación*) is still the most popular one shown by women's groups in Santiago and all over the country. It deals with themes such as the personal changes experienced by women leaving the home to participate in organizations, the relations between men and women and the role of women in society.

> By making videos, we could use our own words, our own language, our own way of seeing.
> *Marina Valdes, Gestación*

Two more videos have been made since *Gestación* under the direction of the workshop. One is on subsistence and the way in which women have survived the recession, the other is on the recuperation of culture and dignity through the process of organization. In both productions PROCESO assisted with the camera work, but the women were involved in direction at all stages from planning to final edit.

Opportunities to "write" the moving image are still very limited in Latin America. Among groups involved in this work, there is a debate about the role of the professional in facilitating the writing process. On the one hand, PROCESO sees the camera work as a neutral technique that helps the direction, rather like the lines on a piece of paper, guiding the newly-literate.

> By professionalization, I don't mean following the formal, classical language of television. But you can't have a single fixed camera view for five minutes, or people won't watch.
> *Herman Mondaca*

There is a danger that anything which fails to match the professional standards of television will be seen as the work of amateurs and rejected by its potential audience. PROCESO make their videos on the principle that certain technical and artistic criteria must be used to prevent such a rejection.

There are other groups who believe it impossible to distinguish any aspect of the production – or "writing" – of video as professional or as a technique. In this view it is essential that the people themselves write their history, regardless of aesthetic criteria. This may well mean the withdrawal of any professional advice. If the product appears amateur or unclear, that is secondary to the authenticity of its origins.

> The people have other cultural codes, including visual ones; another view-point, other styles, other perceptions distinct from those of the communicator and more or less professional; no one better than the people themselves, then, to communicate to the people.[13]

Camera techniques are thus seen as part of the hidden agenda of modern television. Chilean television has made huge technical advances since 1973. Presentation and production are slick and use of modern post-production techniques is widespread. Hand-held camera is never used on the screens. Instead the camera is "hidden", giving an artificial appearance of objectivity, as people are not made aware of the process of filming while watching the product. Cameras in the hands of the people could break these norms, thereby helping to expose, for example, the hidden selectivity of news coverage. Learning to "write" in this way might reinforce peoples' ability to "read".

In the language of literacy, this debate questions to what extent videos written by non-professionals need to have their grammar and spelling corrected in order to be read seriously.

BREAKING THE CULTURE OF SILENCE

A new impact

As the economic recession worsened in the mid-1980s, popular resistance to the dictatorship grew bolder. Large-scale demonstrations spilled over into riots in 1983 and 1986. Pinochet himself was the object of an assassination attempt as the new social movements felt their strength.

> There was a feeling for the first time that Pinochet's rule was finite, that he himself was mortal.
> Raoul

Visual literacy played an important part in breaking the culture of silence. First, it promoted the growth of organizations. Video showings like that in Lo Hermida (which spawned two human rights groups) were repeated all over Chile. Video groups like PROCESO became more skilful in using the medium for organizational ends. One technique was to show a documentary in a public area and video the viewing as well as interviews with viewers and discussions among them afterwards. This new video, of the viewers, would be shown the following month to the same people. Seeing themselves on the screen had a dramatic effect:

> The people feel that they are appropriating the TV . . . and seeing TV again . . . losing their helplessness. Specialist courses are not necessary . . . just seeing the TV inserted in their own reality can produce the "click".
> Herman Mondaca

Video can be responsible for a very rapid conscientization. The mechanics of producing images become clear. Television loses its monopoly as the mouthpiece of truth when moving images are democratized. One viewer responded after seeing himself on the screen for the first time "now I've been on television . . . they're not going to lie to me any more".

Once people realize the way in which the world is presented to them, they are much more likely to try and change it themselves, recognizing that it is their world as much as the world of the presenters. Changing it is suddenly within their reach.[14]

More recently PROCESO have set up a mobile video service for 55 women's groups in and around Santiago. Using a giant screen, they show videos such as *Gestación* to groups of women in the popular *barrios*, sometimes in closed spaces such as chapels, but often publicly, in streets where anyone can join in, watch and participate in the discussions afterwards.

> The screen itself is a novelty. These events play a key role in new mobilizations, just by the mere attendance at a public event breaking down people's fear and giving them confidence.
> *Coty Silva, MOMUPO*

The simple experience of being organized on the streets has been instrumental in overcoming many women's fears of stepping beyond the boundaries of the home into a city controlled by an alien authority in the form of soldiers, armed police and tanks.

As the popular movement gathered strength, video was also important for providing information about events censored by the official media. Some video groups, rather than concentrating on the literacy side of the work, were producing an alternative news magazine. By distributing through unions, political parties, women's groups, cultural associations and of course the Church, these acted as a form of information for the literate. Since 1984, TELEANÁLISIS (now called Nueva Imagen) have produced a video every month, following the protests and demonstrations, national strikes, Church activities, as well as the international news excluded from Chilean TV.

> We started in 1984, because there was no freedom of the press and the TV was so controlled. We wanted to show the images that TV didn't and wouldn't.
> *Claudio, Journalist, TELEANÁLISIS*

These video magazines reached an estimated audience of 50,000 people a month.

The state was not slow in recognizing the significance of video. At first, any videos of public protests had to be shot from parked vans or the top of buildings. There were no laws but rather an inevitable police response and the workers couldn't afford to lose their equipment.

> We wanted to show our images and we didn't want it to be clandestine . . .
> so we started going out into the streets, wearing medical service cards or boy scout cards as identity on our shirts.
> *Herman Mondaca*

Police saw the badges and, reading them from afar, took them as a seal of official approval, a perfect example of the ascendancy of the visual image over the written word. This provided some immunity until the state realized the scale and increasing importance of alternative video. Scare tactics were used. People were followed, received telephone threats, had their houses observed. Newspaper articles were published in which video groups were accused of being subversives, with titles such as "Video: Principal Ideological Arm of the Chilean Left".

> In September 1987 one of us, Mario Nuñez, was kidnapped with four civilians. They were beaten in the face and testicles and questioned about their activities. They searched his house and mine and took some "evidence" ... photorolls and tapes including some of my four-year-old kid. At dawn, the prisoners were released on a road outside Santiago. On the same day, we won a prize in Brazil for one of our documentaries.
> *Herman Mondaca*

Scare tactics were ineffective and the army could do little more because by this stage PROCESO was networked with over 150 organizations. The national movement was too strong. For example, the Catholic Church had video equipment in almost every parish. Repressing video had become an impossible task.

Visions of democracy

> "Of course Pinochet is the construction of an image. He's been constructed by publicity people. And Superman has been constructed by other publicity people. We have been able to use the image of Superman and give the people of Chile the feeling that they are protected. The people in the *poblaciones*, in the slums, said Superman is much stronger than Pinochet. Superman can beat Pinochet."
>
> *Ariel Dorfman (author of "How to Read Donald Duck", speaking about actor Christopher Reeve's visit to Santiago in solidarity with actors who had received death threats)* Made in Latin America, *BBC2, London 1989.*[15]

The 1980 constitution instituted by the military government set elections for 1989. In 1988, Pinochet announced that there would be a Yes/No plebiscite in November to decide whether he should carry on as leader. Effectively this was a tactic, an attempt to avoid full elections. However, legal requirements offered the opposition access to national media. For the first time since the coup, the opposition ("No") campaigners were given daily 15-minute spots on national television. Groups like TELEANÁLISIS and PROCESO suddenly had an opportunity to use the networks themselves.

> The language of the campaign was directed at TV viewers ... not based on arguments or logic, but on visual images.
> *Valerio Fuenzalida*

The polls initially showed a big proportion of indecisive voters. Many of these were people who were frightened of voting no to Pinochet. The government campaign concentrated on showing images of pre-1973 as chaotic, playing on people's fears of disorder. The No campaign was directed at this fear.

The TV spots used the language of advertising to produce the conviction that the "No" was a just position, a happy position, and one of non-violence . . . it created a feeling that to vote "Yes" was non-ethical, an option for aggression and the violation of human rights.
Valerio Fuenzalida

One image was of the police beating an undefended person lying on the ground. Full speed was followed by slow motion of the same sequence. Each blow was circled and amplified with sound effects. The text wasn't saying that those in power must be punished but rather that this must never happen again:

This man is a Chilean [the demonstrator]. So is this man [the policeman]. This man wants peace. So does this man. This man is fighting for what he believes. So is this man. Let them both have what they want. Vote NO!

This was one of very few images dealing directly with violence. The aim was to overcome past associations of the opposition with morose black and white images. The symbol of the campaign was the rainbow.

Without hate, fear or violence, vote NO!
Happiness is on the march.
Campaign slogans

In spite of being broadcast late at night, the No spots attracted record audiences and are recognized as the major factor in the success of the campaign. As the momentum increased the campaign took to the streets. To wear a T-shirt with the image of the rainbow was a sign of a loss of fear. Video was involved here too. PROCESO filmed discussions in villages on the plebiscite and used the mobile video unit to show them.

In the ballot, Pinochet was beaten and the showdown was set for the elections the following year. An alliance of all parties opposed to Pinochet was organized under Patricio Aylwin, a Christian Democrat. In the showdown, more innovation in the use of visual images appeared such as the visual campaign leaflet.

We give a candidate the video equipment and three people in a mobile unit. With this, the candidate can make two videos of publicity for local use. Then, they can show them to the whole district.
Herman Mondaca

Faced with inevitable defeat in the elections, Pinochet made a number of last minute moves to ensure that complete power would not be left in the hands of the new government. One of the bills rushed through Congress involved the privatization of television. Aware of the power of the medium, he sought to ensure that big business – which would remain sympathetic to him – gained control and would retain it even in the aftermath of a lost election.

The future

> Instead of looking down on it, we should get into it, into TV.
> *Gabriel García Márquez*[16]

The new government in Chile presents the same dilemma for the popular movements and for education groups as did the Borja government in Ecuador. Is it worth using the limited democratic space offered by the government to try and open that space further? Or is it better to stay in opposition to avoid the assimilation of any protest?

> We think that TV space must be opened . . . alternative video producers must orientate themselves to fulfil the technical requirements of TV.
> *Herman Mondaca*

> People see many programmes as educational which are not classically so. If we understand this, then we can amplify the educational use of TV, without the title "educational" which alienates people and makes them switch off.
> *Valerio Fuenzalida*

The new government's policy is to democratize the television, creating legal mechanisms so that the national channel is autonomous of government and responsive to the regional needs of different branches of its network, restoring the universities' independent control over their franchises and setting up a new "pluralist and representative" national television council to regulate and supervise broadcasting.

With television genuinely responsive to its audience, the literacy of that audience becomes vital for the success of the democratization. "Active receivers" will be able to articulate the demands that make it their television. As writing develops, the opportunities will exist for different organizations to express themselves through the networks.

> At the same time it's important to maintain our autonomy, not to be dependent on political parties and government but to articulate with them in order to deepen democracy.
> *Herman Mondaca*

> The "No" campaign was made by the middle class using the same manipulative techniques as the *junta*. They did it very well, but will they let the popular classes find their own expression in the future?
> *Coty Silva*

Time will tell what the effect of campaigns based on making and watching television programmes will be: whether they create new forms of participation and organization, or whether, with the military in the wings and the economic situation in the popular *barrios* unchanged, they will merely form part of the social palliative for the de-read democracy which has swept the continent.

NOTES

1.   Freire, Paulo, *Cultural Action for Freedom* (London: Penguin 1972).
2.   British Minister of Trade after visiting Chile in 1980. Quoted in WUS/CCHR, *Education and Repression: Chile* (London 1982).
3.   From *Asi Aprendemos*, an investigation of Lo Hermida, a poor *barrio* of Santiago, carried out by the Santa Maria laundry workshop, 1985.
4.   Director of video group PROCESO in interview with authors, August 1989.
5.   *Lavando la Esperanza*, written by members of the laundry workshop with Taller de Acción Cultural (TAC) (Santiago 1985). Other quotations in this subsection are taken from the same publication.
6.   The Disappeared are a surprisingly large group. It is so common in the Southern Cone (Chile, Argentina, Uruguay, Paraguay) that it has become a verb: I was disappeared, You were disappeared, She is disappeared etc. Few reappear.
7.   National Report 1986, quoted in, *Situatión Educativa de America Latina y El Caribe* (Santiago: UNESCO/OREALC, 1988).
8.   Maria Eugenia Letelier, *Análisis de experiencias de alfabetización en poblaciones de Santiago* (draft), 1989.
9.   Research into television in low-income areas from Fuenzalida, Valerio, *Estudios sobre la Televisión Chilena* (Santiago: CPU, 2nd edn, 1986).
10. The soap opera or *telenovela* in Latin America is slightly different from its European or North American counterpart. It rarely runs longer than 20 episodes and finds its dramatic origins in the melodrama of the radio-soaps, and before them the musical sagas of the continent.
11. Fuenzalida, Valerio, and Maria Elena Hermósilla, *Visiónes y Ambiciónes del Televidente* (Santiago: CENECA, 1989).
12. Derrida, Jacques, *Of Grammatology*, translated by G. Spivak (Baltimore: Johns Hopkins University Press, 1976).
13. Kaplun, Mario, in P. Valdeavellano ed., *Video in Popular Education* (Santiago: CEAAL/IPAL, 1989).
14. An important example of the conscientization achieved by awareness of the techniques of television took place in April 1987 when the Pope visited the country. Channel 13, seen by the Catholic University, were awarded the rights to cover all events. Other channels had to use its footage. This was the first time that the National Channel, with its stricter censorship, was not to provide the source footage for a major news story. Channel 13 took the opportunity of broadcasting all of the Pope's speeches, even those on sensitive issues. The National Channel edited large sections. The Pope's speeches were not especially radical, but for TV viewers in the country it was the first insight into how news coverage could be edited in order to manipulate them. Valerio Fuenzalida believes that this was a key event in the emergence of opposition because it was the first time that it had been expressed on a national level.
15. Christopher Reeve visited Chile in 1988. The quote is an excerpt from a speech given to the Actors' Union and shown as part of *Made in Latin America: 4*, broadcast on British television, November 1989.
16. Marquez has recently written a soap opera and set up a film school in Cuba, recognizing the importance of visual writing.

III

RECLAMATION: LITERACY AND INDIGENOUS PEOPLES

LITERACY AND INDIGENOUS PEOPLES: INTRODUCTION

> Nowhere in the hemisphere . . . do those who identify themselves as descendants of the original inhabitants dominate politically, socially or economically.
> *Roxanne Dunbar Ortiz*, Indians of the Americas, 1984

The Spanish invasion in the sixteenth century was the single most important event in determining the social, political and economic structures of the Latin American continent. Many of today's popular struggles can be seen as a indication of pre-Colombian ways of life. To leave the consideration of indigenous peoples till now is not an attempt at marginalizing the issues but a recognition of their complexity, particularly in relation to literacy. The refugees in Colomoncagua and the *campesinos* in San Antonio de Jura identify themselves with the struggle for indigenous rights against a government that has stolen their land. The residents of San Miguel Teotongo include people who speak more than a dozen Mayan and Aztec languages. The Ecuadorean campaign is really two campaigns, one in Spanish and the other in the languages of the Incas and of the Amazonian peoples. Our aim is now to consider the indigenous issue with the background of economic recession and rural and urban exploitation already clear.

In 1992, there will be celebrations of the 500th anniversary of Christopher Colombus's discovery of the New World. But for many inhabitants of the continent, this is an insult to their history.

> The population of the hemisphere decreased from 100 million Indians to 10 million Indians within a century of European invasion.
> *Ortiz*, Indians of the Americas

Traditionally this has been explained by the accidental spread of disease. In fact, illness was only a part of a more horrific genocide:

> Other killers were principally overwork in the [Spanish controlled] mines, massacres, starvation or malnutrition with the breakdown of subsistence food production, loss of will to live or reproduce, infanticide, suicide and abortion, and massive deportations of slave labour.
> *Ortiz*, Indians of the Americas

For the descendants of the different civilisations that were so brutally destroyed, 1992 could – and should – offer the opportunity to re-evaluate the continuing colonization of their nations in the era of "independence".

8. Guatemala, Cabrican: The New Frontier

THE MAM AND CABRICAN

On the western side of Guatemala's mountainous *altiplano* is the departmental capital of Huehuetenango. From the bus station on the outskirts of town, a cramped minibus will take you to the highpoint where the ruins of the Mayan city of Zaculeu are revealed. The ruins – less spectacular than the view over sunlit, forested mountains – are mostly reconstructions of buildings long since destroyed and the colour of the stone used is the same stained grey as an inner-city tenement block. Behind the Coca-Cola kiosk is a one room museum. Zaculeu was the capital of the Mam people, one of the biggest branches of the Mayan family tree. The museum designers were clearly not over-concerned. The highlight inside is a series of badly drawn pictures that follow the Spanish *conquistador* Pedro de Alvarado on his journey to destroy the city in 1525.

> Of eight million inhabitants [in Guatemala] . . . 68 per cent live in rural areas. Of these 90 per cent are indigenous people (about 4.5 million), the speakers of the 22 vernacular languages.[1]

According to the 1981 government census, the 400,609 Mam speakers make up 18 per cent of Guatemala's indigenous population. One can only marvel at the supposed accuracy of the census in a part of the country where many areas are unreachable by road. Other estimates of the number of Mam speakers range from 680,000 to one million.[2] They live in four of Guatemala's 22 departments. The area now called Cabrican was probably populated by Mam people escaping the Spanish conquest, although there are no written records. Locally, it is told how they settled the densely-forested mountains and cleared areas of land in order to plant maize, the crop at the centre of Mayan culture. Many of the annual ceremonies and celebrations revolved around the planting and harvesting of maize.

> Sown to be eaten it is the sacred sustenance of the men who were made of maize.[3]

Agricultural conditions in Cabrican were hard. The land is poor and largely on steep mountain slopes which will only sustain one crop a year. At an altitude of up to 3,000 metres, frosts are a serious threat. A second source of work was the production of lime, an essential ingredient for the preparation of maize flour from which the mainstay of the diet, the *tortilla*, is made. La Pedrera, a local mountain, has been mined for over 150 years. To this day, the stone is burnt in the large wood-fired ovens that dot the hillsides. Each firing of lime takes 36 hours and uses six or seven whole pine trees.

Once settled, the Mam worked and lived as they had done before the conquest. They maintained their language, beliefs and customs. They lived in adobe houses and wore their distinctive clothes: brightly coloured and embroidered woven blouses (*huipiles*) and lengths of folded fabric as skirts (*cortes*) for the women, trousers and shirts made from woven material for the men. Work was shared: both the land and the quarries were communally worked for the benefit of all the people in the villages. There was no owner.

THE LADINOS

In 1825, four years after the Guatemalan landowning elite achieved independence from Spain, Cabrican was named and recognized as a municipality. It was typical as a last outpost of the administration and even today has the atmosphere of a frontier-town. The 44 kilometre journey from the departmental capital of Quetzaltenango takes four hours by bus: during the rainy season, the road is often impassable. The town, established by Spanish-speaking settlers, is set on a mountain ridge that overlooks the Mam villages, and consists of little more than two streets running between two Catholic churches. A typically vivid turquoise graveyard sprawls over a nearby slope. The inhabitants, and the town as well as the graveyard, bear the *ladino*[4] names of Lopez, Barrera, Ramirez and Vasquez. Horses are tied up in the central plaza outside the tiny Town Hall where births, deaths and marriages are recorded. Beyond these records, written materials are scarce. Neither newspapers nor books are seen outside the textbooks in school. The only map of the region, framed and hung ceremoniously in the mayor's office, is an inaccurate pencil-drawing by the head of the local primary school.

> The *ladinos* see the Indians as irrational beings and tend to treat them in a way which confirms those views.
> *F. Chiodi* (see note 1)

Since the arrival of the *ladinos*, the Mam have suffered systematic racism and the loss of much of their land. In the town, they have been treated as second-class citizens, employed as maids, cooks and cleaners by the *ladinos*.

> In a lot of towns, the Indian kids couldn't play football . . . it was a ladino game, so Indian kids would get beaten up if they tried to play football.
> *Father Ron Hennessy, ex-Cabrican pries)*

The contact between the *ladino* town and the Mam villages is still minimal, the major exception being on market day when villagers converge on the central square, many walking many hours with heavy loads, in order to sell fruit, vegetables and cloth.

The loss of land is an even bigger grievance:

> When an Indian had a good bit of land, the *ladino* mayor would bring the Indian in and put him in jail, insisting that he sign over the land. Before you starved to death or rotted in jail, you had to sign [with a thumbprint]. That's the way things happened.
> *Ron Hennessy*

Forced to subsist from less and less land, most of the Mam have had to migrate every year to the large coffee, sugar and cotton plantations on the rich land of the southern coast. Here they have to work all daylight hours for wages that barely cover their food requirements.

> Life on the farms is very hard . . . the food is very bad . . . the pesticide planes come over while we are working, and eating. . . . There are fleas everywhere . . . a lot of illnesses, like malaria and problems with contaminated water. . . . We work just to survive . . . they give us nothing.
> *Mam villager*[5]

Guatemala is the only country in Central America not to have implemented even a nominal agrarian-reform law. According to a USAID study in 1979, 88 per cent of landholdings are of a sub-family category, that is to say insufficient for the feeding of a family. The only government to have attempted any serious land redistribution, that of Arbenz, was overthrown in a US-backed coup in 1954. Since then, anyone referring to land reform is branded communist by the landed elite and suffers at the hands of the military.

> "School was a place of cultural confrontation."
> *Mario Leyton, UNESCO Guatemala*

The problems of racism also existed in the schools. Given that the Mam population mostly spoke only Mam, it seems absurd that until 1987 Cabrican schools taught only in Spanish, using *ladino* teachers who were foreigners in the villages where they taught. The syllabuses were unrelated to the reality of rural and indigenous life. Most Mam children were either excluded from education altogether or inevitably fared worse than the *ladinos* because of the added difficulty of speaking a new language. Then, even when one or two Mam children did succeed at school, it was likely that they would reject their culture and adopt *ladino* ways. Success meant *castellanización*[6] (becoming assimilated or "Spanishified"), and going on to further education in the capital to gain professional skills that were only of value within *ladino* society. Many parents refused to let their children go to the school which was seen as "their school, not ours". For the teachers, this was further proof of the ignorance and stupidity of the Indians.

> The people in the countryside . . . have been living like animals, and they
> don't want to better themselves.
> *H.G. de León*[7]

The Catholic church was also a *ladino* institution. Although the Mam had been converted to Catholicism, successive priests had refused to let them into the main church. The first Indian to get married in the church at Cabrican (in the 1950s) was put in jail by the sheriff for daring to enter it. In the 1960s, the situation changed because a new generation of priests (inspired by the ideas that later became Liberation Theology) were more interested in the rights of the neglected Mam than the *ladinos*. In Cabrican, Father Thomas Melville (a US priest) turned the church into an almost exclusively Indian one and set up a Mam agricultural co-operative with a truck so that they could compete economically with the *ladinos*, who were furious that such help should be given to mere Indians.

In response to the educational situation, Father Thomas raised funds for the construction of a college for Mam children[8] that would help them with their Spanish, so that they had more of a chance of entering secondary school. The college would also organize Spanish literacy classes for adults.

> He brought in three Spaniards: two teachers and a nurse . . . they had
> classes for children in the morning, women in the afternoon and men in the
> evening.
> *Ron Hennessy*

In 1965, appalled by the lack of land, Father Thomas persuaded his superiors to let him buy land in the north of Guatemala in order to set up co-operatives for the landless. Many left Cabrican with him.[9]

The problem of land worsened through the 1970s. Opposition to the military governments grew and a guerrilla movement gained in strength as more and more people were forced to be involved by sheer poverty and the lack of any alternative. The army response to the guerrilla threat was particularly brutal. In certain areas, dead bodies on the side of the road became commonplace. Massacres of whole villages became a standard counter-insurgency tactic.

> Within barely two hours, they destroyed it [the village], putting women,
> children and the aged to the sword, and killing all who did not save
> themselves by flight.
> *Bartolome de las Casas, missionary, 1524*

For the Mayans, the methods of repression had changed little from the time of the Spanish conquest. Machine-guns and helicopters had replaced swords but the devastation was the same. Internationally, Guatemala developed a reputation as the worst abuser of human rights in the world.

> We must do away with the word "Indian" or "indigenous". Our mission requires the integration of all Guatemalans.
> *President Mejía Victores*[10]

Cabrican was on the edge of the worst conflict areas,[11] but even there the conflict was felt. Twenty-eight people, mostly village leaders, "disappeared" as the violence reached its peak in the early 1980s. Perhaps the most sinister aspect of the counter-insurgency strategy was the extension of permanent army presence to rural areas and the establishment of civil patrols. In every rural community, including the villages of Cabrican, these were imposed by the army. They patrolled the mountains, ostensibly looking for guerrillas. Those refusing to participate were branded as subversives and ran the risk of "disappearing".

The national literacy programme at this time was, not surprisingly, committed to *castellanización*, "adapting" the learner to different work environments and promoting an affirmation of national identity. Methods were mechanical and the programme was ignored by potential learners (see Figure 8.1). Reasons for the failure cited by ministry sources included "the existence of monolingual Mayan groups" and "the lack of motivation amongst the people". By blaming the learners and identifying self-improvement with *castellanización*, the programme failed to reach the people it was aimed at.

The continual attacks on their way of life have had long-term effects on a people who have been blamed by the state for the underdevelopment of the country, who are not allowed to use their own language in school, who are treated as backward, inferior beings and who are killed if they open their mouths to complain. In Cabrican, people were ashamed to use Mam in the town. Many – particularly men – who were more exposed to *ladino* culture, stopped wearing traditional dress. Women had less need to hide their culture as they spent less time outside the home. The Mam language retreated behind adobe walls.

> So we see the change of traditional dress, forced work, the control, the civil patrol. It's all connected, it's part of a plan whose objective, really, is to eliminate the traditional organization that the people have, its structure, its authority, the election of its leaders.
> *Rigoberta Menchu, Mayan leader*

NEW OPENINGS?

In 1986, the army relinquished power to the first elected civilian government since the coup in 1954. President Cerezo, a Christian

Figure 8.1: Imposing Spanish through monologue. An illustration from the Guatemalan Ministry of Education primer in the early 1980s.

Democrat, took office with 67 per cent of the votes, the largest share since 1945. He took control over a country in which that part of the population considered to be in extreme poverty had risen from 63 per cent to 86 per cent in a matter of five years[12] and in which the divisions between army and landed elite on one side, and the dispossessed indigenous peoples on the other, were for the first time under international scrutiny. The new government programme blamed the crisis on these divisions and aimed at creating the conditions for a participative democracy in which the different social forces could all contribute to solving the problems of society.

Cerezo's government was another classic case of the US-inspired strategy of promoting a form of democracy in the region, as a way of legitimizing regimes sympathetic to its interests. As a reward, these regimes could then obtain international credit:

> Twenty-five years ago, when the Alliance for Progress was launched, the whole hemisphere seemed to discover that you could not have long term security without development. Today we are learning a new lesson. . . .
> There is a second connection, that between security and democracy.
> *Eliott Abrams, US special envoy to Central America, July 1986*

The result is not a limited democracy but a regime in which the word "democracy" has been de-read. As in neighbouring El Salvador, power in Guatemala remains in the hands of the army, which continues to use three-quarters of the national budget. In 1986, only 2 per cent of GNP found its way to the Ministry of Education, the lowest proportion in the whole of Latin America (*El Diario de Centroamerica*, 14 February 1988). Cerezo himself is not averse to military power: in 1975, he wrote an article entitled "The Army as an Alternative" in which the thesis that collaboration with the army was necessary to gain power was outlined. An elected civilian leader like Cerezo gives credibility to the regime; this allows the flow of international loans to continue.

Nevertheless, Cerezo's government was the first *ladino* government to recognize the need for a change in education policy that took into account the cultural frontier of the country. In 1987, a semi-autonomous organization was set up to design a literacy programme. The law bringing CONALFA into existence allocated one per cent of the state budget to fund it. A technical team of experienced and committed literacy workers was appointed to produce the materials.

> At CONALFA we thought that it was necessary to have a methodology suited to each community.
> *Hilda Moran de García, Technical Co-ordinator, CONALFA*

The result is a national programme without a literacy primer. Every municipality has a co-ordinator who convenes meetings of local organizations – churches, parents' associations – in each village. Here, animators are chosen who collect information about the needs and interests of the village and develop with the learners a "calendar of themes". For example, in Cabrican, maize-pests appeared as a theme in July while the crop was growing. In classes, animators were responsible for generating dialogue on the themes on the basis of codifications they produced themselves.

CONALFA hopes that organization will develop to tackle specific problems arising out of the literacy classes. For example, the most serious agricultural problem in Cabrican is the erosion of the soil. Trees have been cut down excessively both to fuel the lime ovens and to provide more farm land. Much of this land is on slopes and is farmed without terracing. During the rainy season, without tree roots to hold it, much valuable topsoil has been washed away. If erosion were a theme in the literacy classes in Cabrican, the group could be a base for organizing the introduction of terracing methods and the planting of trees.

> The key to our methodology is that we have adapted ourselves to the
> community and not the community to us.
> *Hilda Moran de García*

The programme should be in a position to recognize the cultures and languages of the country. The literacy law specifically offers "the free choice of the speaker of indigenous languages and Spanish concerning the language in which she/he wants to be literate". With animators from the community there should be no difficulty in fulfilling this provision, and with themes developed with the participation of the learners, the classes should not involve any imposition of an external, alien culture.

A parallel development to the literacy programme for adults was Guatemala's first bilingual education programme for children, developing out of a pilot programme begun in 1984:

> It is the general objective of PRONEBI to provide pre-primary and primary
> education in bilingual–bicultural form to the indigenous school population
> of the country.
> *PRONEBI regulations, Article 4*

With donations and loans from USAID, the programme was operating in 1,000 schools by the end of 1988. PRONEBI trained bilingual teachers and allocated them on request to areas where they were needed. In most (600) of the schools where they worked, they were only teaching the pre-primary year. The syllabus includes literacy in Mayan languages, maths, oral Spanish and civic education.

STATE LITERACY IN CABRICAN

Cabrican today has a population of 12,000, a quarter in the largely *ladino* town and the rest in the 18 villages around. The CONALFA office is prominently positioned near the town square, but usually shut. The co-ordinator for Cabrican and the neighbouring municipality of Huitan was responsible for 17 animators, 10 of whom worked in Cabrican. This is a large work-load for a young teacher straight out of training college, particularly as he was unfamiliar with the villages, many of which are over two hours' walk from the town. He was given four weeks' training; the animators only received two.

There wasn't a single literacy class in Mam in Cabrican. We were told that this was because the learners preferred to learn in Spanish. However when we visited a group of learners with their animator, things looked rather different. Dora, the animator, lived in the town with her father. She moved home from the capital, Guatemala City, after her mother died. As the only remaining unmarried daughter it fell to her to look after her father. The CONALFA job had come up at the right time, soon after her arrival. When we visited, she had been teaching literacy for a year in a village nearby, that is to say an hour's walk down a narrow footpath leading steeply down one side of a ridge that was impassable during the rainy season. There were only 27 families in Xacana Chiquita. They had little land and were forced to migrate every year to feed themselves. We met a group of men outside the school who had just had a village meeting:

– Why is literacy useful to you?
  To take advantage of opportunities.
– Do you remember any of the themes you discussed?
  (No response)
– How is it useful to read and write?
  It's important for cultural life . . . otherwise we have closed eyes.
– In Spanish or in Mam?
  Both are important, but Mam is more useful.
– Why?
  For many reasons. For example, we were sent articles of the constitution [of Guatemala] written for us in Mam, but none of us could understand them.

Before working there, Dora had no knowledge of Xacana Chiquita beyond the land that her father owned near it. She had little contact with the Mam community beyond the maid who did her housework while she was teaching. She could not speak, write or understand Mam, so literacy-teaching was in Spanish despite the villagers' preferences. The migrations destroyed the continuity of the teaching and any possibility of its success in contributing to community organization. A class of over 30 learners dropped to two when the coffee harvest started. It is not surprising that little had been achieved.[13]

But why is it that CONALFA has employed *ladino* animators to work in Mam villages?

> In practice, it is the friendships, contacts and internal cliques that lead to the appointment of animators and some people are just after the money. Here in Buena Vista [another Cabrican village], the co-ordinator contacted the village committee and said he would consult us but the next thing we knew was that someone had been appointed.
>
> *Member of village committee*

Corruption is a pointer to a more general reason. The gulf between Mam and *ladino* cannot be overcome by a *ladino* programme designed, as the Mam see it, by the same state that a few years earlier was arresting and killing them.

> [Municipal co-ordinators] have contact with the authorities in each place: the civil patrols, the military commissioners, the local council.
>
> *Teacher*

The CONALFA network of organizations is the *ladino* – not the Mam – network. The mistrust, ignorance and fear that have perpetuated racism are equally capable of destroying the literacy programme regardless of methodological intentions in Guatemala City. It's not as though the violence has stopped. The army and death squads are still prominent features of Guatemalan society. According to the national press,[14] there were 492 political assassinations during 1988. In Cabrican, two people disappeared and six more were forced into hiding after a group of non-uniformed armed men appeared in the town. At around the same time, the army were burning down areas of forest in the municipality, suspecting that the guerrillas were hiding there.

In the schools, there are further problems. A child from the (*ladino*) town is twice as likely to reach secondary school as a (Mam) village child. Provision in the town is far superior. The primary school is well equipped and has classes of 30 children. Village schools have class sizes ranging from 40 up to 150. The teacher from La Grandeza was to be found in one of the town's many bars after the first day of term crying into a bottle of Quetzalteca: "150 kids and one teacher . . . it just can't be done". La Grandeza is over two hours' walk from the town. The teacher was a *ladino* from another municipality. He travelled home for weekends. We heard many stories of teachers only arriving at the schools to teach on Tuesday, Wednesday and Thursday. On Fridays, they would go home and on Mondays make the journey back to Cabrican.

PRONEBI has had little impact. The Ministry of Education supervisor told us that recently he asked for a bilingual teacher and was sent one who spoke Quiche, another Mayan language, but one which is as unrelated to Mam as French is to Greek. In one village school, there were two PRONEBI-trained Mam teachers. They admitted that they were being used to teach children Spanish so that they were not too far behind when they joined first grade.

> It is a process of rapid *castellanización*.
> *PRONEBI teacher*

At the end of the year, the children can read and write in Spanish but have learnt little of their own culture and certainly can't read and write in Mam.

PRONEBI has little to do with bicultural–bilingual education. In practice it is a more efficient way of trying to integrate Mayan children into *ladino* society. They may gain more qualifications but school itself remains a *ladino* institution. Once again, an ingrained lack of trust intervenes. PRONEBI teachers are not teaching in their own communities. Those in Cabrican came from other Mam-speaking departments and were unfamiliar with the local people. Even the dialect of the language was different. Clearly they would be more effective teaching in their home villages, but:

> The people who make decisions are frightened of letting us ran our own schools.
> *PRONEBI teacher*

ACUMAM

> In the past we [the Mayan people] have been used only as an object of experimentation and investigation. The government gets money in the name of indigenous people: they use us . . . but the money disappears before it reaches us.
> *Mam villager*

Literacy in Spanish

In 1969, a group of Mam people began to organize literacy classes in their villages. Enthused by the education they had received from the Church (under Thomas Melville) and then as students in the state system, they were working in Spanish with the aim of bringing people out of cultural isolation. They used Ministry of Education materials, but soon found the themes and methods to be a limitation. They then managed to purchase time on a commercial radio station in Quetzaltenango, the departmental capital, and started broadcasting their own literacy programmes. This worked well but proved expensive so they prepared proposals for building a small transmitter.

By 1975, the transmitter was built in Cabrican (largely funded by OXFAM), alongside the Indigenous College, the only Mam institution in the town. Before transmitting began, the organizers held a large community meeting to give the people the opportunity to decide what they wanted to do with the new facility. At the meeting they were surprised to find that literacy was not high on the list of priorities:

> Really, the people weren't interested in literacy. They wanted practical help in their lives and didn't see how reading Spanish would help.
> *Pedro, Radio Mam worker*

Radioliteracy

> One cannot say that the Indian is illiterate because he lives in a culture that
> does not recognize letters. To be illiterate, you need to live where there are
> letters and you don't know them.
> *Freire*, The Politics of Education

The rejection of literacy in Spanish forced the workers at the station to re-
think their aims and strategies. They decided that the most serious difficulty
for the people they were broadcasting to was not isolation from *ladino*
structures of power but the slow destruction of their way of life by those structures.
The *ladino* culture was advancing even into the consciousness of the Mam
themselves. Literacy in Spanish could only contribute further to that process. What was necessary was a cultural reclamation to combat the racism of
the *ladinos* by using the radio to promote Mam culture.

> There was a rainfall of ideas and we programmed on the basis of this.
> We identified soil erosion, agricultural techniques, details of pests, cooking,
> healthcare and music as more important than literacy.
> *Virgilio, Radio Mam worker*

Radio Mam started broadcasting and in 1976 extended itself to form
ACUMAM, the Mam cultural association. To ensure that they were
reaching their audience, the workers set up a workshop where radios
could be fixed free of charge. Many of the programmes have contributed practically to breaking the belief that *ladino* ways are more
advanced than or superior to Mayan ones. For example, in agriculture,
the uses of organic fertilizers and natural pest control have been discussed as an alternative to the use of costly chemicals. There are
programmes on herbal medicines and others on forms of nutrition adapted
to the local environment. Through the radio they have taught terracing
methods (used by their ancestors) to prevent the erosion of soil on
hillsides.

Possibly more important even than the contents of the programmes was
the fact that the transmissions were in a mixture of Mam and Spanish. A
language which people had been ashamed to speak in public places was
suddenly being used by the only mass medium in the area. This in itself
has contributed a great deal to reversing the tide of *castellanización* in
Cabrican. In recent years, Mam has left the home and is once more
heard in shops and streets. Traditional Mam greetings are used in the
middle of the town. The frontier has been rolled back to such an extent
that the Mam have even begun to invade *ladino* institutions: Cabrican now
regularly elects a Mam mayor.

Another way of using the radio to democratize society in the municipality
was via the "*campesino* university":

> We organized groups in the villages, and then did 15-minute broadcasts on education, agriculture, youth and women. . . . The discussions in the groups were taped and broadcast. Because it was a bit more formal, we called it the *campesino* university to communicate the idea that you can study without having to do it in Spanish and a long way away. It lasted three years but when the disappearances started, people were frightened to meet and continue this.
> *Ex-ACUMAM worker*

The "university" gave Mam villagers a voice in the same way as literacy could through workbooks or a newsletter. The difference was that the radio could diffuse a purely oral culture. It was concientization without the learning of any techniques beyond overcoming the shyness of speaking into a microphone. ACUMAM's plans now include the setting up of a mobile radio transmitter in a van and the training of local "popular" reporters in each village. The ideas behind the *campesino* university can be extended through this, giving the villagers themselves the opportunity to make programmes in their own villages, recording local events, festivals, debates and sharing their histories, lives and problems with the whole Mam community.

Projects such as this raise questions about whether in a rural area alphabetic literacy is useful at all. If everyone has access to a radio and to the means of producing programmes which will be broadcast by the transmitter, what role can the written word play? Who is to say that a library of tapes cannot serve the same function as one of books? The point is reached again where the concept of literacy has become inadequate. "Radioliteracy" in ACUMAM's work is playing the part of alphabetic literacy. People are learning to "read" and "write" radio programmes. "Written" materials are being produced as a library of recordings.

Mam literacy

In 1984, alphabetic literacy again became part of ACUMAM's work. Fifteen monitors were trained over a three-year period to teach literacy in Mam.

> We have been led to believe that literacy, indeed all education, is only possible in Spanish, but our ancestors had their own system of writing. The reason that we don't have a history of the written word is that our development was abruptly stopped by the *conquistadors*. Our culture and history are not written because they have not been allowed to be written. We have been made to read other people's words.
> *Pedro, ACUMAM worker*

A number of difficulties are involved in Mam literacy. First, most of the pre-Colombian written materials are in European museums, so there is little of the written tradition available to be drawn on. The oppression of the Mayan peoples since the conquest has severely limited the production of new written materials. Bibles and grammar books were produced by missionaries and there are the occasional publications from the US-funded Summer Linguistic Institute. But these are too specialist for use in a rural community.

Even with existing written materials there are difficulties because of the disputes about the Mayan alphabet. In 1988, the government reviewed the Maroquin Institute alphabet then in use. Alternatives available were the Summer Institute's, also largely developed by foreigners, and that of the Mayan Institute, which drew on a range of important Mayan symbols.[15]

> The alphabet of the Mayan Institute was ignored completely and last year [1988], a mixed Summer/Maroquin alphabet was made official. The changes were very confusing.
> *Manuela*

> The official alphabet is a mixture of two gringo versions, which makes it very easy for the gringos to learn our language but very hard for us. The gringos have invaded even our language.
> *Pedro*

In spite of the problems, each of ACUMAM's monitors has a group of between 10 and 15 adult students enrolled in classes. Written materials are produced by monitors and workers at the radio. The themes are practical, chosen by the learners and often related to the themes of past (and future) radio programmes. ACUMAM is becoming a *Tja Nabl*, meaning literally "house of guidance" or – colloquially – a school. Next door to the studio is a room where classes are held. On the floor above, dormitories are being built so that those travelling to the radio station from a long way out can stay the night. There is a documentation centre for all the materials that have been produced.

As well as complementing the radio broadcasts with classes, the promotion of written Mam can contribute to the unity of the Mam people in a way that radio cannot. There are at least 17 recognized Mam dialects. In conjunction with IGER,[16] work has begun on a dictionary of synonyms aiming to unite the variations in the spoken word into a single written form, which will aid communication between all Mam people.

> For example, there may be 17 ways of pronouncing the Mam word for *chile* but the differences are phonetic so we can identify a single spelling which will serve them all.
> *Virgilio*

There are several groups working on this project in the different Mam communities in Guatemala. They expect to complete it within two years. On the basis of the new dictionary, there are plans to develop new materials for adult, primary and secondary education in Mam.

> This is a task for the future. We are building for the long term here,

not for short term ends. We are building slowly.
Virgilio

Children's literacy
The next stage of cultural reclamation, after creating the *Tja Nabl* for adults, is to consider the new generation. Buena Vista is a village of 70 families an hour's walk from the town. In 1985, a group of young people trained by ACUMAM replaced the old village committee. They were faced with no school for their children because government plans had been delayed. Recognizing the urgency, every family contributed 100 bricks, a bag of cement and some roofing tiles. Over two years, the villagers built their own school. Soon after completing it, the community were sent a *ladino* teacher from the Ministry of Education. The teacher was rejected and the committee complained to the supervisor and the mayor, insisting on their right to have a Mam teacher in what was their school.

While the dispute continued, the parents elected their own teacher: a fully-qualified woman from Buena Vista itself. They paid her salary and provided land to the school which is now farmed collectively for food and as a source of funds. Sixty children enrolled in the first three grades of primary school that were offered. It was agreed that all teaching was to be in Mam. The parents involved themselves in the development of the curriculum which is intimately linked to local experience.

> In the past we believed that only qualified people could teach and school was another world, but now we see that teachers are just people who have spent longer at schools themselves and that really we all have something we can share.
> *Juan, parent of child at Buena Vista school*

Practical skills, such as cobbling, carpentry, weaving and sewing are taught to both boys and girls by villagers who have those skills. On school land, the children learn traditional organic farming techniques.

The Ministry of Education continues to refuse to recognize the school.

> Buena Vista can't be official . . . they rejected the *ladino* teacher, and there are laws and norms.
> *Osvaldo Durinio, Ministry supervisor for Cabrican*

By insisting that it is their school, Buena Vista has been cut off by the state system. Legitimacy is provided by the Indigenous College in the town which receives Buena Vista students after their third grade so that they have an opportunity to pursue further education if they wish. For all of them literacy in Mam and their history and culture will have been formative. When we visited the school, all the children greeted us in traditional manner, by putting our hands to their foreheads. All were wearing traditional dress. All of them knew and could write their language.

MAYAN UNITY?

The focus of ACUMAM's work is the rejection of the colonial language, Spanish. What they are attempting is the creation of a regional alternative, to develop Mam as the main local language in order to force the state's recognition of Guatemala as a multi-ethnic nation. Literacy is one of the first steps. A population literate in Mam can set up newsletters, libraries and schools which are relevant to the local people. They can organize independently from the *ladinos*. In rural areas like Cabrican, where Spanish written materials are scarce, the difficulties of creating an alternative to the dominant language are relatively few.

However, as we saw in Chile, alphabetic literacy must not be thought of as superior to other techniques of popular communication. In particular, the literacy class should not be held up as the only effective way of promoting dialogue between people. This idea prioritizes face-to-face inter-personal communication over recorded forms of media and ends up limiting the creative uses of radio and video which, for specific purposes, can be more effective. ACUMAM's work is successful because it recognizes the complementary value of radio and the alphabet: neither is being used at the service of the other. Both are subsumed under the broader aims of their work.

But it is worth questioning the validity of ACUMAM's wider strategy. There are two related criticisms levelled at them. First, some political groups have argued that a cultural reclamation strategy is divisive: there are at least 21 different Mayan languages so that to promote regionalism in Guatemala is to create a cultural isolation of each group that can easily be exploited by a unified, ruling, Spanish-speaking elite. The CUC (the big, semi-clandestine *campesino* union), for example, which organizes *campesinos* against government repression, refused until recently to refer to the indigenous people as such but would talk about the poor or the landless. They considered it vital to learn Spanish because it is the language of communication between different Mayan groups, as well as with the *ladino* poor.[17] Cultural reclamation divides the poor, damaging the possibilities of organizing effectively against the state. Ultimately, this argument becomes an accusation against groups like ACUMAM, claiming that in promoting the value of Mam culture over that of any other, they are being racist.

While ACUMAM recognizes the need for unity between the Mayan peoples, it insists that this is not an argument for teaching solely in Spanish.

> We can learn Spanish, and use it, but still be pure Mam. It is as though you were to learn a foreign language when you needed it . . . but it could never be your own tongue.
> *Pedro*

Spanish is necessary but as a tool for building unity. The 1989 Third

Annual Meeting of Mayan Peoples was held in Cabrican, and Spanish was used for interpreting. Nevertheless, this does not mean that literacy programmes should be in Spanish. The villagers in Cabrican want to learn to read and write in Mam and do not need written Spanish for day-to-day survival in a rural area. Mam literacy teaching, then, is not a means for dividing people but a strategy for a reassertion of cultural identity. ACUMAM is not arguing for the superiority of their language, culture or race and their work is not associated with the oppression, systematic or otherwise, of any other group. Their work is part of a struggle *against* racism.

> Unity can only be built from a position of strength. If we each lose our languages for the sake of unity, we will have lost what we are unifying to defend.
> *Virgilio*

The second criticism of ACUMAM points to its ambiguous role: it is used as a token of the state's tolerance of indigenous groups whilst the work it does is restricted. As one political commentator put it:

> If Radio Mam were to mention land reform, the transmitter would be shut down and half the workers would disappear. The government would blame the guerrillas.

The question is one of strategy. Is the genuine assertion of indigenous rights in society possible only after a significant socio-economic change, such as a revolution? In this case, the cultural work of ACUMAM is merely the little that can be done at times when the popular movements are severely repressed.

> The limits of cultural action are set by the oppressive reality and by the silence imposed by the power elite.
> *Freire*, Cultural Action for Freedom

Alternatively, supporters of ACUMAM would argue that the reassertion of a Mayan identity is a pre-requisite for the achievement of that socio-economic change, that it is only from a position of cultural strength that anything can be done.

> Revolution is always cultural, whether it be in the phase of denouncing an oppressive society and proclaiming the advent of a just society, or in the phase of the new society inaugurated by the revolution.
> *Freire, ibid.*

ACUMAM is not working with any (class-based) revolutionary movements; neither is its work running counter to their objectives. It is clear that conscientization based on the reclamation of pre-Colombian culture and post-Colombian history is of enormous value to a wider struggle. It attacks the racism that forms the bedrock of the way in which the exploitation of Guatemalan *campesinos* is perpetuated and it looks forward to the possibility of a society without that exploitation, drawing on the experience of the Mayan past.

NOTES

1. Eliu Cifuentes, director Pronebi, quoted in Chiodi, F., *Educación indígena en America Latina* (Santiago: UNESCO–OREALC 1989).
2. By the Summer Linguistic Institute and ACUMAM respectively.
3. Miguel Angel Asturias: Men of Maize quoted in E. Burgos–Debray (ed.), *Rigoberta Menchu: An Indian Woman in Guatemala* (London: Verso, 1983).
4. The term *ladino* is historically related to anyone involved with the values of the Spanish. It has come to mean anyone who rejects or was never involved with Mayan culture.
5. For the sake of the security of the people involved we have kept some names anonymous in this chapter.
6. The word means turning people into *castellanó* speakers. *Castellanó* is the variant of Spanish spoken in the Americas.
7. H.G. de León is the co-ordinator of adult education in the Ministry of Education's Literacy and Adult Education programme (in interview with authors January, 1989).
8. The Indigenous College was finally opened in 1972 by the Sisters of the Ascension working in Cabrican. Here the bulk of teaching is in Spanish to comply with regulations, but an equal value is placed on both languages.
9. Thomas Melville recognized that the root problem of the Mam and other Mayan people – beyond the racism of the *ladinos* – was lack of land, which forced them into a never-ending cycle of migration. As a solution he rallied 60 progressive priests and persuaded the Catholic Church to buy large areas of virgin rainforest in the north of Guatemala, first in El Peten and later in the Ixcan. This land was cleared and divided into parcels; co-ordinating committees were organized and advertisements were sent out inviting all Mayan people to begin new, peaceful lives, with land of their own, in a series of co-operatives. People arrived from all over the country: "We walked ten days to get there, carrrying the few possessions we owned. We had nothing to lose. Nothing to leave behind. The promise of land was everything." Each co-operative was planned to be self-sufficient; all rules were decided internally. Maize was planted. Excess produce was taken to the markets in light aircraft by the priests.
10. Quoted in Black, George, *Garrison Guatemala* (London: Zed Books, 1986).
11. The co-operatives in the Ixcan (see note 9) were at the centre of the violence. The rainforest around them offered shelter to the guerrillas. From the start the army accused the co-operatives of growing food for, and sympathizing with, the guerrillas. Army bases were built nearby and soldiers began to threaten co-operative members regularly and steal their food. In 1976 one of the priests, William Woods, died when shot down in his plane. Subsequently people began to disappear. By the early 1980s kidnappings would be followed by the appearance of mutilated and tortured bodies in the fields. Education and health workers were prime targets. In 1981 19 people were murdered by the army in the social house of the co-operative Selva Reyna la Union. Finally the army launched Victory 82: part of the new President's "pacification campaign". Helicopters were sent in, machine gunning

people down. Hundreds of co-operative members were massacred, "leaving the earth burnt and the sky heavy with the stench of blood" (*Nosotros Conocemos Nuestra Historia: Iglesia Guatemalteca en Exilo*, 1985).

12. Government statistics, quoted in *La Politica de Desarrollo del Estado Guatemalteco 1986–7* (Guatemala City: AVANCSO, Cuadernos de Investigación No.2, 1988). "Extreme poverty" refers to the population whose income does not provide for the minimum food basket satisfying energy and protein requirements.

13. The regular migration makes it difficult to develop education programmes amongst all Mayan people. Those from the co-operatives in the Ixcan (see note 11) seemed to have broken that cycle, but only found themselves subject to repression and further displacement. Fleeing from the army in 1982 many spent months, even years in the mountains and forests, eluding detection, before crossing into the area of Lacandonia (where their ancestors had evaded the Spanish) in Chiapas, southern Mexico. Here over 45,000 refugees entered United Nations camps. However, the Mexican government disliked their presence in the sensitive border area, and so the refugees were refused all education provision (which would have been a sign of integration). In 1984/5 the Mexican government forced the refugees to re-locate inland to camps in Campeche and Quintana Roo. These camps could have presented a new life for the refugees, and an end to their incessant displacement and migration. Over 90 per cent were illiterate so education programmes were organized. However, these programmes have themselves now collapsed. The shortage of land available to the refugees, and its poor quality, combined with a cut in United Nations subsidies, has forced the refugees to return to their migratory lifestyle of the past, seeking work in nearby Mexican towns. This has disrupted the education programmes in the camps: "we don't have enough time to learn because we don't have enough land".

14. *7 Dias: La Voluntad de Informar* (Guatemala, no. 16 epoca 11, 24–30 December 1988).

15. For example, for one sound (which also means "sun"), the Marroquin alphabet used the symbol: K' The Summer Linguistic Institute used the symbol: ⊗ . Whereas the Mayan Institute used a symbol more closely associated with the meaning and more in tune with the original ideographic Mayan writing: ※ .

16. Institute of Guatemalan Radio Schools: a non-governmental organization which develops adult-education programmes using radio.

17. The refugees in Maya Tecum, one of the camps in Mexico (see note 13), include Mayan people who speak ten different languages within a community of under 8,000. A literacy programme was planned by exiled teachers, who chose to use Spanish as a language of unity among the groups. In practice the programme taught very few people to read and write but it served an important function in providing basic skills of oral Spanish to previously monolingual groups, aiding communication in the camp. The programme also helped people to reflect on their experiences:

> We lived through so much that we were of course conscious, but our consciousness was broken up. We needed to re-live things to understand them clearly. In the classes we could do this and tie things together . . . make the links. *Interview with refugee, 1988*

In the long term the camp has not united effectively because of the curse of continuing migration (note 13). But faced with life in a multilingual camp within an alien country (where their own tongue is of little practical value), many parents now encourage their children to learn only Spanish. Indeed, given the repression against indigenous people in the past, speaking Spanish is seen by some as a survival mechanism, providing a means of disguise. Spanish alone is taught in the camp's schools, meaning that a generation of Mayan children are now losing their mother tongue (lacking the enclosed village life which would traditionally reinforce it).

9. Bolivia, El Alto: The Language of Power

The Aymara nation, with two million people, is today the third-largest Indian nation in the Americas. The people live on the high plateau which stretches between two Andean mountain ranges from southern Peru, through Bolivia and into northern Chile. They are an ancient civilization but little is known of their history. At 4,000 metres above sea-level, on the shores of Lake Titicaca, the ruins of Tiwanaku stand in evidence to an era when the Aymara civilization thrived. The artefacts include colourful textiles, ceramics and metalwork dating back 3,000 years. However the history has been lost beneath two conquests. First, in the twelfth century the Quechuan speaking Incas, from across Lake Titicaca, expanded into what is now Bolivia. Second, in the sixteenth century the Spanish *conquistadors* arrived, having already destroyed the centre of the Inca Empire in Cuzco. Both waves of colonization encountered strong resistance.

> The Aymara . . . have demonstrated a collective resistance to disintegration on a level superior to that of other Andean groups.
> *Xavier Albó*[1]

While both conquests were successful in terms of economic and political control, both failed to destroy the Aymaran language and culture. In the Bolivian *altiplano* (plateau) Aymaran communities have retained a unique form of social organization.

> The Aymara live submerged in their family and community . . . unable to take decisions, organize their work, enjoy themselves or pray, without others. . . . Decisions will be taken collectively according to a system of authority and a series of norms and ethical principles which are all unwritten.
> *Xavier Albó*

Collectivity is reflected in a remarkable form of rotational democracy in Aymaran villages:

> Equality of opportunity (and lack of opportunity) for each and every person is conceived to be a criterion more important than aptitude for a post. [This] fosters a communal, almost ritual sense of community management by all. . . . The system generates a mystique of "service to the community" in opposition to "power over the community" which is typical of western systems.
> *Xavier Albó*

Mutual help is fundamental to Aymaran communal life. There is an equitable distribution of all resources and obligations. In Aymaran communities there are no beggars.

> Crops are cultivated in family parcels . . . but in the end the land is always controlled by the community.

Alongside subsistence farming of potatoes and *quinua*, families keep herds of llamas and alpacas from which woollen textiles are woven. Living in small adobe brick houses with earthen floors and without windows, they shelter from the bitter climate of the plateau. Temperatures drop to below freezing point every night. The soil is infertile and often frozen solid.

The Spanish invaded this inhospitable land in search of gold. They found silver in abundance in a mountain on the *altiplano*. Both Aymara and Quechua people were forcibly re-located to work in the mines at Potosi where conditions were so appalling that thousands died of suffocation, accidents, diseases and malnutrition. Communal lands were taken over by the Spanish and *campesinos* were forced to work on large estates in conditions akin to slavery.[2] But the climate of the *altiplano* was so harsh that many of the new colonizers chose to live in a vast natural crater overshadowed by the snow-capped mountain Illimani, where they founded La Paz. This became the capital of a large area, stretching beyond the *altiplano* to the Amazon rainforest and fertile valleys in the north and east. The Aymara resisted throughout the seventeenth and eighteenth centuries, at times threatening to overthrow Spanish rule, as in 1781 when Tupac Katari led a rebellion which encircled the crater of La Paz. The rebellion failed and Tupac Katari was captured and pulled apart by four horses tied to his limbs.

Independence from colonial rule was finally achieved in 1825 when Bolivia detached itself from the Spanish empire. But the new country had boundaries unrelated to those of the Aymaran nation. It was the product of a struggle between Spain and the colonial government over who had the right to exploit the resources and people of the area. For those people, the Aymara and Quechua, little changed: they were still manipulated. In post-colonial wars (with Chile, Argentina, Brazil and Paraguay) which left the country land-locked, the indigenous *campesinos*[3] and mine-workers were used as cannon-fodder. Tin mines replaced the silver mines as the main source of income for the country, but the working conditions for miners remained poor. Most died young, from lung disease, gas poisoning or the collapse of tunnels. While the Quechua and Aymara Indians still make up at least 65 per cent of Bolivia's population,[4] until 1952 they were banned from entering the main square in La Paz.

Within a few days of April 1952 Bolivia's history seemed to be overturned. The National Revolutionary Movement (MNR) had won the elections in 1951 but had been deprived of taking office by the army, so they appealed to the workers for support. The tin miners were the most powerful and organized grouping as the mines produced 80 per cent of the country's export earnings. Seeing their chance to overthrow the three families who owned the mines they supported MNR, helping to defeat the army and establish the MNR candidate Victor Paz Estenssoro as President. To ensure their share of power the miners' union FSTMB set up the COB (the Bolivian Workers Congress), and the COB became effective co-governors, forcing MNR beyond their moderate reformist policies. Mines were nationalized and workers' delegates given majority control over them. Universal suffrage was declared (where before only literate people earning above a certain income could vote). The army budget was cut back and soldiers made to work on public services like road-building. A new education code was passed giving all Bolivians the right to education. Agrarian reform was set in motion, which released many *campesinos* from their past bondage as feudal serfs on large estates.

The changes that took place between 1952 and 1956 could have laid the foundation for fundamental adjustment in the position of Aymara and Quechua people within Bolivian society. However, with world tin prices falling, disruption of agricultural exports and compensation costs for ex-mine-owners, inflation appeared and rose to almost 150 per cent by 1956. The MNR turned to the US and to the International Monetary Fund to negotiate a Monetary Stabilization Plan. An emergency loan was given to Bolivia in return for fulfilling various conditions which effectively neutralized the revolution. Public expenditure was cut by 40 per cent and a year later a wage freeze was implemented. The army was re-built. COB, which had always been the dynamic force of the revolution, withdrew its support and encouraged strikes.

The revolution and its defeat have had a dramatic effect on Aymaran *campesinos*, perhaps most significantly by producing repeated waves of migration to urban areas. This has been caused by a series of inter-related factors. First, the *campesinos* freed by the breaking up of the large estates often chose to leave the area rather than wait for the possibility of having land allocated to them through the reform process. As the reform faltered this became more common. Secondly the new education code gave *campesinos* their first taste of schooling. A generation of young Aymarans had their cultural horizons expanded, but there were rarely the facilities in rural areas to explore or realize new ambitions. Images of the city and modern life in school-books were often attractive, and because all the teaching was in Spanish, integration into urban life seemed possible for the new generation in a way that it was not for their monolingual parents. Moreover, those who wished to pursue their education beyond a basic primary level had no choice but to move, as secondary schools were only available in towns.

Perhaps the most fundamental reason for urbanization is to be found in the policies of the military governments that dominated Bolivia after a coup in 1964 led by General Barrientos. The country was turned into an enclave economy for international capital. Under General Banzer's government, during the 1970s, laws were passed guaranteeing majority international investment in the Bolivian economy. The government encouraged the movement of the labour force to areas where big investment projects were under way. The finance made available in the towns and to the agro-industry in Santa Cruz (to the east) contrasted with a pauperization of the *altiplano*: 88 per cent of the government credit for rural areas between 1970 and 1975 was handed to large scale agricultural businesses in the east, while only 0.8 per cent reached the Aymara *campesinos* of the altiplano.[5]

> Migration is a consequence of a whole economic and social formation that gives priority to the assigning of resources to the most capital-intensive minorities.[6]

The agrarian reform ground to a halt. *Campesinos* who had been lucky enough to receive land in the early years found themselves unable to obtain credit or technical assistance to develop it. With no further land available, those with small parcels were forced to sub-divide it to share with children, until there was not enough on which to subsist. A bad harvest was often the final push, forcing people to seek wage labour in the cities.

> The de-campesinization of the traditional rural areas and the access of the *campesino* to modern schemes in the city or in other rural areas will happen only according to the interests of those who control the system. At present the poles of attraction and the zones of expulsion are two sides of the same coin.
> *Albó Sandoval*

Once again the Aymara and Quechua were forced to move by a colonial elite. Just as their ancestors had been forced to work the mines, the new generation was manoeuvred into providing a source of labour far from their villages. The building of rural schools can be seen as in the interests of this manipulation. It provided *campesinos* with a positive image of the city (General Banzer ensured that the rural schools followed urban curricula) and trained them for life there by teaching them Spanish.

EL ALTO

> El Alto is a problem city. Nearly everything is working against it. The climate is cold and dry nine months of the year, and cold and humid the other three. A constant wind punishes it day and night. When it rains it is converted into a quagmire. When it is dry it is one enormous dustcloud.[7]

The migrants who arrived in La Paz found high rents and a shortage of space within the city to build their own houses, apart from on the steep slopes of the crater walls. As a result many settled in the peripheral areas, above the city on the exposed plateau. Using the only resource available, the earth, they built adobe houses, in the same way as they had done for centuries as *campesinos*. As it grew this peripheral sprawl became known as El Alto. In 1950 the population was 11,000, spread in 6 different *barrios*. By 1987 350,000 people occupied 178 *barrios*.

El Alto is a dormitory city for factory workers. Each day 100,000 people go down below to work in La Paz. In the evenings they wait on street corners for the minibuses to take them home. Child conductors shout destinations from bus windows to their largely illiterate passengers. However, many of El Alto's residents find no work, and act as an industrial reserve army, a pool of unemployed whose presence keeps wages down and guarantees an indefinite source of cheap labour. El Alto also serves as a cheap source of food for La Paz, as many residents keep close links with their villages of origin, ensuring a regular flow of fresh agricultural supplies to the city's markets. The atmosphere is something like that of a South African township. Discrimination does not have the legal structure of *apartheid* but the divisions are almost as stark. The population is almost exclusively Indian. Each day people go down to work in the "white man's city". With power centralized in La Paz, El Alto has few resources at its disposal. There is only one hospital, with 30 beds, to serve its 350,000 people. Only 43 per cent of school-age boys and 39 per cent of girls attend school. Housing conditions in El Alto are appalling. Only 30 per cent of homes have toilets, 17 per cent have running water and less than half have their rubbish cleared.[8]

These conditions are partly the product of recession through the 1980s. Industrialization has ground to a halt. Nationally, out of a working population of two million, 800,000 are unemployed. People in El Alto survive through the parallel economy, beyond the regulation of the state, buying and re-selling goods on the pavements of La Paz. Money changers are found on many street corners offering to buy dollars, and an estimated third of these are teachers who, like all public employees, need to supplement their inadequate wages. Other supplements are the food donations. Up to 200,000 Bolivian families are dependent on these, 80 per cent of which come from USAID, mediated largely by the adventist and other evangelical churches, but also by a host of non-governmental organizations. The donations are distributed to groups of women organized into "mother's clubs", and are often linked to work programmes or education schemes. Sometimes they are used deliberately to manipulate people. Political parties use food donations in El Alto in the run-up to elections in order to try to buy votes. More sinister however is the work of the religious sects.

In the last three years over 500 sects have come to Bolivia from the US. The multiplicity of organizations that are now working in El Alto is a big problem

... the original community relations get lost beneath them all.
Arturo Moscoso, director, National Literary and Popular Education Service

EDUCATION FOR EL ALTO

Stemming the tide of migration

In 1982 a new opening appeared in Bolivian politics. The existing military regime was condemned internationally for its involvement in drug dealing (the Minister of Education, Colonel Coca, was responsible for one of South America's largest drug smuggling operations). In subsequent elections, Siles Zuazo – a veteran of the 1952 revolution – came to power with the backing of the COB and the newer united *campesino* movement, CSUTCB (which was organized around land claims). The new government's education policy focused on developing rural schools and setting up the National Literacy and Popular Education Service (SENALEP).

SENALEP was a decentralized public institution, related to the Ministry of Education, but with technical and administrative autonomy. Like the government, SENALEP had close links with the COB and CSUTCB, which had pressed for its creation. Using popular-education techniques it planned to prioritize rural areas and the most depressed and marginal sectors of the population. Most of Bolivia's 1,300,000 illiterate people were indigenous.

> The national elite have always either ignored indigenous people or confined them to folkloric reserves.
> *Arturo Moscoso.*

SENALEP was committed to work towards "bilingual and intercultural education", starting with teaching in the mother tongue. Some people questioned the legitimacy of making Aymara (and other indigenous languages) into a written language.

> The culture is not written. It can be rescued better by discussion and organization than by literacy.
> *Juan Vargas, OXFAM worker, La Paz*

Indeed the very idea of an alphabetically-written language may be perceived as a product of Western imperialism which threatens the original culture.

> When people learn to read and write their memory begins to slide down the pen and onto the paper ... so people no longer recall things in their hearts or minds. ... Illiterate Aymarans can recall events up to five generations ago. The literate Spanish rarely recall more than two generations.
> *Juan de Dios Yapita, director, Aymaran Linguistic Institute, La Paz*

The threat to oral culture is often used as a justification for resisting literacy. But this is to fall into the trap of seeing literacy as a Western

Jichhax kunjamäskis markasaxa

Figure 9.1: SENALEP give *campesinos* **the opportunity to discuss issues like migration in mother-tongue literacy classes.**

technique. It is like suggesting that the Aymara should not use radios even if the programmes are in their own language. A literate people can recall events from more than ten generations past:

> Teaching in the mother tongue helps the individual and the community, valuing their culture, recuperating and dynamizing collective memory, cultural roots and popular creativity. It helps them not to feel frustrated by the avalanche of Western culture that depreciates and marginalizes them.
> *Arturo Moscoso*

For the first time in Bolivian history the indigenous languages were recognized, and the government made a commitment to make them official state languages in the future. Research produced the first united alphabet for written Quechua and Aymara, and this was used to produce primers, the first good quality materials produced on a large scale in indigenous languages in Bolivia. They also produced materials in Guarani, Mojeno and Chiquitano for the smaller indigenous communities of Bolivia (in the east and Amazon areas), and in Spanish for urban communities. A network of volunteer popular-educators was organized in all communities.

> Our system permits the communities to teach themselves with the collaboration of popular-educators who are elected by them and trained by us.
> *Arturo Moscoso*

By teaching in indigenous languages it was possible for dialogue to take place in classes. This had been impossible in all previous adult-education programmes in Bolivia because all teaching had been in Spanish, making participation difficult for people for whom Spanish was a second language. The themes for dialogue in SENALEP's primers included images (like Figure 9.1) which raised the issue of migration among *campesinos*, giving them the chance to discuss the advantages and disadvantages in a structured way for the first time. Equally important was that indigenous people were being offered an education which did not glorify city life and Western culture.

However, SENALEP has had difficulties in implementing its strategy. In 1985, when the materials were ready and a pilot programme was in operation, Siles Zuazo's government was thrown out in the face of 24,000 per cent inflation, brought on by a collapse in world tin prices. Ironically the original revolutionary leader, Victor Paz Estenssoro, took over. Thirty-three years had left their mark on Victor Paz. He closed down tin mines and sacked trade union leaders. Cuts were made in state expenditure, particularly in health and education. Nationalized industries were privatized. Once again international investment was welcomed on any terms and market-forces were given free reign over the economy. SENALEP was stifled by government budget-cuts and yet lost the support of the popular organizations because of its association with the new government. Resistance from other sectors also caused problems. The new alphabet for indigenous languages was not universally recognized. Churches, who had thousands of copies of the Bible already printed in their own version of the alphabet, refused to discard the past. Moreover, a couple of influential linguists continued to promote the superiority of their own alphabets.

The new political climate delayed SENALEP's large scale mobilization until 1988, when 100,000 learners enrolled in 4,000 communities throughout Bolivia. However, this mobilization was weakened by the appointment of a new director in the middle of the year. The new director was an MNR party man, who, according to Arturo Moscoso, "had never read a SENALEP document ... hated the Indians and their culture ... [and] was an ex-paramilitary who had been involved in past coups". A walk-out by SENALEP staff forced his replacement after two months, but not until the mobilization had collapsed to less than half its size. Hopes of stemming the migration to urban areas through this work were also dulled as it was an effort contradicted by other government policies. Closing tin mines had made tens of thousands of miners redundant, most of whom had little choice but to migrate to areas like El Alto.

Aymara or Spanish?

> The choice of language for education can have violent consequences. In South Africa, the Soweto riots of 1976 were sparked off by an attempt to impose the teaching of Afrikaans.
> Alan Murdoch, *Community Education Direct Research Unit (CEDRU)*

SENALEP's strategy is particularly difficult to implement in El Alto. Director Arturo Moscoso admits that "El Alto is one of the hardest places to work because of the diversity of its population and its socio-economic problems." El Alto does not have a stable population or a unitary culture. The recent re-location of tens of thousands of (mostly Quechuan) miners has added to the complex mix. According to Arturo Moscoso, one factor unites all the migrants, whether Aymaran or Quechuan, miners or *campesinos*:

> They are losing their culture and are pressurized to assimilate into Western culture which at the same time refuses to accept them ... so they are left trapped on the margins. With these processes of frustration and acculturation it is difficult to develop our programmes.

In the absence of traditional community networks it is difficult for SENALEP to gain access to illiterate people in the *barrios*. A shortage of staff makes it impossible for SENALEP to do its own groundwork, so it is dependent on non-governmental organizations (NGOs).

> NGOs have the advantage of being able to link their literacy work to

productive projects, which is important in El Alto.
Arturo Moscoso

Working through NGOs gave SENALEP direct access to the women of the mothers' clubs. In El Alto 39 per cent of women have never had access to any education, and 72 per cent are essentially illiterate (statistics from *El Alto Desde El Alto*, UNITAS). They suffer from a triple subordination, owing to their culture, their gender and their poverty. Seven out of every ten illiterate people in the urban areas of Bolivia are women.

One *barrio* where SENALEP has worked in El Alto is Cosmos '78. This is an area populated largely by Aymaran miners who had been working as a co-operative until cuts in state subsidies made it impossible for them to repair a broken generator. Here SENALEP has co-ordinated with an NGO called CEBIAE.[9] The main group in Cosmos '78 consists of 30 women who link learning to read and write with educational work on nutrition and other aspects of health. During 1987–8 they did a course to learn to read and write Aymara. The women have some positive memories of the experience:

> It was worth our while learning in Aymara because before we were losing it, mixing it with Spanish and getting it all wrong. The language we were using in the city was not the same as back home in our village.

> We learnt to tell the tales our grandmothers told and it helped us to see whether what we are doing now is following our ancestors or not.

However, other women in the group were dubious about the value of learning in Aymara:

> It was not very useful.

> We have forgotten most of it because there is nothing to read in Aymara. The only book I've ever seen in Aymara is the SENALEP workbook.

> What is the point of learning to read and write in Aymara? It is not a written language. It is not used when we go and do business. It will not help us get a job or make money.

There are no national newspapers in Aymara, nor any popular magazines. After some initial enthusiasm the attendance at classes dropped.

> Not many of us learnt . . . a lot of women just came to meet each other or learn about health.

> Some women would come one week and not the next . . . there are too many other pressures.

Eventually CEBIAE were forced to re-evaluate their policy in the light of their experience.

> Teaching Aymara was too slow, it was difficult to keep the attention of the women.
> *Rosaria, CEBIAE teacher*

A migrant who is seeking work and social status in the city does not have a strong motivation to learn Aymara. This puts us in a dilemma. We consider it important that people valourize their culture and language, but we have ended up concluding that teaching them in their own language is not necessarily the best way of achieving that goal.
Gustavo, CEBIAE teacher

CEBIAE decided to stop teaching in Aymara and to switch to Spanish. They now use the workbook produced by SENALEP for marginal urban communities, which is in Spanish. But this too is flawed.

The materials were mostly out of date: talking about inflation and the times of Siles Zuazo.
Rosaria

Part of the problem is that although the group is made up only of women, the primer has few themes explicitly relating to the women's lives. Moreover, whereas the materials produced in the Aymaran language are full of themes of cultural relevance to the Aymaran people (for instance, drawing on their myths and encouraging discussions of their history, their traditional medicine, their language, their values and their sense of identity), the materials produced in Spanish for use in areas like El Alto have no reference to the Aymaran or Quechuan culture (focusing instead on various aspects of city life, including the struggle for services, the right to work and the nature of Bolivian democracy). There is no attempt to grapple with the complexity of issues faced by the migrants and there are no codifications on the problems of assimilation. Eighty-five per cent of SENALEP's work is in rural areas, an indication of a failure to address urban indigenous reality.

In SENALEP's vision there is an Aymara culture based in rural areas and a Western culture in urban areas. Their materials fail to recognize the crossover between the two. In rural communities traditional forms of organization have adapted to enable participation in national unions. Equally, in urban areas, *barrio* organization is rooted in the mutual-help mechanisms of the village. In the community councils, people of traditional authority work together with the younger generation of leaders. An urban Aymaran culture is evident throughout El Alto. The traditional dress of the Aymaran resident is merely the most visible representation of this. Festivals celebrated in the villages have been transposed and adapted in the *barrios*. Although the printed word is lagging behind, the battle for the electronic word in Aymara is being won. Several regional radio stations now broadcast in Aymara and there are two television channels that have regular programmes in the language. Small-scale local radio stations have also been set up in different *barrios* to broadcast programmes in Aymara.

In 1989 Aymaran mobilization in El Alto won the area the right to its own council, so it is now a city in itself rather than a disregarded peripheral area of La Paz. The institutional structures now exist through which the Aymaran people can have a say over the allocation of resources in their communities. Although the resources are not yet available, the success of the "municipalization" fight was itself the product of concerted organization by the *barrios* of the indigenous city, using traditional methods of collective decision-making. Evidence that the networks of support continue to exist is clear in the lack of crime, drug addiction or violence.

> In a crystalline way El Alto illustrates the impoverishment of many Latin American cities . . . but it is different . . . the deficiencies and desperations have not been converted into social delinquency.
> *Sandoval and Sostres*, La Giudad Prometida

An urban indigenous culture is possible in El Alto in a way that it is perhaps not in other Latin American cities – for example Mexico City, where migrants speak over 50 indigenous languages, or Lima in Peru, which is built on the coastal plains far from the home of the Quechuan people in the mountains. In El Alto the majority of migrants speak Aymara and they are migrating to an area which is of historical (and continuing) importance to their culture.

> The atmosphere of El Alto and the values of the people, are still firmly within the Aymaran code.
> *Xavier Albó*

SENALEP is not alone in its failure to recognize people in marginal urban areas as truly Aymaran.

> A resident who lives in El Alto told us that when he registered his first son in the notary's office the clerk noted him down as *mestizo*. When he came to the same notary for his second son he was put down as "white". With the third son the notary wrote down *mestizo* again. This time the father of the children made the notary aware of his inconsistencies. The notary suggested that the best thing to do was to register nothing. The resident thought for a moment and made another proposal: he suggested to the functionary of the civil registry that he should re-inscribe his three sons as "Aymaras".[10]

The failure to recognize the composite nature of culture in the whole of Bolivian society is SENALEP's downfall. There is no original Aymaran culture. Like all cultures it is constantly evolving. For centuries there have been Aymaran people living in towns. Their language is not necessarily tied to the agricultural life which forms the basis of SENALEP's only primers in indigenous languages. They have made no attempt to produce materials in the indigenous languages based on urban themes. By treating Aymaran culture as all or nothing SENALEP risks marginalizing those in rural areas by denying them access to the language of political power. Meanwhile it also risks promoting assimilation of migrants into the dominant Western culture in urban areas, contrary to its stated aims.

The language of power

> Literacy is of no use if it does not empower us. Spanish is the language
> of power and we must adopt it if we are to assert ourselves and seek
> change. The government have a glorified ideal of preserving our culture, but
> only we can do that and only from a position of power. We don't want to
> preserve our poverty.
> *Spoken at a meeting of the Centre for Self-Managed Development, 1986*

In 1983 two Argentinian women set up an NGO in La Paz called
the Centre for Self-Managed Development (CDA).[11] They decided to
work with women, who were perceived as the lynchpin for community
development and through whom the work would reach families and *barrio*
organizations.

> We are not against men, but women are the axis . . . the nucleus around
> which everything rotates. Women are the best means for disseminating
> information and knowledge to neighbours and children.
> *Margarita Callisayo, CDA director*

By linking themselves to the mothers' clubs in *barrios* of El Alto and La
Paz, CDA sought to "design, plan and implement large scale processes of
popular education", aiming at "a profound democratization of systems of
power". The organization rejected any tendency to professionalization of
their work, seeking to employ only Aymaran women who lived in *barrios*
like those of El Alto. These women from the grassroots set up a Nucleus
of Women's Education within each mothers' club, aiming to use the
meeting-space to replace the women's dependency on external aid with
self-management, which would give longer-term solutions to fundamental
problems like infant mortality. A CDA survey revealed that 208 babies out
of every thousand died in El Alto.

After early consultations CDA decided that their highest priority should
be the development of literacy in Spanish. The choice to work in Spanish
is central to their philosophy. Many Aymaran women in rural areas are
monolingual, with no use whatsoever for Spanish, whereas their husbands,
who have more contact with the towns are more likely to know the
language. When families are forced to migrate, women can encounter
many problems. It is necessary to know Spanish to survive.

> The fact is that Spanish is the official language. If people do not know it
> they are easily deceived . . . they find it hard to orientate themselves and are
> easily manipulated.
> *Margarita Callisayo*

In every dimension of public life in La Paz, Spanish is the language of
power. It is used in all aspects of government administration, in offices and
businesses, for documents, forms and negotiations. It is the language of
the education and legal systems. Newspapers, magazines, advertisements,

warnings, roadsigns, timetables and even maps are all in Spanish. Literacy in Spanish is essential for successfully negotiating city life. To learn it is the first step to empowerment.

The most fundamental reason for teaching in Spanish is that the women themselves request it:

> The women want Spanish . . . every time that we ask them they always say they want Spanish. The women are adults, they won't lose their own language. Besides, other mechanisms retain culture. Cultural values are given within the family, and have lasted generations, since before the *conquistadors*. These values will not be lost easily, but they are more likely to be lost if the women cannot stand up for themselves and assert their rights . . . in Spanish.
> *Margarita Callisayo*

Teaching in Spanish does not necessarily mean devaluing the Aymaran culture. *Castellanización* is more than just the teaching of a language, and can be avoided if the materials are culturally relevant to the learners. In 1984, CDA set up 56 Women's Education Nuclei, mostly in El Alto, involving 6,500 Aymaran women. Through participative investigation with these groups a primer was prepared. The women themselves chose the themes that were to be covered and the specific generative words around which discussions would focus. Photographs were taken by the women, of the women, based on identified themes. These were used as codifications in the primer.

The primer moves from the concerns of individual women ("I am a person and nobody has the right to *knock* me down"), through to the family ("in my family everyone *gives* something"), the nucleus ("to *participate* is to *change* our lives"), the *barrio* ("if we work together with the community *council* we will advance") and finally to the country ("*we want* a free and just Bolivia"). The primer, called *We Are Able*, finishes with histories of two women who were important Aymaran leaders who fought the Spanish in the eighteenth century: Gregoría Apaza and Bartolina Sisa. The intimacy of the primer's images, together with the immediacy of the themes and the fact that most of the groups using the book are co-ordinated by Aymaran women, all signify that Aymaran culture is not depreciated or devalued by CDA's work (see Figure 9.2). Indeed, rather than contributing to the pressures upon Aymaran culture, the process of learning literacy in Spanish may strengthen that culture, giving Aymaran women the chance to meet, reflect on their lives and develop skills which will enable them to organize a collective response to the new world that surrounds them.

One of the success stories of CDA has been in Viacha, where 45 women have been meeting every week for three years. The women meet outdoors, sitting on the ground with occasional winds whipping up dustclouds as they talk. Some come with babies wrapped on their backs, but most children are cared for in a crèche run by young boys,

La pobreza no nos impedirá la superación.

Figure 9.2: "Poverty will not hold us back" – from the CDA primer, *We Are Able*. It is possible to empower Aymaran culture even though teaching in Spanish.

which CDA has set up to free the women for one afternoon a week. Whereas most were illiterate when they arrived, all the women have now completed a ten-month literacy course (except for three new members who are presently doing it). For these women, literacy has been the base for all subsequent work.

> If we had not learnt to read and write it would have been difficult to learn other things.[12]

> During the literacy course we prepared a study of our neighbourhood so that we could see what problems we all shared, and what work we needed to do next.

As with most of CDA's nuclei, literacy classes were the first building block.

> We have learnt a lot about pregnancy and our bodies which we did not understand before. I used to be frightened of doctors, but now I know when to use one and when not to, so I feel less dependent and much less scared.

> We have done many things with our organization. We have mobilized this area for vaccinations, we have cleared litter and built roads. Once we went to an assembly with all the other nuclei and we filled a whole stadium. All us women together . . . we felt so strong.

> Now we are starting a vegetable garden to improve our diets and maybe to sell some things in the markets. We had to dig a well and build a wall to protect the garden. Soon we will be planting carrots, lettuce, tomatoes, radishes, celery and turnips.

Sadly, the experiences of Viacha are not typical. In other *barrios* CDA have encountered many problems, especially economic ones.

> The choice is becoming increasingly clear: women have either food or education, not both.
> *Margarita Callisayo*

Year by year women are forced to work longer hours to survive. Nowadays housework often fits around 16 hours a day selling on the streets of La Paz, the profit from which is measured in pieces of bread. It is not possible to plan more than a day or two in advance. The very economic conditions that make it important for women to learn, deprive them of the time to do so. In such circumstances CDA has difficulty sustaining commitment from the women. Few will stay in a nucleus for more than a year. In 1988 over 85 per cent of those who enrolled were new members. Although this means that CDA is reaching a large number of different women it also means that they are failing to consolidate their work. What is learnt in one year may be largely lost by the next. Co-ordinators are also deserting CDA: at the peak there were 2,000 but now they number less than 250.

From its early days CDA has struggled against the dependency of the mothers' clubs on food donations. In an attempt to break with the short-term charity mentality of so many non-governmental groups that work in El Alto, CDA have tried to promote self-managed development from which people can build their own future. However, they have failed. The women need the donations to feed their children; without them they starve. In May 1989 CDA set up a new group in the *barrio* of Kollpani. In July 1989, asked why they had joined the women responded "Some of us have come to do weaving, one or two for literacy, but most of us have come hoping for food. . . . We have come here to collect food donations." Once the women fully realize that CDA are against charitable donations many leave the groups.[13]

Despite the limitations of CDA's work, it is clear that their policy of teaching literacy in Spanish is more popular amongst the women of El Alto than the teaching of Aymaran. Those who learn to speak the language of power at least have the tools to be able to assert their rights. But it is by no means simple. Behind the language of power lies a culture of power, embedded in a social and political system that dominates and exploits the Aymaran people in a way that can be described in both race and class terms.

> In European theory class and race seem contradictory and it seems to many people that they must recognize one or the other. Here the correlations are strong. A high percentage of Aymara and Quechua people have clear class identities.
> *Xavier Albó*

If the Aymaran culture is to flourish it must and will be done by the Aymaran people themselves, whose first immediate struggle is to overcome their poverty. Doing this necessarily involves challenging the political system that sustains the economic crisis.

> The issue in Bolivia as in South Africa is perhaps one of democracy and majority rule for the Indians and Black Africans respectively, and minority rights for settlers.
> *Roxanne Dunbar Ortiz*, Indians of the Americas

The assertion of racial and cultural rights is an essential part of the struggle against oppression in Bolivia. As in Cabrican, Spanish is the most effective language in which to assert these rights, but using it does not signify the abandoning of indigenous language and culture.

What is charitable?
Prospects of an assertion of indigenous rights in El Alto are bleak.

> Now a husband, wife and their dog can form a project and get money from international organizations to implement it. It's just a matter of learning the tricks, producing the right reports and evaluations . . . even if it is all lies, because the funding bodies have no understanding and never check up.
> *Arturo Moscoso*

Many middle-class Spanish speakers in Bolivia have set up projects as their own particular contribution to helping the Aymaran people in El Alto. Each group is possessive of its project, working in isolation, jealously guarding their space and unwilling to share any experiences or knowledge with other groups. As a result, levels of understanding tend to be low and projects fail – though the co-ordinators of the agencies simply do a re-evaluation and come up with another project. The projects take little account of the organizational structures already existing in El Alto and can in fact damage them. The supposed beneficiaries of the projects rarely have any opportunity to contribute to decisions on how and where money is to be spent.

CDA was an attempt to counter this, but despite their emphasis on self-management they have not become effective practitioners of it. The organization has a vertical, centralized structure. At the *barrio* level there is a low level of active participation. Groups are poorly organized with handfuls of women dotted about learning different things. Those who are following the workbook *We Are Able* do so mechanically and methodically. Discussion is rare, despite the evocative themes. Women learners often look up to the co-ordinator as a figure of authority who is to be listened to in silence while co-learners do not merit the same respect. The nuclei have become passive and fail to develop self-management. Individual women are given individual skills but are not encouraged to organize or assert their rights. As a result, none of the CDA women in El Alto has succeeded in joining the local councils of each *barrio*.

Many of the NGOs and evangelical churches who work in El Alto give food donations without any attempt to build awareness or organization among recipients.[14] Food donations by evangelical sects are, in practice, a means of buying their way into communities. Food-for-work programmes (such as clearing litter) make no attempt to motivate or engage with people concerning the work (for instance, discussing the links between litter and disease or the importance of hygiene), so in practice the tasks are not done when the incentives are no longer there. Even groups who link their work with basic health and education projects can be questioned. As the Bolivian government continues to privatize the economy, it is estimated that over 40 per cent of education nationally is now in private hands and 80 per cent of that is run by the Church. Nationally at least 60 per cent of health care is provided by NGOs; in El Alto the figure, according to Juan Vargas, is closer to 100 per cent. Clearly the Church and NGOs can provide little more than emergency cover for health and education. But by alleviating the extreme consequences of government policy – by accepting the responsibilities themselves – they legitimize the continuation of that policy. On a more sinister note, they effectively boost the army budget, which is one of the only areas of expenditure not to have been cut.

The Aymaran people have become guinea pigs for those who want to organize their communities for them, without any respect for the existing community organizations. El Alto abounds, in the words of Juan Vargas, with "a lot of people who think they are Columbus and pretend they are discovering things". In this context Aymaran people who wish to work for themselves have difficulty getting recognition. They are forced to play the elaborate funding-game which pressurizes them to present everything in neat project proposals rather than ongoing programmes, making it difficult to respond to changing needs and demands. These problems have recently been exacerbated by the influx of "Sendero money": funds that international agencies had committed to the Andes, which they cannot invest in Peruvian villages for fear of guerrilla attacks (the Peruvian guerrillas call themselves Sendero Luminoso) on aid-agency workers. Bolivia is now swamped by organizations with lots of charitable money and no understanding, making it ever more difficult for Aymaran people to find their own solutions to problems.

> True generosity consists precisely in fighting to destroy the causes which nourish false charity. False charity constrains the fearful and the subdued, the "rejects of life", to extend their trembling hands. Real generosity lies in striving so that those hands – whether of individuals or entire peoples – need be extended less and less in supplication, so that more and more they become human hands which work and, by working, transform the world.
> *Paulo Freire*, Pedagogy of the Oppressed

NOTES

1. Albo, Xavier, *Desafios de la Solidaridad Aymara* (La Paz: CIPCA, 1985).
2. The land and the people living on it were shared out among the *conquistadors*. The *campesinos* on each vast estate (*encomienda*) were required to pay tribute to its owner. In return they were converted to Christianity.
3. The Aymara and Quechua identify themselves as *campesinos*. The term *indio* (Indian), apart from sanctifying Colombus's original error (he thought he'd found a western route to India) is historically a racist term of abuse in Bolivia.
4. Statistics of the 1976 census concerning the mother tongue of people show 38.4 per cent (1,594,000 people) speak Quechua and 27.9 per cent (1,156,000) Aymara. This however is not necessarily a measurement of how people would identify themselves, which is perhaps the best way of measuring the size of the Indian population. Census details are taken from Xavier Albó, *Lengua Y Sociedad en Bolivia* (Instituto Nacional de Estadistica, 1976).
5. Calderon-Dandler, *La Fuerza Historica del Campesinado* (La Paz: CERES-UNRISD, 1984) quoted in *Mujer Indigena y Educación en America Latina* (Santiago: UNESCO/III, 1989).
6. Sandoval, Albo and Greaves, *Chukiyawa: La Cara Aymara de La Paz: volume 1: El Paso a la Ciudad* (La Paz: CIPCA, 1981).
7. Chukiagu Marka, quoted in Sandoval and Sostres, *La Ciudad Prometida: Pobladores y Organizaciónes Sociales en El Alto* (La Paz: Systema/Ildis, 1989).
8. Figures from *El Alto Desde El Alto* (La Paz: UNITAS, 1989).
9. CEBIAE is Centro Boliviano de Investigaciónes y Acción Educativa. Most people only ever know the acronyms of such organizations.
10. Sandoval, Albo and Greaves, *Chukiyawa: La Cara Aymara de La Paz: volume

3: Cabalgando Entre Dos Mundos (La Paz: CIPCA, 1983).

11. When founded in 1983 the organization was called Autogestión Educativa. They changed their name to CDA in 1986. For the sake of consistency and clarity we use CDA throughout.

12. This and the following quotes come from a meeting in July 1989 with the women of the CDA nucleus in Viacha.

13. In a similar way SENALEP has suffered. Discovering that many of their groups were only meeting to distribute food donations, SENALEP demanded that the women do two hours of literacy twice a week. Widespread failure to fulfil this requirement meant SENALEP made cutbacks in La Paz, ending up with just 20 groups out of an original 70.

14. There are some who see the work of NGOs and evangelical sects as part of a pre-meditated plan by the US, who seek to dissolve all grassroots organizations in Bolivia to pave the way for making the country into a secure US base in South America. The borders that Bolivia shares with Chile, Argentina, Brazil, Peru and Paraguay make it strategically important, and suitable for playing an equivalent role to that played by Honduras in Central America.

10. Nicaragua's Atlantic Coast, Karata: Miskitu Dialogue

> Dialogue with the people is radically necessary to every authentic revolution. This is what makes it a revolution, as distinguished from a military coup. One does not expect dialogue from a coup – only deceit (in order to achieve legitimacy) or force (in order to repress). Sooner or later a true revolution must initiate a courageous dialogue with the people. Its very legitimacy lies in that dialogue. It cannot fear the people, their expression, their effective participation in power.
> *Paulo Freire*, Pedagogy of the Oppressed

In the case-studies so far in this section, the goals of indigenous peoples and those of the revolutionary movements have converged: both involve the overthrow of an oppressive regime and the recognition of people's rights to self-determination. While there are substantial differences in strategy, there is no clear conflict of interests. On the Atlantic Coast of Nicaragua, the eastern half of the country, the opposite seems to be the case. Since 1981, many of the Miskitu have been ostensibly fighting to overthrow a revolutionary government as auxiliary forces in the Contra War. The situation is a complex one. It is too simplistic to argue that the Miskitu were just tools of US imperialism. Equally facile is the argument that the revolution in Nicaragua was a Pacific Coast revolution which was only interested in continuing the historic oppression of indigenous peoples by "Spanish" states. Literacy is critical to the analysis because the war was started by a literacy campaign and bilingual education may well have been an important factor in ending it.

NICARAGUA'S OTHER HALF

To begin to make sense of the interplay of interests here, it is necessary to understand who the Miskitu are. In the tenth century, a group of Amazonian Chibcha Indians migrated north to the shores of the lake now known as Lake Nicaragua. Displaced by other migrating groups, they followed the waterways into the dense jungle of the Caribbean coast of what is now Nicaragua and Honduras. Here they continued their semi-nomadic lifestyle living largely by fishing from the coastal seas, lagoons and rivers, and supplementing their diet by hunting. The difficult terrain left them undisturbed by the arrival of the Spanish *conquistadors* on the Pacific Coast who failed to penetrate the unfamiliar rain forest.

During the late-sixteenth century, the same coastal seaboard provided an ideal base for French, Dutch and British pirates to attack Spanish galleons returning home full of Andean gold and silver. Pirates traded axes and guns for the Indians' knowledge of the area which provided them with safe shelters and food. The trading posts expanded as the settlers became aware of the resources of the territory: initially timber and fruit. The Chibcha group who developed links with the Europeans became known as the Miskitu.[1] Subsequently, Africans were brought over as slave labour by the British in order to extract the valuable resources more cheaply. The Miskitu, mixing freely with pirates, traders and Africans, developed a unique composite culture and a language which owed something to all of these roots.

> The objective of British foreign policy in the sixteenth, seventeenth and eighteenth centuries was basically to try to diminish the strength of the Spanish Empire.
> *Ray Hooker*[2]

The British government saw the flourishing trading posts as a way of claiming the wealth of the area and of using it strategically as another thorn in the side of their colonial competitor. In 1687, they declared the whole area a protectorate of the British Crown, naming a Miskitu leader as the king of Mosquitia in a crowning ceremony in Jamaica.[3]

> It's not that Britain loved the Indians more than the Spaniards did, because in the United States, the British practically wiped out the original population ... It served British interests to gain the support of the natives ...
> *Ray Hooker*, Nicaragua

The Miskitu operated as a buffer class, given weapons and power so that they could defend the new Protectorate from incursions by the Spanish and quell any disturbances by other indigenous workers and African slaves. They were of use to the British throughout the region.

> They [the Miskitu] have always been, and still are, in the place of a standing army; which ... maintains the English in firm and secure possession, protects their trade, and forms an impenetrable barrier to the Spaniards, whom they keep in constant awe.
> *Long, 1774*[4]

> The British fomented hatred of the Spaniards. That is, the British taught the native population to hate the Spaniards. Now the Spaniards on the Pacific Coast also taught the people there to hate the natives of the Atlantic Coast region. So we had two European powers teaching the local populations to hate one another.
> *Ray Hooker*, Nicaragua

British control over Mosquitia declined throughout the nineteenth century. Nicaragua was declared an independent state in 1838, splitting the Miskitu nation into two parts along the Nicaragua–Honduras border marked by the River Coco. However, the capitals of both Nicaragua and Honduras were on the Spanish-speaking Pacific Coast. With few representatives on the Atlantic Coast, national sovereignties and the new boundaries were largely meaningless. The real challenge to both British and Miskitu hegemony over the Coast came from the interest of US companies who set up economic enclaves to exploit its resources. These self-contained enclaves were isolated from any government administration and had their own company shops to supply all the material needs of the workers. The Miskitu lost their special relationship with the British as they became labourers in the enclaves. Meanwhile, the Afro-Caribbean Creoles took over administrative posts because they were the only people who could communicate with the gringos.

Church and Communities

> With the Moravian church, the communities were formed. People were
> semi-nomads and became sedentary. The community can be dying but they'll
> still build that white church.
> *Mirna Cunningham*[5]

The forests of the Coast were rich in hardwoods, particularly mahogany, which companies wanted to extract efficiently and in large quantities. To do so they depended on groups like the Miskitu who knew where to find the best trees. To establish fixed sources of labour and to promote the Protestant values of hard work, the British sent Moravian church missionaries to areas of the Coast that they controlled. Once established, the Moravians spread their influence over the whole region, community by community as more missionaries arrived.

> There was a ray of light that founded the church. People were inside and a
> strong wind came and blew out the candles. People cried and sang for joy
> as the light beamed down on them. This made people choose to live and die
> here because it was seen as a sign.
> *Moravian pastor, Karata*

The Moravian church set up the first schools in the region. Teachers were trained in English and are still remembered in some villages:

> I had three-years English teaching by a man from Jamaica.
> *Village elder, Karata*

Moravians also translated the Bible and hymnal into Miskitu. In this way the church helped to maintain the Miskitu language and provided a sense of cohesion to the community. The pastors were in a powerful position as the source of most information about the world beyond the village.

There were 80 people living on the edge of Karata lagoon when, in 1875, an English Moravian called Smith arrived to found the mission. Karata is now one of the less remote communities, close to the small port of Puerto Cabezas; but the journey from the port still involves a three-hour canoe ride along a river lined with mangrove swamps and across a large lagoon. The first sight is of a small beach with the distinctive Moravian spire rising behind it. Coming closer, the fishing canoes and nets appear. The houses remain hidden until you walk through the coconut palms into the village. There are 55 wooden huts, built on stilts, housing around 300 inhabitants.

> This village is really one big family.
> *Charlie, sub-director Karata school*

The homes surround a green where a makeshift baseball field has been marked out. There is no electricity. Two murky wells at one end of the village supply the freshwater needs of the whole community. A broken-down bridge leads from the village to what used to be the port where boats from the lumber companies would load their cargoes.

> There used to be a gringo company that took out mahogany . . . Karl Bunson. I think he was Danish. The small boats arrived to pick up the wood that we cut with axes and carried on our backs . . . they took it to the big ships in the sea . . . There was a gringo with blue eyes. The gringos came and went overseeing the Miskitu workers but they didn't live here.
> *Village elder, Karata*

By 1884, Karata was known as the old mahogany pier, a place where paid work could be found. The church was the seed around which the community grew. It is remembered as a good time by the older people in the village:

> The companies treated people well, there were shops with shoes and clothes and food which provided us with what we needed. They respected the Miskitu.
> *Village elder, Karata*

However, while the shops provided goods, it was in many cases instead of wages, a way of more cheaply extracting the rich resources of the forests.

In 1894, the British were finally forced to pull out of the Nicaraguan part of Mosquitia by the nationalist Pacific Coast government of Zelaya, but they left land titles to the communities.[6] Karata, in addition to the land of the village itself, was given the land where they grew crops – "a day's boat journey away" – and another large area where their cattle grazed. Successive Nicaraguan governments failed to recognize these communal rights. In 1921, the government of Chamorro granted a concession of 50, 000 acres to the Bragman's Bluff lumber company, a subsidiary of Standard Fruit, for timber-cutting and lumber. The US company built the port of Puerto Cabezas on Karata's grazing land and the Miskitu living in communities around, including Karata, were considered "squatters on company lands".[7] The sawmills of Bragman's Bluff used the pine that the hardwood exporters had left untouched. Judging from the memories of the old people in the village, it was at around the same time that the companies left Karata, after depleting the local forests of hardwoods.

> In the past there was a lot more here. But then a hurricane came and destroyed a lot of the old village . . . in the 1920s.
> *Village elder, Karata*

The community declined in size. People who had migrated to work in Karata moved on to the new port. Karata was left with few inhabitants and a useless wooden pier as the only remnant of the boom years. Those remaining reverted to their traditional means of existence: fishing. The lagoon is rich in shrimp and fish. The name Karata itself is a Miskitu word meaning "the place where Kara grows". Kara is the plant from which the people manufactured the fibre for sewing their canoe sails and making their harpoons. The presence of the nearby port provided a market for their fish and shrimp, which were exported to the United States, providing the fishermen with dollars to spend in shops in Puerto Cabezas. They supplemented their diet with harvests from small plots of yucca, cassava, rice and plantain that they maintained on the other side of the lagoon.

> Things were better then, there was more freedom, more friendship. We could travel to our farms without being frightened.
> *Farmer, Karata*

Somoza and the Coast

Unlike on the Pacific Coast, the rule of the Somoza family brought no new repression to the people of the Atlantic Coast. They simply gave US companies free rein to continue exploiting the gold, silver, wood, fish and turtles of the area. The only state representative in each village was a judge nominated by villagers. Most civil functions (for instance, the registrations of births, marriages and deaths) were carried out by local leaders. The dominant influences in Karata remained the Moravian church and the companies in Puerto Cabezas.

However "Somoza-time", as it is referred to in Miskitu, did bring a number of changes. During the 1960s, companies all over the Coast began to move out, leaving behind them widespread deforestation and contaminated rivers.

> All governments are the same. They took so much wealth from here and left us with nothing. We can only cry to God . . . maybe they'll give us a bit of help . . . but then they leave.
> *Comandante Hercules, Miskitu fighter*

The advent of planes and motorboats made the Coast more accessible to the capital, Managua. Although there was still no road, a good deal of migration to the region took place during Somoza-time. The landless Pacific Coast *campesinos* who arrived were Spanish-speaking *mestizos*.[8] Partly to supply these migrants the national government took over the running of Atlantic Coast schools. But there was another, underlying aim: in the new schools, Miskitu was banned. In addition, a pilot *castellanización* literacy project was initiated in the River Coco region (on the border with Honduras), promoting the Spanish language and culture. The result was that many people were ashamed to speak their own language. Another Pacific Coast import was the Catholic Church which arrived in some communities (though not Karata) with *mestizo* migrants, causing considerable tension.

> When I was a little girl, we would go to the Moravian church on Sunday and then we would go with stones with the pastor and stone the Catholic church. That was the morning service. In the evening service, the Catholics would stone us. . . . I tried to go to the school and was not admitted because I was Moravian.
> *Mirna Cunningham*

In Karata, a school was built in 1975. Two teachers were brought in from Puerto Cabezas, both *mestizo*, who used Spanish texts printed in Managua, with themes (for instance transport using cars and trains as examples) that were irrelevant to the reality of the students. Many students dropped out simply because they couldn't understand the teachers' language. Under Somoza, the historical conflict between the two halves of Nicaragua, fomented by imperial powers and exacerbated by national governments, was felt for the first time in every village of the Atlantic Coast.

RACE AND REVOLUTION

The Sandinista victory in 1979 had a very different meaning for the people of the Atlantic Coast. There was only a handful of FSLN members there and there had been no fighting to overthrow the Somoza regime. For many, it represented no more than a change of government in Managua. Until the Sandinistas built the all-weather road from Puerto Cabezas to Managua in 1982, it was easier to travel from the Atlantic Coast to New Orleans than to the other half of the country. Even now, although the distance is only 700 kilometres, the uncomfortable journey by land takes at least two days in a truck.

The new government had a high profile on the Coast. They set up branches of the new ministries and extended state social services.

> Revolutionary government cadres, with much enthusiasm but with a certain lack of knowledge of these people's history, wanted to change everything overnight. Without giving much thought to the consequences, we wanted to

develop on the Atlantic Coast structures and projects similar to those on the Pacific.
Tomas Borgé[9]

The Sandinistas, based in Puerto Cabezas, had little contact with the surrounding communities. In Karata, the immediate benefits were only for the fishermen who traded in the port. Fishing nets were provided and the state subsidized gasoline supplies for the long motor boats that took the fish to Puerto Cabezas to be sold. Recognizing the need for greater communication between the revolutionary state and the villages, the Sandinistas created a mass organization for the peoples of the Coast. MISURASATA (the Miskitu, Sumu, and Rama Sandinista Alliance) was formed from organizations of indigenous groups which under Somoza had little power (the Sumu and Rama are two of the smaller indigenous groups on the Atlantic Coast). The new body became the link between the communities and the FSLN.

> Everything done by the government for the Atlantic Coast was done by MISURASATA; the vaccination campaign, the opening of schools . . .
> *Mirna Cunningham*

Local branches of MISURASATA played a similar role to the Sandinista Defence Committees on the Pacific Coast. The difference was that MISURASATA activists were, for the most part, not Sandinistas. They had no history of working within the revolutionary struggle. In addition, they had an extra role: that of interpreting the new aims, policies and ideology through languages which had few words to give substantive meaning to revolutionary slogans that had developed out of the euphoria of the Pacific Coast victory over Somoza.

A Crusade in Languages?

For the Sandinistas, the Literacy Crusade, as the "second revolution", had particular importance on the Atlantic Coast. If national unity on the Pacific Coast meant building a dialogue between urban and rural areas, on the Atlantic Coast it signified forging a dialogue across a historical, cultural and linguistic divide that over 140 years of Nicaraguan independence had done little to bridge. Success depended on establishing a relationship of trust between the Coasts and an acceptance that both had something to learn and something to teach.

Difficulties were inevitable. When the crusade was announced in September 1979, MISURASATA leaders started demanding that a plan be developed for a parallel crusade in indigenous languages: Miskitu, Sumu and English. If the classes were to be more than the learning of techniques, it was clear to them that literacy in the mother tongue was necessary in the communities. It was difficult to discuss their own reality in a foreign language which many didn't speak and very few spoke naturally. To make the revolution theirs, and not an external imposition, fluent discussion was essential. However, demands for a campaign in the languages were initially rejected.

> There wasn't resistance, but a lack of comprehension.
> *Hazel Lau, MISURASATA leader*

Sandinista leaders saw the languages of the indigenous minorities as "linguistic prisons"[10] that people had to be freed from. The implication was that Spanish was the language of modernity, of development and of liberty. Underlying these assumptions was a perception not far removed from that of the Guatemalan Ministry of Education (see Chapter 8). To be Indian was to be backward, an obstacle to progress. Dubious educational arguments were used to justify the position:

> It has been proved that a Miskitu who learns to read and write in Spanish can read perfectly in his own language while those that learn to read and write in Miskitu cannot read in Spanish.
> *Ministry of Education report, 1983*

This suggests that literacy is purely a technique, ignoring the methodological principles on which the crusade was based. It is paradoxical that a revolutionary government took on the idea of using the colonial language as a means of unifying an independent nation.[11]

The MISURASATA leadership, Steadman Fagoth, Brooklyn Rivera and Hazel Lau, mobilized the communities of the Coast against Managua's decision. After seven months, they convinced the Ministry of Education that a crusade in Spanish would be rejected and that it was therefore in the revolution's interest to have literacy in indigenous languages. A decree was passed and a technical team set up to develop materials in Miskitu, Sumu and English. The team was headed by Brooklyn and Hazel who developed a primer admirably adapted to the reality of the revolution as well as to that of the Coast. For example it included themes on the two most important Sandinista figureheads:

> We thought it was right to use the theme of Sandino but according to the experience of the coast . . . Carlos Fonseca [Founder of the FSLN] was the second theme because, in 1973, Fonseca sent a team here to study the reality of the coast and how to incorporate it into the political platform of the FSLN.
> *Hazel Lau*

Differences from the national materials centred on specific themes on ways of life such as fishing and boat-building, as well as a theme on MISURASATA itself. In Miskitu, the major difficulty was deciding on which variant of the language to use. Communities on or close to the seaboard such as Karata use a variant with more roots in English. Those on the Rio Coco, on the border with Honduras, have a larger

Spanish influence on the language. It was decided to use the criterion of "originality", searching for the oldest form of a word in an attempt to try and distil a pure form of the language.

Mestizos in Puerto Cabezas were worried that the Miskitu were planning to use the crusade to revive their old hegemony over other Coastal peoples. The Ministry of Education on the Atlantic Coast, dominated by *mestizos*, campaigned throughout the Coast against MISURASATA. They claimed that there would be no literacy in Miskitu and that people should join the crusade in Spanish which had been launched on the Coast for the *mestizo* population. In Karata, some villagers joined the Spanish crusade not realizing that later they would be able to learn in Miskitu.

> The *brigadistas* came from other parts . . . had some strange ways. I learnt a little, but I've forgotten most of it . . . most people weren't interested, they couldn't speak any Spanish.
> *Fisherman, Karata*

As well as using a certain amount of deceit, the Ministry in Puerto Cabezas told Managua that a crusade in languages would be politically dangerous, giving too much control to MISURASATA. A fear spread in Managua (where the coast was still little understood) that a crusade in languages, far from promoting dialogue between the Coasts would promote demands for a separate state, particularly by Miskitu leaders. With the materials ready for printing, MISURASATA faced a second battle with Managua. The only printing facilities in the country were on the other side of the country. The organizers sent the drafts to Managua but it took over two months of phone-calls and meetings to arrange for the materials to be printed and returned.

FROM LITERACY TO WAR

> I think it will be a long time before our people have an experience like the crusade in languages was here . . . it's the first time in the Americas that an indigenous organization has used the whole organization of the state as part of a national programme.
> *Hazel Lau*

Literacy work in the communities began in June 1980. In Karata, there were eight *brigadistas* who taught 53 adults to read and write in Miskitu. It was the first time that their lives under the enclave economy could be discussed (the following comments come from a meeting in Karata in April 1989):

> In Miskitu, we could talk about the revolution . . . how it might change our lives . . . and what we should demand of it.

> It was good . . . now nearly everyone reads. The materials went from easy to difficult so the old people turned up all the time.

> It was such a big change . . . In Somoza-time, we weren't allowed to even
> speak our language in school. . . . In these classes we were learning to write
> it.

As the crusade gathered momentum, the conscientization within the
communities gave the leaders of MISURASATA the confidence to seek
a more active role in national affairs. Steadman Fagoth, who represented
MISURASATA on the Council of State, wanted to push things further.
As the only Miskitu leader based in Managua, he was in a position to
manipulate his power and present demands without backing from the
communities. For example, he pushed for a seat on the ruling "junta
of national reconstruction"[12] and he unilaterally presented proposals to
legalize Miskitu communal lands, based on a map which would have given
the Miskitu 48 per cent of national territory. The issue was a sensitive
one to a government worried that separatist demands from Coast leaders
would be exploited by the US in their plans to overthrow the Sandinista
revolution. Somoza's ex-National Guard was already being trained by US
advisers in Honduras, but demands for a separate state would have given
them a much stronger cause for intervention. Quite apart from possible
US manipulation, the proposals were totally impractical. They would have
left the *mestizos* of the Coast, around half its population, with nowhere to
live.

The Sandinistas rejected the demands outright. Anticipating trouble,
they arrested the whole MISURASATA leadership and initiated a
thorough investigation of the organization. They discovered that Fagoth's
office in Managua had been receiving funding from the US embassy. Two
weeks later, the leaders were released on bail pending further investigation.
Both Steadman Fagoth and Brooklyn Rivera fled the country to join the
counter-revolutionary forces assembling in Honduras. However, it was not
until the incident at Prinzapolka that large numbers of the Miskitu joined
them.

> We had decided to present the plans for the legalization of communal lands
> at the ceremonies to celebrate the end of the Literacy Crusade in languages.
> *Hazel Lau*

On 22 February 1981, in Prinzapolka, a seaboard community down the
coast from Karata, Sandinista soldiers entered the Moravian church
where the *brigadistas* of the crusade in languages had gathered to receive
certificates and to find out if the communal lands were to be returned
to them. The soldiers had gone in to arrest one of the organizers of the
crusade. A fight broke out and eight people died, four soldiers and four
Miskitu. This is seen in Karata as the spark for the conflict: soldiers had
entered their church and killed their people.

> Two *brigadistas* from here were teaching in Prinzapolka. They were at the
> ceremony when the Sandinista soldiers went in. Afterwards they fled and

hid. The pastor of the Moravian church [in Karata] spoke on their behalf to the Sandinistas and arranged for their safe return to Karata. However, the Sandinistas had plans to get them.
Teacher, Karata

In '79 and '80 we had no problems with the Sandinistas. They had given us literacy classes and opened up the school. Prinzapolka was where the problems started. They didn't want us to learn in our own language.
MISURASATA delegate, Karata

Everyone on the Coast wanted to get rid of Somoza but when the new government started killing our people in Prinzapolka, there was fighting here.
Fisherman, Karata

Before Prinzapolka, there was no talk of separatism here. . . . The government struck first, they killed our race, so everyone had to arm themselves.
Comandante Hercules, Miskitu fighter

It is certainly true that Fagoth was building links with the opposition parties and the counterinsurgency movements preparing for attack from Honduras, but Fagoth only represented a small part of MISURASATA. His group of fighters, aligned with Somoza's ex-National Guard, went on to be renowned for the horrific abuses they inflicted on their own people. Brooklyn Rivera, on the other hand, only became involved with the Contras as a result of his arrest and after the events in Prinzapolka when he declared that political solutions had "no resonance in the communities".[13] The Sandinista action could not have been better calculated to turn the Miskitu against the revolution.

Anti-communist ideology, as propounded by the Moravian Church, has a long history on the Coast, one reason why the abortive Bay of Pigs invasion of Cuba was launched by the US from Puerto Cabezas. Attacking unarmed people in a church was a gift to pastors' rhetoric against the Sandinistas. The Moravians felt threatened both by the Catholicism of the revolution and, paradoxically, what they assumed to be its atheism. The pastors mobilized people in the communities to fight against the revolution, exploiting a historical parallel with Prinzapolka. In the 1930s, Sandino (the inspiration for the Sandinistas) was organizing attacks on the lumber companies in Puerto Cabezas. Some of his soldiers, identifying the Moravians with the companies, killed a Moravian church missionary, burnt the pastoral house and destroyed all traces of the property. In 1931, as in 1981, many Miskitu fled into exile in Honduras.[14]

Perhaps the biggest paradox of the developments leading to the war was that, as Brooklyn Rivera admits, the Miskitu became embroiled in a struggle against the very movement that had made their organizations a reality:

Of course, the revolution made this whole movement possible. The fervour of the revolutionary triumph injected into the soul, heart and atmosphere that everyone could participate. Before there was no incentive . . . we were just asleep.

War in Karata

For the people of Karata, the war years meant hardship, the blame for which they pinned on the Sandinistas who seemed directly responsible. While it was the US who mined Puerto Cabezas harbour and started an economic blockade, the villagers blamed the Sandinistas for the loss of their prime source of income. Now they could only sell shrimp to the state which could not provide the dollar-income that they were used to. The journey to sell the fish became hazardous anyway. There was fighting around the lagoon and anyone in the area was suspected of being a Contra by Sandinista soldiers who didn't know the Coast. It was too dangerous for Karata's fishermen to sail out at night in order to cast their nets for a dawn catch. The sowing of crops became impossible. On the long journeys up-river, they needed to take guns with them to protect themselves from the wild animals on their farms (which were no more than clearings in the rain forest). Sandinista patrol boats would instantly suspect that the people in the canoes carrying rifles were Contras. For six years, they planted nothing.

As on the Pacific Coast, compulsory military service alienated most people in Karata. Men preferred to remain in hiding without work rather than accept the draft. So most of the soldiers in the area came from the Pacific Coast. These soldiers saw no clear distinction between the Contras who had once been members of Somoza's National Guard and those who were Miskitu, fighting for an indigenous cause. Worse, most soldiers regarded the Miskitu as reactionary, counter-revolutionary people who were aligned with the Contras even if they were not activists. To the Miskitu themselves, the appearance of soldiers from the Pacific Coast heightened their feeling that the conflict was a racial one. Karata was one community singled out for suspicion by the Sandinistas because of the two *brigadistas* who had fled from Prinzapolka. The isolation of the village (where the main sources of information during the war were the Moravian pastor and the counter-revolutionary radio, broadcast in Miskitu from Honduras) prevented any alternative interpretation from gaining currency.

It was specific personal incidents which destroyed any vestiges of trust in the Sandinistas:

The Sandinistas killed my cattle.

Sometimes they fired bullets into the air through the village just to frighten the people.

The Sandinistas accused us of giving food to the Contra. But this is a lie. If the Contras arrived we had to give them food and if the Sandinistas arrived we had to do the same.

A load of soldiers arrived at the farm and took away my husband and two children who were working there. Then they burnt the house on the farm. I travelled to Managua to find out what happened. The people there said it was a lie. . . . Now I am sure that they were murdered.

When you have a war people disappear and there's no way to find out . . . who can tell them? If we can't tell them here or in Managua then no one can. Maybe they were in a farm, working, and the Contra came in and killed them; maybe they were caught in crossfire . . . maybe they're in Honduras. . . .
Mirna Cunningham

Disentangling the truth here is difficult and probably impossible. For example there were cases of Contras dressing as Sandinistas and terrorizing areas. There was clearly a problem of communication in that the Sandinistas had no network within communities like Karata to counter the type of information spread by MISURASATA through the Moravian churches. The point here is that regardless of where the blame really lies, 12 men disappeared from Karata over two years and the people blame the Sandinistas. Seven youths left the village to join the Contras at this time. One of them, Comandante Hercules, became a leader on the Contras' southern front.

I am the survivor of 26 combats and of 16 ambushes. I am a guerrilla and I am good in the mountains . . . I can kill.
Comandante Hercules, translated from Spanish

I me myself kill plenty of dat man [Sandinistas] . . . I couldn't pardon dem kind o' people. I couldn't use my bullet to dem . . . I had to use my knife. It is a war . . . you can't love one another. You fightin' . . . Fightin'! You no' gonna keep dem in jail.
Comandante Hercules, in Creole

A NEW DIALOGUE?

It's a question of building something over so many bodies because of a war that . . . the people in the communities do not understand because of the way they have been manipulated.
Mirna Cunningham

As early as 1983, a re-evaluation had started. A government delegation in July admitted that the Ministry of Education and the government had been escaping their responsibilities to provide bilingual–bicultural education by blaming MISURASATA and saying that the crusade in languages was a counter-revolutionary plot. In the light of the war, the enormous damage it was doing to the revolution, and the threat of direct US invasion, it was absolutely vital to rebuild some kind of dialogue with the communities of the Atlantic Coast.

If we had sat down to discuss these problems in 1981, surely the situation
would not have been the same as what happened.
William Ramirez, Sandinista leader

A series of studies was commissioned by ministries considering how to adapt
the revolution to the reality of the Coast. One of the first consequences was
that bilingual education was freed from its associations with separatism
and recognized as crucial to educational success on the Coast.

The strategy developed was a complex one. In order isolate the US
from the Miskitu Contras, the Sandinista government had to recognize
what was legitimate in MISURASATA's demands. The first step was to
recognize its own errors and develop a dialogue without threatening the
unity of the national state: not an easy task when the two sides were at
war and there was a history of hundreds of years of mistrust. Central to
it was the development of a new Statute of Autonomy for the peoples of
the Coast:

> The autonomy we want is our freedom. We want it as before with our
> ancestors, when our leaders ruled us . . . or in the time of Somoza. . . . We
> know that the indigenous people were always below the government but
> everything was free. . . . We lived by our work.
> *Comandante Hercules*

> One of the problems we have is the paternalistic pattern that existed in these
> communities . . . We won't have autonomy until we stop thinking that change
> comes from outside.
> *Mirna Cunningham*

During 1984, working groups began exploring local ideas of autonomy.
A two-year process of consultation began, operating in a similar fashion
to the conscientization of the crusade in languages, except that this time
the Sandinistas were in direct contact with the communities, with no
intermediaries.

> In 1981, these things we are talking about now were taboo and we didn't
> touch them. We were terrified to speak of autonomy because we did not under-
> stand it. And we didn't understand it because no one understood the Atlantic
> Coast. Today we speak of this naturally. . . . The struggle of the Indian people
> themselves has caused us to reflect, has led us to question ourselves, to ask
> ourselves about their attitude, which we sometimes even considered irra-
> tional. . . . We must study these attitudes, not shut our eyes to reality.
> *William Ramirez, Sandinista leader*

Commissions of Peace and Autonomy were set up by the government in
consultation with community representatives. The Autonomy Law which
arose out of these consultations was unique in the Americas, guaranteeing
not only cultural, linguistic and religious rights but also the ownership,
use and transfer of communal lands according to customs. It prevented
any one group (Miskitu, *mestizo*, Sumu, Rama or Creole) from gaining

ascendancy: the rights were granted not to communities or peoples but to individuals free to determine their own racial identity.

> If it succeeds, it will set indigenous and other ethnic struggles ahead by 25 years. If it fails, or is made to fail, it will set those struggles back just as far.
> *Member of the Autonomy Commission*

> Autonomy is an example for North America and the whole world.
> *D. Rojas, Chair of World Council of Indigenous Peoples*

The promise of autonomy lies in the possibility that for the first time in nearly 500 years of oppression by imperial and post-imperial powers, indigenous languages could genuinely become languages of power. Spanish will remain the national language, but the regional councils, to be elected in 1990, will include representatives of all the different peoples of the Coast and will operate using interpreters for all the languages. The role of bilingual education is not a side-issue here but at the centre of the transformation projected by proponents of the autonomy process.

The Ministry of Education is not talking about a transitional bilingualism (like PRONEBI in Guatemala), in which the mother tongue would be used ironically as the most efficient way of teaching Spanish and therefore, in the longer term, of replacing Miskitu language and culture. Neither is it interested in teaching Miskitu just as a separate subject. If maths, natural and social sciences continue to be taught in Spanish, then the Miskitu language will remain underdeveloped, without the words for political, technical and scientific concepts. This would leave it as it was historically, a language only used within the family and the church. The Sandinista bilingual programme aimed to break this marginalization, making Miskitu into a language of science, work and political power through permanent bilingualism, starting with bilingual literacy. The idea is that not only Miskitu, but all the languages of the Coast will become languages of power through a step by step increase in their use by schools, ministries and other institutions.[15]

The following are specific aims of the bilingual–bicultural education programme (as taken from Ministry of Education documents, April 1989):

- to stimulate in children the use of maternal languages in daily communication in and outside the classroom as a way of valourzing ethnic identity;
- to promote the recovery of cultural traditions, forms of organization and mechanisms of development in terms of reaffirming their identity in the context of national life;
- to develop in children the ability to observe, analyse and understand the natural world surrounding them, and to value the resources offered by nature;
- to foster in children the use of scientific methods and the linking of theory with practice so that they can actively participate in the transformation of society.

BUILDING AUTONOMY

From the outset, some people saw the Sandinista strategy as a way of ending the war without really conceding anything. Others felt that the new autonomy law and the bilingual programme were what Miskitu leaders like Brooklyn Rivera and Hazel Lau had been asking for all along.

> Now we have a legal status that every indigenous group in America would like. In 1981 we had a plan which was classified by Managua as separatist. I say that that plan was the same Autonomy.
> *Hazel Lau*

> The Autonomy Law came from the thinking of Brooklyn. But the government only goes so far, doesn't put it into operation as it should be.
> *Delegate of Peace and Autonomy Commission, Karata*

Peace

> We want peace, dialogue, no more blood. War is not an option any more.
> *Ex-soldier of YATAMA (Contra grouping) at Unification Assembly 1989*

> We no wan' dialoguin'. We'll return to the mountains. If dey is such men dat wanna fight, we is such men dat'll fight.
> *Comandante Hercules*

The war is not over yet. In April 1985, a ceasefire was agreed on the basis of talks on autonomy. Talks broke down, partly because Brooklyn was paid by the US government to walk out of them. The indigenous struggle had, through its leaders, become subservient to US interests. But after the autonomy process was initiated, soldiers began to take up the amnesty offered by the government. Pro- and anti-dialogue factions appeared in the communities, in the refugee camps in neighbouring Honduras, and among the Miskitu Contra.

> Six fighters from our village came back from Honduras and are now working in Puerto Cabezas. Two refugees stayed there but only because they found work. Few people are fighting now.
> *Peace and Autonomy Commission delegate, Karata*

One Miskitu Contra from Karata is still fighting:

> Although the US doesn't help us as much as before, we will work out the way to fight communists. It could be for 100 years but it'll be worth it if we achieve our ends.
> *Comandante Hercules*

Of an estimated 40,000 refugees in Honduras, over 30,000 had returned by April 1989.

> In Honduras we weren't allowed to cut a tree down so we could plant;

we weren't even allowed to leave the camp. We came back because we're Nicaraguans. Here we are free.
Miskitu woman

With the exception of Steadman Fagoth's hardline forces most of those who were fighting have also returned. The destruction of schools, clinics, sawmills and bridges is for the moment over, a first precondition for the success of the multi-racial state. Autonomy has successfully undercut the language of those fighting in Honduras whose arguments have lost their basis in indigenous struggles and are reduced to anti-communist rhetoric and a defence of the free market.

Although there is relative peace, military service remains. The youth of Karata are still in hiding, unable to look for paid work or positions of responsibility in Puerto Cabezas and can only farm their land secretly. This has had an interesting side-effect. Most of the people in control of government and ministries are women because the men have been fighting or in hiding from conscription for years: a case where a conflict of race and class interests has benefited women.

The men are in hiding but they believe that they can come out of the bushes and take over . . . Even some women believe that . . . Everyone should be represented [on the regional council]. I think we have to make an effort to have men represented on it. They should feel that they're represented too!
Mirna Cunningham

No woman's going to tell me how to do my job . . . she likes her power . . . she won't stop talking.
Ex-director of Karata school talking about the co-ordinator of the Ministry of Education Zonal Office

Autonomy

We no wan' their autonomy . . . we no wan' politics-law. Politics-law can' do nuthin'. What is politics is lying. I want my right. I no want these politics.
Comandante Hercules

We're trying to build a bridge of trust between those people and the government of Nicaragua. You can easily build a bridge of confidence in Karata if you can go in there with a new school, with clean water, with motorboats. But we don't have anything so you have to say "Believe us because we are working for peace". I think a little bridge has already been built.
Mirna Cunningham

People's memories cannot be eradicated by the new developments in a short time. After the experience of the war, there is a feeling in Karata of wait-and-see. The reluctance to fulfil military service is one factor which inhibits participation in the changes. Some are suspicious that this is not real autonomy because they have seen no social benefits since the dialogue began. The people of Karata have no new wells, no electricity and not even a generator. The nominal health post is still in the process of being built and it is difficult to imagine a time when it will be well supplied.

> This year is the first year [1989] that we've been able to plant crops on our land. Things are better now. But costs are too high: people don't have enough to eat and the foreign aid doesn't arrive here because they don't see the poverty outside Puerto Cabezas.
> *Village elder*

Others feel that Autonomy is just a Sandinista word to replace Revolution and that if real autonomy were implemented, the Sandinistas would clamp down on it in the same way as in 1981:

> If I have doubts, they are that they'll give us rights to participate but in their way. Autonomy for me is not this but rather the freedom to develop these rights in our own way.
> *Fornes Rabonias, MISATAN co-ordinator*[16]

The government blames the slow progress on that wait-and-see approach, because for them, autonomy is what the communities make of the legal framework given to them. They accept that the major problems are economic ones: but the US trade embargo prevents free trading and leaves the Sandinistas without the finance to implement the necessary social programmes with the communities. To produce more, the area needs investment, but to invest, the government needs production. The same catch exists on the Pacific Coast but on the Atlantic side it is more severe as there is so little infrastructure – a legacy of hundreds of years of neglect. Many Atlantic Coast villages do not have electricity, running water or paved roads while these are common features of even small villages on the Pacific side. This is paradoxical: the Atlantic Coast is still rich in resources including timber, gold and other minerals. The most critical task of autonomy is to correct the economic imbalance, giving the Coast's peoples rights over their own resources, even if this is at the cost of weakening the Pacific Coast's economy.

> Autonomy does not mean separation. In other words, the fact that autonomous regions can exist will not contribute to dividing the country, but rather to strengthening national unity.
> *William Ramirez*

The tentative communications between the Coasts can best be pictured through the road which unites them. Closed for five years by Contra road-mines and blown-up bridges, it is now open again but the journey still involves taking a ferry across one river and fording many small streams. Building stronger links requires not only economic investment, but also dialogue, otherwise the road will always be vulnerable to attack. It will continue to be vulnerable if the dialogue is not authentic, if either Coast asserts power over the other, believing that it alone is the teacher, and the other the learner. Autonomy cannot be defined or imposed by either side.

A new language of power?

Bilingual education is now underway for the first three grades of primary school in Karata. There are four teachers, all of whom come from the village. There is no doubt that the materials are similar to many materials designed to integrate people more effectively into a Spanish culture. However, primary schoolchildren in Karata are literate in both languages and the backdrop of the autonomy process changes the whole context of the programme.

> Bilingual education is the one good thing the Sandinistas have done. Before, the language was dying. Bit by bit, people who left would come back and not want to speak Miskitu. I was ashamed of speaking Miskitu in the Moravian college. Now, we are proud of our language.
> *Teacher, Karata*

> Now Miskitu is more widely used, people feel free to speak it in the market and in offices . . . the government radio uses all the Coastal languages and has opened things up more, though here, very few people listen to the radio because its so difficult to get batteries.
> *Head teacher, Karata*

However, within the communities, there has also been a great deal of resistance.

> Bilingual education is necessary. The problem is that when kids go to secondary school, they have problems if they've been taught in Miskitu. The young want to learn Spanish more than Miskitu.
> *Teacher, Karata*

Many parents rejected the use of Miskitu in school at first. They said that their children didn't need to go to school to learn Miskitu because they could do that at home. Paradoxically, the bilingual workers justified themselves by saying that using Miskitu was the best way to learn Spanish. With adult literacy, there have been similar problems as learners want to go on to qualifications in Basic Education – in Spanish – for jobs that at present need Spanish teachers.

> I want to study to be an auxiliary nurse but it is difficult because I need sixth grade to do it. It would be better if our books were in Miskitu but it would create problems for travelling to different places where only Spanish is spoken.
> *Learner, Karata*

The new modular structure to adult education, launched in 1989 (see Chapter 3) should be flexible enough to enable local production of relevant reading materials in Miskitu. This will depend more than anything on the alleviation of the economic crisis. For example, printing facilities are still not available in Puerto Cabezas. The series of Miskitu modules already produced have been printed in Managua. At present, there are 12 workers who, with limited resources, are doing everything from writing and planning materials to training and supervising teachers for the whole of the North Atlantic region. They also have to do military service.

> The technical team feel overworked so they don't have time to study . . . we need more training. Our teacher training school is not a bilingual centre but we need teachers to be trained bilingually so that they can go out and teach it. It's another step. . . . We're building from nothing . . . it will be three generations before things can change completely. . . . It's just beginning.
> *Mirna Cunningham*

Nevertheless, the decentralization of the Ministry of Education has created the potential for Coastal languages to be used throughout the education system, both for children and adults, and in formal and popular education.

Within Karata, people's support for literacy in Miskitu is tied to how much faith they have in the autonomy process. Those who distrust the Sandinistas will, paradoxically, cling to Spanish (the language of the Sandinistas) as the only means of survival. On the other hand, those who believe that autonomy is not another deception are keen to learn in their own tongue in order to contribute to ensuring that the communities have a stronger voice in the new Councils. But it will take a long time to build up confidence. If employment on the Coast requires education in Spanish, then students are forced to reject mother-tongue education. Autonomy aims to change this dependence but the difficulties are enormous. The legal system provides one of many examples. If court cases are to be held in different languages, then either many interpreters are required, or the law has to be translated, clerks have to be able to record in the Coastal languages, lawyers have to be educated in the languages and judges have to come from the communities. For Miskitu, Sumu and Creole to become languages of power, interpreters are not enough because effective power will still remain in the hands of Spanish speakers if Spanish is to remain the language into which everything else is translated. However, with only 12 workers to implement changes in all institutions, the task is one that will necessarily take many years.

A measure of what has been achieved can be gathered from the Unification Assembly in May 1989. Delegates from the whole region and from military groups that have taken amnesty converged in the community of Sisin, inland from Karata, to discuss how to implement the elections the following year. While the briefs for workshop discussion had been prepared by government workers, the discussions were extremely lively. It is not an insignificant advance to have Sandinista and ex-Contra leaders sitting under cashew-nut trees discussing what only a few years earlier people were dying for. This was a practical test of how an autonomous assembly might function. Both the conference brief and discussions were in indigenous languages (mediated by many interpreters). A broad measure of agreement was reached. If this was the Miskitu dream in 1981, then they have achieved it. Barriers to further progress are seen by Miskitu and Sandinista as no longer ideological. The revolution and the self-determination of indigenous peoples have proved themselves to be more than compatible. Remarkably, the Miskitu have used an imperialist power – the US – to gain the first victory in the continent for indigenous peoples.

Election results

North Atlantic Autonomous Council
UNO (United Nicaragua Opposition; US backed)   – 2
YATAMA (Indigenous organization)   – 22
FSLN (Sandinistas)   – 21
National Assembly, representatives from the North Atlantic
Mirna Cunningham   – FSLN
Daniel Edwin Tate Jerry   – UNO
Alfonso Smith Warman   – PSC (Social Christian party)

Miskitu monologue
Not all the Contra believe that they have won the war for their autonomy. Comandante Hercules, viewed as a lunatic in his own village, continues trying to rally support in the school, the only indoor meeting place in Karata.
Translated from Spanish:

> "My mother is beautiful. All men love her. But my father betrayed her. My step-father came and he promised to teach us to read and write so that he could live with my mother . . . but he didn't. He raped her and put her in prison. What else could we do but go to the mountain and fight? Now our eldest brother Brooklyn must come . . . our brother who comes from our mother's loins . . . to be in our presence always. All of us, the indigenous people, want him to come. My father was Somoza. My stepfather is Daniel Ortega. My mother is the Atlantic Coast. I want my mother . . .
> The Sandinistas are deceiving the poor indigenous people . . . because we have small brains . . . they use the indigenous people . . . put them against one another. They don't keep their promises. If the Sandinistas didn't promise so many things we wouldn't want them, we wouldn't fight. Somoza didn't promise anything and it was alright.
> Here are the sharks and the black tigers waiting for Brooklyn. If he comes back, they'll kill him so that the indigenous people can advance no more."

Translated from Creole:

> "We no wan' false autonomy. We wan' true autonomy. We not politicians. We no studied politics, no. If dey not give us the rights we fight.
> Dem Sandinistas, dey sell things expensive . . . and change the money. How

many times dey done dat? In my thirty years I never heard of the US do dat. Dat never happen. But dey Sandinista deceive people. Suddenly their money no worth nuthin'.

Money is sometin' delicate . . . money kill my brother . . . money can kill the mother, can kill the father . . . can make you kill your brother. Dat's the trouble we have right here. With money. Dere is no work here.

Trust kills you . . . If I take my hat off, someone can put a snake in it. . . . Every mornin', I have to shake out my pants to check I got no snakes. . . .

Problems and trouble, dey the two brother twins. Problem is the smaller brother, trouble is the heavier brother, the older brother."

Asked for his advice on Thatcherism:

"If you havin' trouble with your government you must get some people together . . . get dem people to go up to the mountain . . . fighting . . . like guerrilla . . . you must fight dat government . . . and kill dem. Dere is no other way."

NOTES

1.   The word Miskitu is of uncertain origin. The Chibcha who remained aloof from the Europeans are now known as the Sumu.

2.   Hooker, Ray, *Nicaragua: The Sandinista People's Revolution, Speeches by Sandinista Leaders* (London: Pathfinder Press, 1985).

3.   An insight into the relevance of the monarch to Miskitu society can perhaps be drawn from the name of one of the Miskitu dynasty: King Old Man I.

4.   From Bourgois, Philip, "Ethnic Minorities" in Thomas Walker (ed.), *Nicaragua – Five Years on* (Praeger, 1985).

5.   Mirna Cunningham: Presidential Delegate Minister to the North Atlantic Region (in interview with authors May 1989). "Communities" is the word used for the small villages on the Atlantic Coast.

6.   See the Harrison–Altamirano Treaty of 1905, between the US and Britain.

7.   Dozier, Craig, *Nicaragua's Mosquito Shore: The years of GB and US presence* (CIDCA, 1985).

8.   *Mestizo* means mixed race. It is similar to *ladino* in Guatemala but without the same derogatory connotations.

9.   Quoted in Hooker, *Nicaragua*, op. cit.

10.   *Ethnic Groups and the Nation State* (Nicaragua: CIDCA, 1984).

11.   Guinea Bissau offers an interesting comparison. After the revolution they chose to launch a literacy programme (with Paulo Freire's support). They used Portuguese, the colonial language, rather than Creole (against Freire's advice). See *Pedagogy in Process: Letters from Guinea Bissau* (London: Writers and Readers Publishing Cooperative, 1978).

12.   The government until the 1984 elections in which the FSLN won 69 per cent of the votes.

13.   Quoted in Jane Freeland, *A Special Place in History* (NSC and War on Want, 1988).

14.   Wilson, John, *Obra Morava en Nicaragua: Trasfondo y Breve Historia* (CIDCA, 1975).

15.   For a good exposition of these arguments, see Susan Norwood, *Bilingualism and Bilingual Education in Special Zone 1* (CIDCA, 1985).

16.   MISATAN is one of the myriad groupings of the Miskitu, formed in response to pro- and anti-dialogue factions at different moments of the peace process.

APPENDIX: THE LIFE OF PAULO FREIRE

Paulo Freire was born into a middle class family in the Brazilian town of Recife, in 1921. Through his youth, in the Great Depression of the 1930s, he suffered malnutrition and poverty despite the relative wealth of his parents.

> As a child I had associated with working class children and peasants.

But unlike most children in the north-east of Brazil, Freire was able to attend and complete secondary school. He went on to Recife University to study linguistics. Here Freire met Elza, another teacher, whom he married in 1944.

> My linguistics studies and meeting Elza led me to pedagogy. I began
> to develop certain pedagogical ideas along with historical, cultural and
> philosophical reflections.

Freire took up a post as a Portuguese school-teacher in Recife. In the late 1940s, under the influence of his Catholic mother he became active in Church movements as a way of addressing the injustices which he saw around him. Before long he was made aware of the contradictions involved in charity work, in which the benevolent middleclasses would do things for the poor but not with them. At the end of the day the caring bourgeois would return home to food and comfort, far away from those whom they sought to help.

> We decided not to keep working with the bourgeois, and instead to work
> with the people.

Through the 1950s Freire lived and worked in the *barrios* of Recife, learning the street language and the ways of life. Increasingly his work focused on the teaching of adult literacy, a critical issue at a time when illiterate people were not allowed to vote.

> I found literacy to be the most important issue, since the level of illiteracy
> in Brazil continued to be extremely high. It seemed to me profoundly unjust
> that men and women were not able to read and write.

Freire began to develop a new approach to teaching literacy based on the meetings he held between parents and teachers.

> I tried to see the meetings as forums for critical thinking about what is
> real and concrete.

Freire realized that the discussions that were the basis of his work with parents, could just as easily be used as the basis for teaching people to read and write. Rather than teaching reading letter by letter, he saw the value of whole sentences and words, and the importance of discussion as the way into teaching them. He formalized his experiences into a doctoral thesis which he completed in 1959. This was so well received that he was appointed Chair of History and Philosophy of Education at Recife University. When in 1962 an adult literacy programme was launched in Recife he was appointed co-ordinator. This was his first opportunity to practise the ideas that he had developed on a large scale. He set up "culture circles" in which literacy was tied to critical consciousness-raising through dialogue.

Following the success of his work in Recife, Freire was appointed head of the Brazilian National Literacy Programme in 1963. In this position he hoped to emulate the work of the Cuban Literacy Campaign which had almost eradicated illiteracy between 1960 and 1963. Freire planned 20,000 culture circles, with the aim of eventually reaching 2 million illiterates across the country. A thorough eight-month training programme was initiated for the co-ordinators in each state. But the high profile of his work brought problems. Rapidly he was accused of attempting to "Bolshevize the country" and of encouraging subversion.

> My political ideas, fortunately, did not benefit and continue not to benefit the interests of the dominant class.

In 1964, Freire's work was abruptly stopped by a military coup instigated by officers who feared any shift of power away from the traditional élite of Brazilian society. Freire was arrested and imprisoned.

> I was jailed precisely because of the political nature of education.

Released 75 days later, he was exiled to Bolivia which itself suffered a coup, forcing him to move on again, this time to Chile.

> No one goes through exile without being strongly marked by it. It envelops you as a being. It shakes you up physically and mentally.

In Chile, the Christian Democratic government of Eduardo Frei welcomed Freire and appointed him as a consultant to a team working on adult basic education. While he worked to link the literacy programme to agrarian reform in Chile, he also wrote up his Brazilian experiences (later published in English as *Education for Critical Consciousness*) and went on to weave his practice into a theoretical framework. The result was *Pedagogy of the Oppressed*, which gained him international recognition and an invitation to Harvard as a Visiting Professor in 1969. Articles from his period in the US were published as *Cultural Action for Freedom*.

As a consultant to the World Council of Churches in the 1970s, Freire participated in conferences and seminars in many countries, including Iran, India, Australia, Italy, Angola, Mozambique, Tanzania and Papua New Guinea. He continued to be involved practically in Guinea Bissau where he was invited to assist in preparing a literacy programme for the post-revolutionary society (see *Pedagogy in Process: Letters from Guinea*

Bissau). In 1980 Freire once again contributed to work in Latin America, helping the Ministry of Education in Nicaragua to design their National Literacy Crusade.

As democracy returned to Brazil through the 1980s, Freire was able to return to his homeland after almost 20 years in exile. Nevertheless he continues to travel widely, to participate in seminars from Havana to Dundee. He also continues to write though not all of his recent works are yet available in English. A good and accessible collection of articles is to be found in *The Politics of Education: Culture, power and liberation*. The value of Freire's work to schools in the West is particularly explored in a book with the radical US educator Ira Shor (*Education for Liberation*).

Based in São Paulo Freire has aligned himself with the newly-formed Workers Party. In recent years this party has gathered strength, first winning municipal elections and then, contrary to all expectations, nearly winning the 1989 national presidential elections under the leadership of Luis da Silva, popularly known as Lula (who won 48 per cent of the votes in the final run-off). Freire's contribution (as well as being secretary of the local Workers Party) was to organize literacy work in the poor *barrios* of São Paulo, linking his conscientization work, more than ever before, to a specific political organization.

> The other day I talked with Lula after a television conversation where a very good intellectual said to him: "Lula it is a surprise for me, because I know you do not have time to read, but still you speak very seriously about the historical moment of Brazil, especially the situation today."
>
> Then, Lula said: "I really don't read."
>
> I said to him after that I disagreed with him. I said: "Lula, you are for me one of the best readers of Brazil today, but not readers of the word, readers of the world. That is, you are reading the history we are making every day. You are understanding it, grasping it to the extent that you are making it also. Please, don't say any more that you are not reading. You can say that you are not yet reading books. But you are reading history."

AFTERWORD

Conclusions are usually attempts to close a text: to tie up the ends of a narrative and set an agenda for future work. The nature of this book, which seeks to maximize the role of the people in the communities where we worked, precludes our right to set any such agenda. However, in the light of the case-studies, it becomes possible to consider those questions which would have been too abstract for the introduction. What is literacy? Why is it important at all?

The common sense view of literacy is as a technique: the learning of the alphabet and the ability to use it. However, the role of these techniques in development projects can be called into question. In rural areas where the written word plays a minimal role, the techniques of literacy seem marginal to the needs of the people. Literacy campaigns in such communities are likely to promote migration to the cities. The skills being taught are only considered valuable in an urban environment. But within that environment, literacy skills are not enough to guarantee employment or adequate housing. They can even be counter-productive since they can make people more vulnerable to manipulation, whether through advertising, political propaganda or the promotion of cultural assimilation.

As a reaction to this technicist approach, many popular-education groups have linked the teaching of literacy techniques to the development of a critical consciousness. This can be misconceived. Often the teaching of the alphabet is rather clumsily grafted to a process of political consciousness-raising. The techniques themselves become almost irrelevant and it is common in such classes for students to comment that the political discussions are all very well but have nothing to do with reading and writing. If conscientization is detached from the techniques, then conscientization is reduced to the imparting of a political perspective. This de-reading helps to explain why so-called Freirean methods have been used by Ministries of Education who are not interested in the liberation of the oppressed. In this conception of literacy, the teaching of the alphabet can be linked to any ideological position.

Some of the popular-education groups highlighted in this book have a more coherent, alternative view of literacy. It is one which starts from the empowerment of the learners in which literacy is seen as their ability to express their own needs and desires using whatever techniques are most relevant. The development of a critical consciousness (conscientization) thus harnesses techniques in order to be able to actualize itself. Practically, this has a number of implications. First, it means that in different concrete circumstances, the techniques most relevant to empowerment will be different. The reading and writing of television, video and radio can be more relevant than the alphabet in societies where communication is less dependent on the written word. Secondly, it leaves literacy teaching secure from the charge of ideological manipulation, since it is the learners themselves who set the political agenda for dialogue based on their own experience rather than on any theoretical ideological position. Thirdly, and perhaps most importantly, if literacy is to enable learners to express their needs effectively, it must in practice be linked to organizational structures that will give those demands a collective voice. These structures can be a state which responds to the written demands of its people, as in Nicaragua, or an NGO that is engaged in fighting for the rights which the learners have articulated in the literacy classes (for instance, the CNTC in Honduras).

Conceived in this way, literacy is an indicator of the level of democracy in a society. Democracy (rule of the people) can be assessed in terms of how much participation there is in decision-making procedures. Literacy is what makes that participation possible. But this cannot be easily quantified. It is not a statistic to be collected by experts with pre-conceived notions and fixed measuring tapes. There is a strong sense in which only the learners can define their literacy level. If it is a measurement at all it is a measurement of the nature of the relation between the learners and the world in which they live. Only the learners can characterize that relationship and judge the effectiveness of the techniques they have for making their voices heard.

Index